THIRTY-FIVE

mm.

PHOTO TECHNIQUE

Miniature Camera Practice

H. S. NEWCOMBE F.R.P.S.

Fourteenth Edition

THE FOCAL PRESS
London and New York

CONTENTS

A QUARTER OF A CENTURY AGO   7
Introduction to 35 mm. work. Early troubles

THE ADVANTAGES OF THE 35 mm. SYSTEM   8
Comparisons. Suitability for various tasks

THE SEARCH FOR THE IDEAL 35 mm. CAMERA   19
Main features of miniature cameras

CURRENT CAMERA TYPES   22
The principal groups of miniatures compared

THE PRECISION RANGE-FINDER MINIATURE   23
Focal plane shutter cameras and their scope

THE CONVERTIBLE LENS CAMERA   25
Using some between-lens shutter cameras

THE SINGLE-LENS REFLEX   26
Screen focusing and its variations

THE DIAPHRAGM SHUTTER REFLEX   28
More popular reflex cameras and their specifications

THE TWIN-LENS MINIATURE REFLEX   30
An unusual camera type of some interest

WHICH WILL SUIT ME BEST?   31
Factors that should influence the choice

DIRECTION OF SHUTTER MOVEMENT   34
The effect of focal plane shutters on moving subjects

WHAT OPTICAL EQUIPMENT IS AVAILABLE?   35
The range and scope of miniature lenses

CONVERTIBLE AND ADJUSTABLE LENSES   39
Special methods of obtaining alternative focal lengths

THE BEST OPTICAL OUTFIT   40
The requirements of different users. How they can be met

COATED LENSES   42
What they can and cannot do

RANGE-FINDERS   44
The principles employed. Description of the different types

VIEW-FINDERS   49
Their purpose and peculiarities. Parallax

SIMPLIFIED 35 mm. CAMERAS   54
With and without exposure automation

HOLDING THE CAMERA   59
Recommended methods—and why

LOADING 60
How to refill cartridges, cassettes and camera

SHOOTING 63
Sequence of operations. The desirability of method

THE IMPORTANCE OF THE LENS HOOD 64
What it does and why it is necessary

DEPTH OF FIELD 66
What it is. The advantages of the miniature

DEPTH FOCUSING IN PRACTICE 72
How to secure adequate sharpness. Examples

PERSPECTIVE, ETC. 77
What governs perspective. How it can be controlled

THE CHARACTERISTICS OF FILM 86
Speed, colour sensitivity, contrast, grain, latitude

TYPES OF 35 mm. FILM 92
The basic types compared

FILTERS—THEIR USE AND MIS-USE 94
Their task. Correction and emphasis. What to choose

THE NEED FOR CORRECT EXPOSURE 105
Latitude. The characteristic curve

THE USE OF EXPOSURE METERS 107
The principles involved. How to use the meter

THE CONFUSION ABOUT FILM SPEEDS 111
Systems compared. Recommended speed ratings

HANDLING THE FILM 121
The need for care. Methods. Faults due to handling

HANDLING SHORT ENDS 122
Removing part exposed films from the camera

THE VARIABLE INFLUENCE OF DEVELOPMENT 123
The effect of different types of developer. Temperature

THE MYSTERY OF "GAMMA" 129
A frank explanation. "Hard" and "soft" films

SUITING THE FILM TO THE DEVELOPER 131
Three film types processed in three types of developer

FINE GRAIN V. GOOD DEFINITION 133
Energetic developers for maximum resolution

COMMONSENSE PROCESSING CONDITIONS 138
How to get good results. The ideal darkroom

DEVELOPING TANKS 140
Types in use. Methods. Agitation

FIXING, WASHING, DRYING 142
The theory and practice of negative finishing

HOW DO YOU STORE YOUR FILMS? 145
Flaws due to mishandling, and their avoidance

RECOMMENDED DEVELOPER FORMULAE 147
The best tested formulae grouped in three basic types

POST DEVELOPMENT FORMULAE 157
Faults; their identification and cure

TOURING WITH A CAMERA 162
Requirements of the pedestrian, cyclist and motorist

PANORAMS 179
How they are made. Panoram heads. Hand held panorams

WATERSIDE AND MARINE PICTURES 182
Exposure problems, composition. Focal length and lenses

PICTORIAL WORK 192
Composition. Simplicity. Suitable subjects. Exhibiting

PORTRAITURE 207
Methods. High and low key. Lighting. Backgrounds

AT THE SHOWS 225
Lighting. Film. Exposure. Methods. Handling apparatus

ACTION PHOTOGRAPHY 231
Suitable subjects. Shutter speeds to arrest motion

FLASH WITH A MINIATURE 248
How to use flash bulbs and electronic flash

COLOUR PHOTOGRAPHY 254
Lighting and contrast. Latitude. How to assess the exposure

ENLARGING ROUTINE 267
Outline of the process

ENLARGING EQUIPMENT 268
Types of enlargers compared. Diffused v. condensed light

CONTACT PRINTING 275
Strip prints for filing. Simplified exposing

THE IDEAL DEGREE OF ENLARGEMENT 276
The extent to which pictures should be enlarged

THE CHOICE OF PRINTING PAPER 281
Surfaces. Contrast grades. Paper tone capacity

PRINT EXPOSURE AND PRINT PROCESSING 287
Methods. Formulae

PRINT QUALITY 288
Getting good "blacks". Exposure, development

CORRECTIVE PRINTING 293
Dodging. Shading. Flashing

CREATIVE PRINTING 305
Tone separation methods

GETTING CLOSER STILL 309
Reproduction, macro, micro

THE TECHNIQUE OF THE ILLUSTRATIONS 314
Tabulated technical data

A QUARTER OF A CENTURY AGO

BACK in the relatively early days of 1925, I acquired my first Leica. It was then a distinct novelty, and I was much intrigued with its handling. It was one of the early models in which the lens was in a Compur shutter and in its way it did me yeoman service. A little later I changed it for one of the new models which had a focal plane shutter, as I found that this handled more easily.

At the time I started using the Leica, I was doing the bulk of my photography with a 3¼ x 4¼ reflex, and I derived a lot of enjoyment from using the Leica on those various odds and ends for which unpacking the quarter-plate camera seemed hardly worth while. My new small camera produced what I then thought were some really remarkable results: pictures which enlarged up to about 4 × 3 in. and were in some cases *almost* as good as those taken with the larger camera. Still, I could not count on consistently getting this sort of quality, and therefore the Leica continued to be very much of a second string. In fact, within a few months, I became rather tired of it when I found I could not *quite* equal the work done by the larger instrument. At one stage I was on the point of entirely giving up Leica photography. It was only the chance examination of a number of pictures that had come over from the Continent that made me realise that there was, perhaps, after all something in miniature photography, and that if my results were not up to the required standard it was hardly likely to be the fault of the camera.

It must be remembered that in those days there were very few photographers in this country with whom to discuss problems arising in the use of such equipment, and the only books on the subject required laborious translation

7

from their native German. But either through obstinacy or personal pride I did not like the idea that the Leica had "got the better of me", so I really settled down to try to learn why some people could do good work with the camera, while my own was only mediocre. At last, after a year of painstaking work, I discovered that attention to a number of small technical details made all the difference between *good* Leica photographs and the type which I had hitherto been turning out. Finding myself at last able to produce reasonable pictures, an interest and affection for the miniature camera was born which I am glad to say has not waned, and now I am probably doing 90 per cent. or more of my work with 35 mm. apparatus, although I still sometimes enjoy using other and larger instruments for special purposes.

THE ADVANTAGES OF THE 35 mm. SYSTEM

THUS the position changed. The range-finder miniature, once just good enough for odd jobs, became my chief photographic tool and the larger instrument took the place of secondary equipment reserved for special use. I have never, I believe, offered the opinion that the 35 mm. camera is *better* than every other design; rather would I say that it is more versatile than any other individual camera, and to our everlasting shame, nearly all precision 35 mm. cameras (at the time of writing this book), have been of foreign origin.

There is, of course, still much to be said for the larger camera. The type employing sheet film or pack and a ground glass focusing screen does undoubtedly appear at first sight to offer advantages in the ease with which the picture can be composed and sharply focused, and for serious commercial photography of architecture, machinery, still life and similar

The scope of the miniature camera is almost unlimited. Small and unobtrusive, combining ample depth of field with extreme lens speed, it can be used at a moment's notice in almost any circumstances.

Page 9. AN ANXIOUS MOMENT—An example of work by normal lighting possible only with the fastest lens.—F. H. Sharman.

Page 10. A POLICEMAN'S LOT—The type of picture that occurs only once, and must be captured on the instant. The perfect reason for always carrying a "35".—C. C. B. Herbert.

Page 11. OUT OF THE WINDOW—An interesting study available only to the 35 mm. camera with its immense depth of field.—Paul Wolff.

Page 12. THEATRE—Another outstanding example of the extreme depth of field given by a wide angle lens.—Felix H. Mann.

Above. THE STATUE—Careful composition with the variable view-finder and a very long focus lens.—Unknown Photographer.

13

Page 14. PENGUIN—*A long focus shot that concentrates the interest on the subject by portraying it on a large scale and eliminating unwanted background detail.*—Erich Auerbach.

Page 15. QUITE A HANDFUL—*The type of subject for which a close focusing attachment is invaluable. Even at this range the depth is adequate.*—Erich Auerbach.

Above. GOING DOWN—*A happy series like this can best be made with a "35".*—Hugo van Wadenoyen.

work I do not think that the miniature will ever compete with it. Against this, however, must be put the weighty bulk of the sheet film camera and the fact that it must be used on a tripod.

The 35 mm. camera is small and compact. I, too, have heard hundreds of people at different times laughing at the miniature camera enthusiast with his outfit of almost suitcase dimensions, but I think that very few of the scoffers have bothered to think just how much luggage would be involved if the large camera user were to carry an equally comprehensive range of equipment. A great deal of the value and pleasure of miniature camera work undoubtedly lies in the fact that a large range of accessory equipment *is* made for it, and that most of this is so small that to carry a really extensive outfit becomes a practical possibility.

The miniature camera of the type that we are considering takes anything up to 36 exposures at one loading, and its film material is inexpensive. This may perhaps encourage promiscuous "shooting", but, if it does, at least it increases the choice of negatives from which to make the final picture. And although the very fact that there *are* 36 pictures on the strip is sometimes proffered as a disadvantage, in most cameras a portion of the film can easily be removed for development before the entire film is exposed if this is desired.

Enormous advantages to the miniaturist accrue from the use of 35 mm. film. The perforated edge of this standard motion picture stock provides a ready means of transporting the film safely through the camera. Developments in cinematography have resulted in improvements of this material following fast on one another, in colour sensitivity, speed, and fineness of grain, all of which are vital to us.

A constructional feature of the best precision miniature cameras is an all-metal design eliminating bellows and securing extreme rigidity and mechanical accuracy. This very much helps to make the miniature a competitor on level terms with larger instruments for the majority of subjects.

But the miniature camera has, I think, won its popularity

17

almost entirely because, shortly after its introduction, a method of automatically coupling a range-finder with the focusing mount of the lens was evolved. There are good miniatures which employ other means of focusing, e.g., the reflex mirror which I shall come back to shortly. I feel, however, that the coupled range-finder is to be preferred, on balance, for a number of reasons which will be discussed in the next chapter. But I offer this remark as a purely personal opinion, and there may well be many reasons why my own personal choice and that of the reader may be at variance.

The things on which I insist, if a 35 mm. camera is to be able to compete with larger apparatus, are:—

It must be of good design—and made with suitable precision, and be in perfect optical and mechanical order.

It must be used with the most suitable film material for the tasks in hand.

And—perhaps above all—the photographer must devote the requisite care to his part of the work, at the time the exposure is made, and in the subsequent processing operations.

We are dealing with *small* negatives, on which we shall crowd an immense amount of detail. If we are to get all this back again in the form of a technically perfect enlargement, we cannot afford to leave anything to chance, nor to be slipshod in our methods.

Those willing to pay this small price for the joy of using such fascinating equipment will soon learn that the modern miniature is capable of competing on level terms with the majority of larger cameras. They will also realize that this system of photography possesses a degree of versatility that cannot be equalled.

The success of the 35 mm. camera is based on its compact size, its unparalleled range of equipment, the large load of sensitised material it takes and the quality of that material, the rigid precision design and the unfailing method of range-finder focusing.

The wide scope of the "35" is indicated diagrammatically on the following page, and it is interesting to note for how many different subjects the miniature is well suited, in comparison with larger sizes.

18

IN ALL the earlier editions of this book we have studied the comparative merits of the two first leaders in the 35 mm. field—Leica and Contax—in detail, and have made less detailed reference to the variety of other types of instrument.

During the last few years there have been any number of fresh contenders for pride of place—some of them introducing completely new systems. The time has now come to take stock of what is available, to consider the different methods of doing the same thing, to discover what their respective merits really are and to see which of the systems will most nearly approach perfection *for our particular requirements*.

I am not going to take sides. I cannot. There is so much to be said in favour of the different methods that are now available—for focusing, view-finding, shutter speed selection, and everything else—that the final preference and choice must necessarily be personal to a degree. I have already indicated that I am exceedingly happy with my Leica, and expect to continue in that frame of mind; but that does not infer that I have anything but admiration for some of the newer designs, nor that *my* choice of camera will necessarily be the best one for *you*.

Before discussing classifications of complete cameras, let us look first at the features that make up the camera. There we have four main groups that represent aspects in which modern miniature cameras differ: focusing systems, lens systems, shutter systems, and exposure systems.

Focusing systems in 35 mm. models are the range-finder (usually coupled with the lens) and the reflex screen.

With the range-finder you measure the subject distance by adjusting a lever or ring until a double image fuses into one; occasionally you have to line up the two halves of a split image. The control movement of the optical instrument that is the range-finder is linked to the lens focusing mechanism; so that once the range-finder image is clear and single, the lens is also correctly set.

On the reflex screen you see the image and can check directly whether it is sharp. It is the lens which forms the visible image and projected via a movable mirror in front of the film. Provided the ground glass screen, film plane, and

19

mirror are correctly aligned (which is a comparatively easy matter), the focusing system cannot go out of adjustment as there is no mechanical linkage. Moreover, the screen shows the image sharpness irrespective of the lens used, at normal distances or close-ups, even with supplementary lenses. The screen also shows the exact field of view of the lens.

Focusing on the screen is comparatively slow—especially in weak light. Many modern reflex cameras therefore incorporate a special range-finder device in the screen which shows even an out-of-focus image clearly, but *split in two*. While the image is out of focus, the split halves in the centre of the screen are out of alignment. They join up when the focus setting is right. See also p. 44.

On inexpensive 35 mm. cameras the focusing system simply consists of a distance scale. The subject distance is then set on the focusing mount of the lens by estimation.

Miniature camera lenses may be fixed or interchangeable. The provision of alternative focal lengths immensely increases the versatility of the camera. I shall come back to that in due course.

The classic way, used from the very beginning on miniature cameras, is to take out the whole lens and replace it by another one of a longer or shorter focal length. The lens is in this case mounted in a screw or bayonet fitting in front of the shutter. Such completely interchangeable lenses are found on the best precision 35 mm. models, and range from the ultra-wide angle units of less than an inch in focal length to telephoto lenses as long as 20 inches or more.

Another way is to design the standard lens in such a way that only the front part of it is removable. The rear components remain permanently in the camera—usually behind the shutter—and form wide-angle or telephoto lenses with alternative front units. These *convertible* lens systems were popular for a time in certain miniatures of more compact types. Their drawback is that the alternative front components are rather bulky, and the range of focal lengths limited.

The two main shutter systems in use are the focal plane and the diaphragm shutter. The former consists of a pair of flexible blinds, usually fabric, but more recently ultra-thin stainless steel ones have come into use as well—which move across the film close in front of it. The first blind

20

uncovers the film, and the second one covers it up again. At slow shutter speeds (longer exposure times) the time interval between the first and second blinds is the actual exposure time. At fast speeds the second blind starts to cover up the film before the first one has uncovered it fully. What we get then is in effect a slit moving across the film to expose it. By making this slit very narrow, the effective exposure can be really short—as little as 1/1000 second.

The diaphragm shutter consists of a series of metal leaves, mounted between or just behind the lens elements. These leaves open outwards and close again during the exposure. Until recently, diaphragm shutters were limited to a maximum speed of 1/500 second: some of the latest types however claim to give exposures of 1/1000 second.

Apart from their construction, the main difference between the two shutter systems is that the focal plane shutter is invariably an integral part of the camera; while the diaphragm shutter is a separate unit. Often it is not even made by the camera manufacturer. For that reason high quality diaphragm shutters may be found on comparatively inexpensive cameras: focal plane ones are nearly always associated with higher priced precision models.

The main advantage of the focal plane shutter is that it is completely independent of the lens mounting. That provides the greatest versatility in the use of interchangeable lenses: the shutter is always out of the way. A diaphragm shutter must be as close to the lens as possible for maximum efficiency; that limits the range of interchangeable lenses that can be used. It is in fact the main reason why convertible lens systems came into being.

The diaphragm shutter has the merit of exposing the whole negative at once instead of piecemeal. So flash synchronization is simpler (p. 248). Also, the proximity of the shutter to the lens aperture controls makes coupled exposure systems easier.

Exposure systems, finally, are concerned with methods of determining the correct exposure (p. 105) for a picture, and with setting it on the camera in terms of a combination of aperture and shutter speed. Two developments have taken place in this field, after countless years of exposure calculators and exposure meters (p. 107). One of these steps forward was the exposure value system—a way of assigning simple values to whole series of combinations of aperture and shutter speed. All aperture-speed combinations corresponding to the same exposure have the same exposure value. Aperture and speed controls are, moreover, cross-coupled, so that you can set an exposure by a simple control, and once the exposure is selected you can choose alternative combinations without changing the actual exposure.

The second step, following from this, was to couple the exposure setting with a built-in exposure meter. That led directly to the automatic miniatures. Two types exist: the semi-automatic exposure control in which the act of adjusting the exposure meter sets the lens aperture; and the fully automatic system where the exposure meter itself *actually selects* the correct camera settings according to the prevailing light.

CURRENT CAMERA TYPES

THE various features described above appear on present-day 35 mm. cameras in ever-growing permutations and combinations.

To clarify the position to some extent I would like to outline just what is available for selection at the present time: so that you may decide which type is most likely to appeal to you—for your specific form of picture making. For convenience we can group 35 mm. cameras in the following basic forms:

(*a*) The coupled range-finder type, with focal plane or diaphragm shutter and *interchangeable* lenses where the whole lens is removable. Examples are the Leica, Contax, Ambi-Silette, Canon, Nikon, Prominent, etc.

(*b*) The coupled range-finder type with diaphragm shutter and *convertible* lenses where one part of the lens is interchangeable. Examples are the folding Retina models.

(*c*) The single-lens reflex pattern, incorporating a focal plane shutter and interchangeable lenses. Examples are the Alpa, Exakta, Pentax, etc.

22

(*d*) The eye-level-reflex instruments such as the Bessa-matic, Retina Reflex, Contaflex, etc., with diaphragm shutter and interchangeable or convertible lenses with removable front lens components.

(*e*) A variety of models of the above groups employing a greater or lesser degree of exposure automation, where a built-in photo-electric exposure meter indicates—or in some models actually sets—the exposure and stop required.

(*f*) The multitude of simpler instruments with fixed lens which range from the basic camera without exposure meter, or range-finder; to models which incorporate one, or even both, of these desirable features. The exposure meter may again be coupled.

Now let us examine them in detail.

THE PRECISION RANGE-FINDER MINIATURE

THE salient features of this camera type, which includes most of the well-known top-class miniatures of today, are the film transport system, the shutter, and the optical system of lens and range-finder.

The film loading and transport are perhaps the most standardised features. Usually a rapid winding lever advances the film by one frame, tensions the shutter, and advances the film counter. One swing of the lever (occasionally two) thus gets the camera ready for the next shot—an essential point for instant readiness. Older cameras—and even a few more recent ones such as the Leica g series—use a winding knob, which is a little slower.

The film counter sometimes counts exposures backwards from No. 36, finishing up at No. 0 to indicate that the film is finished. It thus shows the number of exposures still remaining on the film—the argument being that this saves some mental arithmetic while shooting. Not all photographers—nor all camera makers—are convinced of that, so plenty of present-day miniatures still keep on counting forward from 1 to 36—my own preferred method.

The internal part of the film transport consists of a

23

sprocket wheel which engages the film by its perforation holes and pulls it forward through the camera. The film winds itself up on the take-up spool—usually built-in, but occasionally removable. Some cameras with removable take-up spool permit the use of a film cassette on the take-up side. This does away with the need for rewinding the film after exposure—you can cut off the exposed portion of the film at any time in broad daylight (since the cassette is light-tight) for processing. For easy access to all these internal features and for loading most miniatures have a hinged-on or removable back—the Leica with its removable base plate being a salient exception.

All the above features of film winding and transport are by now fairly consistent on most miniature cameras irrespective of type—in other words they are also to be found on reflex, automatic, and simple models.

Range-finder miniatures with fully interchangeable lenses have a wide range of alternative lenses of different focal lengths, especially when the camera is fitted with a focal plane shutter. There the lens can never interfere with the shutter mechanism or components, and such models may take lenses from less than 1 inch (21 mm.) up to 20 inches (500 mm.) or even longer in focal length. Normally lenses up to about 135 mm. are automatically coupled with the range-finder on insertion in the camera. Longer focal lengths are rarely coupled, mainly because the focusing accuracy of the range-finder is no longer adequate at intermediate distances (i.e. between 25 and several hundred feet) where long focus lenses still need precision focusing. Reflex housings or attachments are therefore mostly used with the extreme tele lenses to check the image sharpness directly on a ground glass screen—as in a miniature reflex camera.

Extreme tele lenses are not suitable for use with range-finder miniatures having a diaphragm shutter. The shutter has to be immediately behind the lens, otherwise it cuts off part of the picture area. The practical limit is usually around 180 mm.—which may or may not still be coupled with the range-finder.

With the majority of precision miniatures the lenses are fitted in bayonet mounts—certainly on those models carrying diaphragm shutters—but a few still use a screw thread.

The outstanding feature of the precision range-finder miniature camera is the fact that it is the basis of a complete photographic system. The Leica was, and still is, the most famous example of how an astounding range of accessories can be built up around a camera to cope with almost every imaginable photographic task. Apart from an extensive range of interchangeable lenses, there are extension tubes, bellows focusing units, reflex attachments, copying gear, and other close-up devices; also extra rapid winding attachments, photomicrographic adapters, and other units.

THE CONVERTIBLE LENS CAMERA

THIS camera type arose in the first place from attempts to provide interchangeable lens systems for comparatively inexpensive instruments. Though popular in a few models, the convertible lens miniature is becoming less common—possibly because recent lens designs make cameras with interchangeable lenses available at comparable prices.

Such a camera nearly always has a diaphragm shutter—that is a shutter situated *between* the components of the lens. Because the shutter is so placed, it will be evident that the back cell of the lens is sited *inside* the camera body, and could not be removed for changes of focal length without opening the camera (which naturally would fog the film).

To get over this seeming impasse, the lens designers have adopted a system in which the *rear* element of the lens can become a common part of three or more different lenses of various foci. The change from, e.g., a 50 mm. lens to one of, e.g., 35 or 85 mm. focus involves nothing more than removing the existing *front* lens component and replacing it with another "front" lens.

Where a range-finder is fitted, it is of course coupled to the standard lens. However, a long-focus lens requires *more*, and a wide-angle lens requires *less*, camera extension to cover the focusing distance from, say, infinity to 5 feet. So it will be obvious that the range-finder can no longer couple with the long-focus or wide-angle lenses, but can only indicate the distance of the observed object on a focusing scale. And herein lies, to my mind, the gravest disadvantage of this system.

Focusing with alternative lens units thus becomes cumbersome. Assuming that a long-focus lens is in use, we have to measure the distance of the subject by focusing the camera front in the usual way, and then *note the distance reading* on the *standard lens scale*. We then refocus the camera front so that this precise reading is against the appropriate index *on a separate "long-focus lens" scale*—which may be on the camera itself or on the lens. The procedure with the wide-angle lens is similar.

THE SINGLE-LENS REFLEX

THE "true" reflex cameras as exemplified by the *Exakta* and the *Alpa*, of course, overcome the difficulties just mentioned. These instruments generally are fitted with a focal-plane shutter operating just in front of the film, as in the precision range-finder miniature.

Cameras of this type are basically a box, on to the front of which the lens is fitted in its own focusing mount. As focusing is carried out by inspection on the screen there is no difficulty in determining sharp focus or the amount included in the picture, whatever lens is in use.

All reflex cameras (except twin-lens models) suffer one disability: that is the disappearance of the focusing image just before the exposure is made. This is inevitable. The mirror reflecting the image on to the focusing screen has to be got out of the way to allow the light from the lens to have uninterrupted passage to the film, before the shutter commences its travel. To get over this, a number of current single-lens reflex models, especially from Japan, feature an "instant-return" mirror, in which the mirror mechanism is spring-loaded so as to shoot back into its viewing position immediately after the exposure. In this way the black-out of the screen is restricted to a fraction of a second.

A drawback of every reflex that has existed over the years has been the fact that, if you use a small stop, say $f11$ (for reasons of depth of field or other purposes), you can only get a very poorly illuminated image on the focusing screen. However, many of the lenses now in use on such cameras are available in "pre-set" or "automatic pre-set" mounts. With the first mentioned, the diaphragm can be pre-set to the aperture it is intended to use; and the lens *kept at full aperture during focusing*. The stop is then set to the pre-selected point by *feel* (usually by moving a lever, or turning the iris ring until it comes up against a positive stop) at the position corresponding to $f11$ or $f6.3$—or whatever has been chosen in advance.

In the "automatic" variation of this system the iris control ring is spring-loaded, and there is a coupling of some sort between the iris operating ring and the shutter release button. After focusing at full aperture, the act of pressing the shutter release permits the iris to close to the pre-selected stop. This takes place a split second before the exposure.

Most reflex cameras are designed so that the focusing image is observed from above, on a horizontally disposed screen; 35 mm. models are designed so that the general arrangement of the camera is horizontal because the film passes from side to side of the body. With a reflex camera used normally (horizontally) the image on the screen is the right way up—but the wrong way round (laterally reversed—as is natural in any mirror reflection). If the camera is turned on its side to take a *vertical* picture, we run into some inconvenience; as the image is then *inverted* (like that on the focusing screen of an old-fashioned field camera).

Fortunately, this drawback is overcome on many current models with the aid of an optical "roof-prism" assembly, usually referred to as a *pentaprism*. This can be fitted over the focusing screen, in place of the usual hood on a number of cameras—and is incorporated as an integral part of the design in others. The pentaprism keeps the image the right way up and the right way round, irrespective of whether the camera is used normally or turned on to its side.

With a pentaprism we look through a magnifier eyepiece at the upper rear edge of the camera, using it at eye-level (like a range-finder model) instead of at waist- or chest-level.

Modern single-lens reflex models incorporate further improvements in the focusing screen. To provide an evenly bright image over the whole screen, the latter usually incorporates a Fresnel "field lens". This distributes the light uniformly over the screen area.

For even greater brilliance some reflexes do not have ground glass surface over the whole screen but only carry a central ring of ground glass. This is then used for observing the sharpness of the image.

Finally, most present-day reflex screens incorporate a split-image wedge range-finder mounted in the screen (p. 20) to provide both screen and range-finder focusing, according to which is more suitable for the subject being taken.

In the most advanced cameras of this group the whole finder system may be interchangeable. Thus the waist-level hood and screen can be replaced by an eye-level pentaprism unit, and alternative screen units may also be available with or without range-finder, or with special features such as clear spots for "aerial" focusing—a useful aid for special applications such as photomicrography.

THE DIAPHRAGM SHUTTER REFLEX

THIS camera, which is a combination of the best features of at least two of the preceding types—if not all of them—has jumped into popularity during the last few years. Typical examples which have been extremely well received are the Zeiss *Contaflex*: the Kodak *Retina Reflex*, and the Voigtlander *Bessamatic*.

In basic design these models employ an eye-level pentaprism finder, which is very similar to the finder system of the modern focal plane shutter reflexes. Normally, this finder system is not interchangeable (there are one or two exceptions to this), but it almost invariably incorporates a split-image rangefinder of the built-in wedge type.

Essentially this type of instrument is also designed round a diaphragm shutter. Lens changing thus works on

28

the same principle as with rangefinder miniatures carrying such a shutter: the lens is either convertible with the rear component permanently built into the shutter (Contaflex, Retina Reflex), or the whole lens is mounted interchangeably in front of the shutter (Retina Reflex S, Bessamatic). For the users of these "popular" reflex cameras the limited range of focal lengths available (i.e. limited by the use of the diaphragm shutter) is no serious handicap.

The diaphragm shutter brings with it two further advantages. The first is the close coupling possible between the aperture control and the shutter tensioning and release mechanism. The second is the scope for automatic exposure control systems.

Reflex cameras of this type therefore almost always have an automatic aperture mechanism. The lens aperture is wide open for viewing and focusing, being kept thus by lever acting against a spring. The latter tends to close the iris as soon as the lever is released —which takes place on pressing the shutter release button. The degree to which the lens iris closes down is set by another mechanical stop—the perfect pre-selector iris diaphragm. And it is fully automatic, too; on tensioning the shutter, the aperture opens up again to its full extent.

As the shutter also is open during viewing, a camera of this type needs separate protection of the film against light—there is no focal plane shutter blind immediately in front of the film. Its place is here taken by a special "capping" plate which closes the film aperture light-tight all the time the mirror is down for viewing. During the exposure the capping plate then moves out of the way of the optical axis of the lens immediately after the mirror.

All this shows that the internal mechanism of a reflex camera with diaphragm shutter is far from simple—possibly even more complex than in the case of a focal plane shutter camera. The operations that take place between one shot and the next in fact fall into two sequences: the winding sequence and the release sequence. The winding sequence begins immediately after the exposure as you work the transport lever or knob to get the camera ready for the next shot. Apart from advancing the film and film counter, the winding mechanism first brings down the mirror and capping plate into their viewing positions, tensions the shutter mechanism, opens the lens aperture fully, and *opens the shutter*, keeping it open. Now you can view and focus the image on the reflex screen.

The release sequence comes into action when you press the release button. This first closes the shutter, and releases the spring-loaded iris diaphragm so that the lens stops itself down to the pre-selected aperture. At the same time the mirror and capping plate fly up out of the way of the image forming rays, and finally the shutter *opens again for the appropriate exposure time* set on it, and closes once more. All this, from pressing the button up to the moment of opening the shutter for the exposure, takes only a fraction of a second—somewhere in the order of 1/50 second! To keep all this functioning reliably thus needs an appreciable amount of precision. The shutter is of course specially designed for this reflex operation, though similar in performance and all other respects to the standard shutters made by the same manufacturers.

The spring-loaded diaphragm is by comparison a simpler matter, especially on reflex cameras with convertible lens systems where the iris remains permanently on the camera together with the shutter.

This spring-loaded iris is also the basis of the automatic exposure control systems fitted on the more advanced models. What happens here is that the mechanical stop of the pre-selector mechanism is controlled not by the aperture setting ring, but by the exposure meter needle. After setting the shutter speed desired, pressing the release button locks the meter needle in the position it has reached under the influence of the light falling on the meter cell. At the same time the spring-loaded iris is released, and stops at the point determined by the position of the meter needle—the lens stops itself down automatically to the correct aperture.

THE TWIN-LENS MINIATURE REFLEX

WHILE single-lens reflexes are very popular, twin-lens models are very rare. One or two were produced before and during the war, but never became successful.

One more recent design that shows some promise is the Agfa *Flexilette*. This resembles a single-lens reflex in general design, but has two lenses one above the other: to form the image on the film, and to form the finder image on the screen. The two lenses are mounted close together on a circular panel, surrounded by the aperture and shutter speed rings. During focusing the two lenses move forward and back in unison, thus assuring perfect sharpness on the film whenever the image is sharp on the screen.

One advantage of this design is that it does away with much of the complicated mechanism required to present the image on the screen one moment, and to throw it on the film the next. There is no need for pre-selector iris systems, and the image is visible on the screen all the time. On the other hand, lens interchangeability is more of a problem (the Flexilette lens is not interchangeable); it would involve removing and replacing both lenses at the same time. Time will tell whether this new attempt to make such a camera system popular will be more successful than the previous ones.

WHICH WILL SUIT ME BEST?

ALTHOUGH 35 mm. cameras nearly all yield negatives of the same size, they vary in weight and bulk. A simple model may weigh around 16–20 ounces, a reflex with advanced features up to twice as much. In other words, the more facilities we enjoy, the greater the bulk, and the weight. But even so a host of refinements may be had without any very serious increases.

I suppose that the greatest difficulty that a newcomer to 35 mm. work has to face, in choosing his new camera, is that of deciding between the basic range-finder instrument, and one (with or without range-finder facilities) in which the picture is composed and focused on a reflex screen.

What are the pros and cons? In my personal experience I am convinced that it is easier to focus accurately by means of a range-finder than it is on a *small* reflex screen. With any range-finder we determine the point of sharp focus by examining a small field area in which we see *two* images of the object under examination at all times except when it is correctly focused. Even if we are not blessed with perfect eyesight there is seldom any difficulty in establishing whether we can see one, or two separate images.

The only possible objection to the reflex screen is that one secures sharp focus by the rather negative approach of focusing the lens backwards and forwards, watching the transition of the image from unsharp to sharp. My own feeling is that the true range-finder is more rapid—and in the hands of anyone whose eyesight is imperfect—infinitely more certain. That, however, is a personal opinion; and judging by the growth in popularity of the reflex design, it is not everyone's view.

As we have seen, some of the reflex models also provide a split-field range-finder image in the centre of the screen. This would seem to offer the best of all possible designs; but before we accept it completely as the whole answer to the problem, it is well to consider just how and why a range-finder works; and here I refer the reader to page 44 for a detailed explanation. For the moment I merely wish to make the point that while the accuracy of a normal range-finder depends on its base-length, the device on the screen of a reflex is what I would call an "artificial" range-finder. There a pair of "opposed" prisms on the screen give a double image at all times except when the rays are exactly focused on the screen. Because of this difference in optical method employed, such a range-finder does not give as much *separation* of image as the orthodox pattern; and it is consequently more difficult to determine precisely when the two images have come into exact alignment.

This is not intended to be a damning criticism of the reflex system which has so many advantages, more particularly in the pleasure derived from viewing and composing the picture on a full-size screen. But I do criticise the current design of some reflex screens, where the *only* area of ground glass on which one can focus by normal methods is in the form of a small ring surrounding the range-finder spot. This, in my opinion, is far too small an area for easy, accurate focusing.

It will have been noted that we find both diaphragm and focal plane shutters (p. 21) in modern cameras, and it may

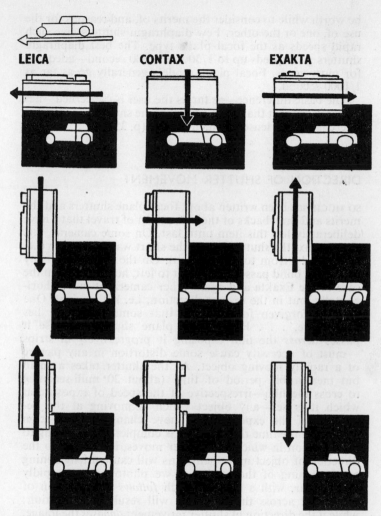

LEICA　　　**CONTAX**　　　**EXAKTA**

The subject as seen by the photographer and his camera (top). Image distortion is caused by focal plane shutter exposing the film in strips: it varies according to the direction of shutter travel in relation to object movement. The drawings are exaggerated for the sake of clarity.

be worth while to consider the merits of, and reasons for the use of, one or the other. Few diaphragm shutters give such rapid speeds as the focal plane type. The best diaphragm shutters give speeds up to 1/300 or 1/500 second—adequate for most needs. Focal plane models generally go as far as 1/1000 second.

The basic difference—as far as the user is concerned—lies rather in the fact that, with a focal plane shutter the range of interchangeable lenses is much greater (p. 35).

DIRECTION OF SHUTTER MOVEMENT

SO MUCH has been written about focal plane shutters and the merits and drawbacks of their direction of travel that I have deliberately left this item until last. On some cameras, e.g. the Contax, the shutter moves the short way of the film (i.e. downwards, from top to bottom). On the Leica and many others the blind passes from right to left, horizontally, in the case of the Exakta and again other cameras it moves horizontally, but in the reverse direction, i.e. left to right. One may be forgiven for thinking that some advantage lies somewhere. . . . Every focal plane shutter—because it passes *across* the film exposing it progressively in strips —must of necessity cause some distortion in any picture of a rapidly moving object. As the shutter takes a small but measurable period of time (about 20 milli-seconds) to cross the film—irrespective of the speed of exposure at which it is set—any object which is moving at the beginning of the exposure will have changed its position slightly by the time the exposure is completed. According to the direction in which the shutter moves, in relation to the direction of object movement, this will cause a lengthening or shortening of the image. If we photograph a rapidly moving car, with a shutter which *follows* the direction of movement across the film, this will result in elongation; while if the direction of shutter movement *opposes* the image, the result will be a shortening. Should a vertical shutter movement be employed (or a horizontal shutter camera be held on end) such distortions as these will be of an oblique

34

nature. The amount of distortion so caused by any but the most rapidly moving objects is relatively slight. Still, it is worth bearing in mind that to hold the camera in such a way as to elongate the object generally conveys a better impression of its speed in the final print.

When applying this rule, one must also remember that the image on the film is upside down and laterally reversed—so that the movement inside the camera is exactly opposite to that of the actual object.

WHAT OPTICAL EQUIPMENT IS AVAILABLE?

THE most impressive fact about the more advanced range-finder miniatures is the range of interchangeable lenses available for the camera. I have already hinted at the immense scope of such an optical outfit, and now I propose to examine the actual lens types and their applications in more detail.

As already mentioned, the range is greatest for cameras with a focal plane shutter; there is virtually no limit—other than optical complexity and size—to the focal lengths that can be fitted, since no part of the camera interferes with the lens. An only reservation applies to reflex models: where the distance between the rear of the lens and the film must be sufficient to accommodate the moving mirror. For that reason certain ultra-wide-angle lenses either cannot be fitted to miniature reflex models at all, or require special lens designs to provide a greater clearance.

The standard lens of most miniature cameras has a focal length of 5 cm., or occasionally 4.5 cm. Such lenses come in two distinct types: medium speed units with a maximum aperture of $f2.8$ or 3.5, and high-speed lenses of $f1.4$ to $f2$.

The 5 cm. $f2.8$ and $f3.5$ lenses are usually 4-element designs—comparatively simple lenses but of high optical correction which at this aperture is still perfectly feasible. Famous designs of this type are the *Elmar* of the Leica, the *Tessar* of Zeiss cameras, the Schneider *Xenar*, Agfa *Solinar*, Voigtlander *Color-Skopar*, to name but a few. With the advent of rare-earth glasses, lenses of similar performance have even become possible with only three components; these are generally found on less expensive cameras.

To provide greater scope in poor light conditions, 35 mm. cameras soon began to appear with standard lenses of maximum aperture $f2$ and larger. Three- and four-component designs are no longer adequate to offer acceptable sharpness and evenness of illumination at such speed; most of these lenses are therefore 6- and 7-element constructions, or even more complex. Current examples are the Leitz *Summicron* and *Summilux* (the latter, aperture $f1.4$), the Zeiss *Sonnar*, Rodenstock *Heligon*, Schneider *Xenon*, and others derived from these.

Even $f1.4$ is not the limit of lens speed; a few Japanese lens makers have managed to produce lenses of $f1.2$ and $f0.95$ aperture—though not without some sacrifice in quality.

The alternative lens units available can for convenience be classified in four or five groups. Among the lenses with shorter focal lengths than the standard one we have wide-angle and ultra-wide-angle units. Among the longer focal lengths we can distinguish between semi-long focus, long focus, and extreme tele lenses. (Tele or telephoto lenses on the one hand and long-focus ones on the other are identical in application, though they differ in optical construction.)

Most wide-angle lenses for 35 mm. cameras have a focal length of 3.5 cm. and a maximum aperture ranging between $f2.8$ and $f4$. In addition to their use as a means of including a considerably greater angle than the normal lens, these lenses offer, thanks to their short focal length, a very extensive depth of field. As an example, focused on 20 ft. and stopped down to only $f5.6$, everything more than 10 ft. away will be sufficiently sharp to allow considerable enlargement of the picture. This characteristic also makes the 3.5 cm. lens particularly valuable to the tourist or anyone who wants to secure unposed pictures in the street, native markets, etc.—in short, candid photography. For example, by pre-setting the lens to say 12 ft. and $f5.6$, satisfactory definition is available from 8 to 30 feet, thus making the use of the range-finder unnecessary.

For work in poor light, even wide-angle lenses of high speed are now available. Maximum apertures here reach

f2 and even larger in the case of some Japanese lenses.

While a 3.5 cm. lens with its image angle of 64° is already an appreciable advance on the 45–47° taken in by the 5 cm. lens, ultra-wide-angle lenses go considerably further still. The most popular ultra-wide-angle lenses have a focal length of 2.8 cm., with maximum apertures between f5.6 and f2.8. Such a lens is a valuable standby for technical photographers, especially for covering broad expanses in architectural photography.

For extreme angles a few manufacturers have produced lenses with a focal length of 2.1 cm., covering a 90° angle of view. Examples are the Leitz *Super Angulon* f4 and the Zeiss *Biogon* f4.5. These are decidedly specialist units and represent to date the limit of angle of view available on normal precision miniature cameras. The use of such lenses requires some care, since they are liable to give rise to a certain degree of distortion; this is not a fault of the lens design, but an inevitable result of covering such an angle on a flat negative. In practice this distortion shows itself in the "spreading" of the image near the edges of the field.

A focal length of 2.1 cm. is also beyond the limit of what it is possible to design for single-lens reflex cameras. In such cameras the space between the lens and the film is insufficient to permit the movement of the reflex mirror. One camera, the *Contarex*, gets over this problem by fitting its 2.1 cm. lens only when the mirror is raised; the screen is not then available for focusing, and a separate view-finder has to be used.

The purpose of a long-focus lens is the direct opposite of the wide-angle one: it covers a narrower angle of view, and shows the subject matter on a larger scale. The magnification of such a lens is simply its focal length divided by the standard focal length. Thus a 9 cm. lens has an effective magnification of $9/5 = 1.8$ times, a 20 cm. lens has a magnification of 4 times, and so on.

The first group of long-focus lenses—the medium long-focus units—usually have a focal length of 8.5 to 10 cm., covering an angle of 29° to 25°. Usually maximum apertures are around f2.8 to f4. This focal length is ideal for portraiture, as well as for outdoor work (candid shots from more distant viewpoints, landscapes, etc.). Such a long-focus lens is in fact the most useful second lens in a miniature camera outfit. A few 8.5 and 9 cm. lenses are also available with speeds of $f2$ or even $f1.5$, and are valuable for theatre and press photography where we have to deal with poor light conditions.

The second group of long-focus lenses usually covers units with a focal length of 13.5 cm. On most miniature cameras that represents the longest focal length that can be coupled with the camera range-finder, and it is also the longest focal length available for most cameras with interchangeable lenses mounted in front of a *diaphragm* shutter. The reason for these two limitations is that with increasing focal length the focusing movement necessary for small distance differences becomes much greater, and exceeds the accuracy with which a range-finder can focus distant subjects. In the case of diaphragm shutters the optical centre of the lens is so far forward as to risk vignetting.

In its applications the 13.5 cm. lens, with an image angle of about 19° and a magnification of 2.7 times emphasises the special points of the 9 cm. lenses. It is useful for large head portraiture, sports, and nature study. When employing a long focus lens it is essential to hold the camera very still while exposing, as the lens amplifies any shake or movement in direct proportion to its own magnification. So use a tripod whenever possible; and if the camera *must* be held in the hand, use exposures not slower than 1/125 second. On many miniatures the 13.5 cm. lens protrudes some distance in front of the camera, and may carry its own tripod bush to balance the camera and lens assembly more evenly.

With the focal lengths of 20 cm. (sometimes 18 cm.) and above we come into the realm of the extreme telephoto-lenses. These are specialist units, invaluable for really distant landscapes, long-range sports and nature photography, and similar applications. A 20 cm. lens has an angle of view of about 12° and a magnification of 4 times linear (*16* times in area)—the more comprehensive miniature camera outfits often include focal lengths up to 40 or 50 cm. Even longer focal lengths are available from specialist firms, as much as 100, and even 200 cm.—over 6 feet!

In construction, most of these units are true telephoto systems which makes them more compact than a full long-focus lens of the same focal length, but they are still so big

38

that long-range photography with them involves fitting the camera to the lens rather than the reverse! Some 100 and 200 cm. optics are "mirror lenses"; that is to say, they employ spherical mirrors (rather like astronomical telescopes) instead of, or in addition to, glass lenses.

With telephoto systems of this type, even in the more usual focal lengths of 20 to 50 cm., any form of range-finder focusing is out of the question. They are ideal with reflex cameras, since the focusing screen still indicates the correct field of view and sharpness. And since screen focusing is the only practical way of working with such lenses, special reflex housings are available even for range-finder cameras. These housings fit directly in front of the camera body, and in turn take the lens. The housing incorporates a full-size ground glass screen on which the image appears right side up, and in a size corresponding to that on the negative. A magnifier is provided on top of the reflex screen; sometimes alternative magnifiers incorporate a pentaprism system for eye-level viewing of a right-way-round image.

As these reflex housings act in a way like extension tubes, they are also useful for close-up photography at very short range (p. 309). Also, some of the medium and longer focus lenses designed normally for use directly on the camera are available in special short mounts for fitting in front of the reflex housing to provide a focusing range from infinity downwards.

CONVERTIBLE and ADJUSTABLE LENSES

AS ALREADY indicated, the range of focal lengths with a convertible lens system—i.e. where part of the optical components are permanently built in—is limited. They usually comprise, in addition to the standard lens, a wide-angle unit of 3 or 3.5 cm., and a tele unit of 7.5 to 8.5 cm.

A different approach to alternative focal lengths is now becoming popular, using lens attachments. The most obvious one is a monocular—half a binocular—mounted in front of the camera lens. The idea is not of course new, but monoculars of this type have in recent years appeared of sufficient precision to be used in this way without appreciable loss of image quality.

So-called afocal attachments, working on a similar principle, have also appeared in Japan for other focal lengths. These again simply fit in front of the camera lens, and magnify or reduce the image on the film.

Yet another innovation in this field is the variable focus lens. This is a single lens system of some complexity, which permits the focal length to be adjusted *without changing the lens*. This idea has been taken over from motion picture and television work; one of the first miniature camera variable focus or "zoom" lenses is the *Zoomar* for the *Bessamatic* and other single-lens cameras. This has a focal length range from 3.6 to 8.2 cm., with a maximum aperture of $f2.8$. Using this lens is really simple: you watch the image through the reflex finder (a reflex camera is almost indispensable for such a system) and adjust the focal length until the image appears in the desired magnification and covers the field required.

THE BEST OPTICAL OUTFIT

THERE *is* no "ideal" optical outfit in a universal sense of that word. What may best suit my needs may be far from perfect for yours. Everything depends on the particular type of work that one is most likely to do. I would, therefore, like to try to classify the needs of representative camera users, and to indicate what lens equipment seems in my experience to form the collection that will most usefully cope with the subjects likely to be met.

It is hard to find headings to embrace all types of miniature workers, but the following should serve as a guide. If one's particular interests embrace two or more of the subjects mentioned, it may involve the purchase of possibly only one additional item to give equal facility in both or all fields.

40

Advertising: as the advertising photographer is likely to be called on to illustrate almost anything, he can hardly have too comprehensive an equipment and may want almost any optical combination at any time.

Architecture: speed is seldom of serious importance; the need is for utmost definition and the possibility to reproduce the subject on almost any scale at almost any distance. Several wide-angle and long-focus lenses are thus useful.

Clinical work: speed, and the finest definition, are the two prime requisites, with the need for securing large-scale pictures of small detail at a reasonable distance. A range of long-focus lenses is thus most useful.

General snapshooting: in its most usual form, pictures at home of the family and friends, holiday souvenirs, etc., taken perhaps by a busy man who may derive little pleasure from the purely technical side of the hobby, but to whom good sharp pictures of his friends and activities are of the utmost value; his needs imply that the equipment should be simple, efficient, and sufficiently unobtrusive so as not to interfere with his other activities.

Landscape: calls for a reasonable degree of versatility, to take care of perspective; speed is of secondary importance.

Mountaineering: light weight and a choice of angles to deal with distant detail, and to include sufficient of a nearby massif seem to be the principal requirements.

Nature and animal photography will involve fast lenses for use in poor light, and long focus equipment to deal adequately with small objects or quarry at a distance.

Portraits: require a reasonably long focus lens for large heads—possibly the ability to soften definition and, of course, a good fast lens for general work.

Press photography: the skill and enthusiasm of the operator will largely govern the size of the outfit in this case; like the advertising photographer the pressman can seldom have too wide a choice at his disposal, but convenience may dictate working with a compact outfit consisting of a standard, wide-angle, and high-speed medium long-focus lens.

Record and document copying: definition and readability are the prime requisites; normal focus lenses will probably meet all needs.

Sailing and marine photography: lenses of normal and moderately long focus are useful, so is a wide angle, if pictures are taken in which part of one's own ship is included as a foreground.

Sports photography: requires fast lenses capable of the best definition, and a long focus lens is almost an essential.

Technical and industrial requirements are difficult to generalise—remarks *re* "Advertising" and "Press" largely apply.

Theatrical pictures (including photography in streets and buildings by artificial light): demand above all "speed", and a fast lens of longer focus is also valuable.

COATED (OR "BLOOMED") LENSES

THIS new development, for which extravagant claims are sometimes made, is new only in application. As long ago as 1892 it was discovered that a lens which had discoloured by exposure to the elements, passed more light than one which was colourless.

Attempts were made to create this "bloomed" condition artificially by exposing lens surfaces to the action of chemical solutions or fumes, and in at least one experiment, by depositing soap bubble films on the surface of the glass.

These early experiments confirmed that artificial blooming had certain advantages, but they could not be carried out satisfactorily on a commercial scale, and the surfaces so treated were by no means always permanent.

Because of the difficulty in producing a coating which will stand up to handling, cleaning, etc., many early "coated" lenses were treated only on their internal surfaces. But the majority of lenses now made are "hard" coated on all surfaces and are sufficiently robust to withstand *careful* cleaning by normal methods.

Just what coating or blooming does, seems to be insufficiently understood, and I think that some clarification is desirable.

When a ray of light strikes a glass surface—as in a

lens—only some 94 or 95% actually *enters* the glass, the remaining (say) 5% being reflected (the precise amount involved depending on the "refractive index" of the glass itself). When the (95%) light *emerges* from the glass a similar loss again occurs: and with a lens containing some six or eight surfaces, this loss at every successive glass-air surface ultimately reduces the amount of light that emerges to form the image, to possibly only 70% of that which reached the front surface.

Broadly speaking, light, passing from air—which has a refractive index of 1—into optical glass—the index of which may be 1.5 or 1.6—has difficulty in entering this denser medium; but by coating the surface of the glass with a transparent film of a *lower* index the light enters more easily, the amount lost by reflection is reduced, and the transmission correspondingly increased.

The gain in speed is perceptible, but it is not as great as some of the fantastic claims that one hears. It can be calculated with sufficient accuracy if the number of surfaces are known.

With optical glass in common use, a surface reflection of 5% or 6% is normally to be expected. When these glasses are coated, the amount reflected is usually only about $1\frac{1}{2}$ or 2% of the incident light; so that it will be seen that a lens with say 6 glass-air surfaces (e.g. *Elmar* or *Tessar* types) will probably transmit about 70% of the incident light normally, and about 89% when coated, representing a speed increase of about 25%.

Obviously the more glass-air surfaces a lens has, the greater the proportionate gain in speed, when they are all coated; and with a complex objective of large aperture, the gain may be considerable.

Because more light passes through the lens, and less is reflected, there is less stray light inside the lens, and consequently less wasted light to emerge in diffused and scattered form to degrade the brilliance of the negative: while similarly, "flare spots" resulting from internal reflections between the various glass surfaces, are almost eliminated; a very considerable advantage when taking pictures which include any unscreened light source.

Coating, in its modern form, consists of volatilization of a

43

mineral salt—usually magnesium fluoride, under conditions of extremely high vacuum. The film thus deposited on the glass surface is built up gradually until its thickness is one quarter of a wavelength of the light for which the maximum transmission is desired; (about four millionths of an inch). The thickness of the coat is determined by its colour, and the optimum performance is achieved when this becomes plum-purple as seen by reflected light. Little or no colour is however visible when looking *through* the lens, and coating has absolutely no adverse effect on the colour correction of the lens, or on its colour rendering. Colour transparencies made with a coated objective possess *purer* colours than when an untreated lens is used, because of the considerable reduction in scattered light.

It is worth noting that practically all the new (post-war) lenses are supplied coated in the process of manufacture.

RANGE-FINDERS

WHATEVER make of camera is involved, the basic principle of any normal range-finder is the same.

In some cameras it takes the form of a transparent mirror and another reflecting surface; the first fixed, and the second movably controlled by, and directly coupled to, a wheel inside the camera against which the back of the movable part of the lens mount bears. Adjustment of the lens thus governs the angle of the moving mirror, and when the two images reflected from these mirrors are seen to be in coincidence, the camera lens is in precisely that position that will ensure a sharp picture.

In another design the same effect is secured by two fixed reflectors, and an ingenious arrangement of two movable prisms, in front of one of them, the movement of the prisms, connected to the lens mount, bringing the two observed images together when the lens is in the right position.

Whatever the exact method applied, the result is the same; although it may take one or two different forms. In many cameras (e.g. Leica) the movable image in the range-finder has to be *superimposed* on the fixed image. In other

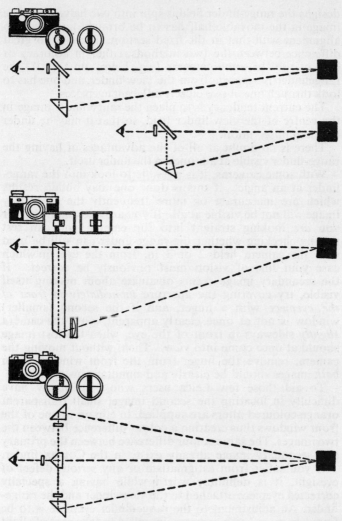

Basic differences in construction between three types of coincidence and split-field range-finders. Note how image of a flagstaff appears to the eye, before and after accurate focusing.

designs the range-finder field is split into two halves, and the image in the movable half has to be brought laterally into alignment with that in the fixed section. There is no great difference between the two methods, either in accuracy or ease of use. In some cameras (e.g. Leicas up to IIIf) the rangefinder is *separate* from the view-finder, and one has to look through one of two closely adjacent eyepieces.

The current tendency is to place the range-finder image in the centre of the view-finder field, so that it may be under constant observation.

There is no doubt at all of the advantages of having the range-finder visible at all times in the finder itself.

With some cameras, it is possible to look into the range-finder at an angle. If this is done one may obtain results which are inaccurate or more frequently the secondary image will not be visible at all. If you are uncertain whether you *are* looking straight into the camera you can test this by checking whether the range-finder can still be used with the camera held 2 or 3 in. from the eye; in which case your line of vision must obviously be correct. If the secondary image seems obstinate about making itself visible, try covering the aperture *immediately in front of the eyepiece* with a finger, and if the second (smaller) window is not at once clearly apparent, move the camera *slightly* sideways in front of the eye, when the lost image should at once come into view. Then, without moving the camera, remove the finger from the front window when *both* images should be clearly and simultaneously visible.

To aid those few Leica users who consistently have difficulty in locating the second image, small transparent orange-coloured filters are supplied, to clip on to one of the front windows thus creating a colour difference between the two images. The same colour difference between the primary and secondary image already exists in the Contax finder.

If you suffer from astigmatism or any serious defect of eyesight, it is definitely worth while having a specially corrected eyepiece attached to the view-finder and the range-finder. An adjustment to the range-finder eyepiece is to be found on most Leica cameras, intended to take care of slight variations in eyesight so that any user can set the range-finder. Some cameras have this built in. Almost everyone

46

derives some advantage from this when taking readings of very close objects at, say, between 3½ and 7 ft.

Camera users sometimes seem to be doubtful as to the accuracy of their range-finder: in most cases entirely without reason. I am frequently asked to test range-finders which are suspect; and where the user has been carrying out such tests for himself, I have generally found that he is most careful to test at distances of, for example, 4, 5, 7, and 10 ft., and a suspected discrepancy of perhaps an inch at any of these readings is almost invariably pointed out as a serious fault. With cameras such as Leica, Contax, etc., in which the range-finder mechanism is constructionally above reproach, I have, however, normally found that if the range-finder is correct at infinity (∞) it is almost invariably right throughout the whole scale. An infinity test consists of nothing more than viewing, for example, a flag-staff at say 400/500 yards with the lens pre-set at the infinity mark; when, if the range-finder *is* in perfect adjustment with that lens, the two images must appear as one. In almost every case, this may be taken as an assurance that the range-finder is correctly adjusted throughout its range. My own practice is to make an infinity test whenever I am about to take a photograph. It takes only a second or two and it leaves me entirely happy in the knowledge that my camera is right. With some instruments even a relatively small bump may have upset the range-finder without the owner knowing about it.

Focusing by range-finder hardly wants explanation, other than that already given, but if any difficulty is experienced with objects which have few pronounced features for examination, try to find a *vertical* line or edge for use when the camera is held horizontally: and *vice versa*. The separation between the images is then more obvious.

Although the coupled range-finder has done more to make the 35 mm. miniature a practical proposition than has any other single feature it is a mistake to become an absolute slave to one's range-finder, and I would urge every miniature camera user to adopt the press photographer's method of knowing what certain "set" distances look like: for example, 15 or 20 ft. It does not take very long to accustom oneself to "hit off" these distances within a very small margin of error, and while the use of a range-finder may make the photographer too conspicuous under certain circumstances, it is easy to pre-set the lens at, for the sake of argument, 15 ft. and to walk up to within that distance of one's subject and take the picture without reference to range or perhaps even the view-finder. Depth of field (see p. 66) should take care of any small error.

When photographing moving objects, it is virtually impossible to keep the object in focus all the time, but it is easy to pre-set the lens to a convenient distance that the moving object will pass; and then, viewing the object in the *range-finder* instead of the view-finder, to release the shutter at the moment the two images become one.

As already indicated, even single-lens (and one twin-lens) miniature reflex-cameras nowadays have a range-finder system built into the focusing screen. While this range-finder image is similar in appearance to that seen in a split-image range-finder, the mechanical and optical principles are entirely different. (See page 45.)

To start with, the "screen" range-finder has no moving parts at all. It consists of a pair of optical wedges let into the under side of the focusing screen, with the inclined surfaces crossing in the plane of the focusing surface. If the image from the lens is in exactly the plane of the screen surface, the view across the range-finder wedges is continuous; when the image is out of focus, it is split across the wedges with the two halves displaced. Provided the screen is accurately positioned with respect to the film plane, the range-finder is always accurate—it can never go out of adjustment. And since it uses the image formed by the camera lens, no coupling problems ever arise: the moment any interchangeable lens is mounted on the camera, it is automatically coupled with the screen range-finder.

Due to the inherent features of this system, there is no "base length" as such of the range-finder. Optically, the diameter of the lens aperture corresponds roughly to the base length of a conventional range-finder. The larger the lens aperture, the more accurate such a range-finder becomes. On stopping down, the split-image rangefinder generally becomes useless when the lens aperture becomes smaller than the length of the wedges in the screen. One or both the wedges simply go dark, with no image visible. Such screen range-finders must therefore be used at the full aperture of the camera lens—which makes pre-selector diaphragm systems almost essential.

VIEW-FINDERS

AN essential part of any miniature camera is an accurate view-finder. We have the range-finder to ensure a sharp image; the view-finder is there to define picture area. Every camera has this "built in", usually in the form of a tunnelled optical finder through the upper part of the camera body, in which the area included by the standard 5 cm. lens is clearly indicated. Although this finder is usually quite small, the image which is seen through a negative lens is crystal clear, and there is little or no difficulty in determining exactly what will be in the picture.

Most modern optical finders show the image in almost full visual size (i.e. on the same scale as seen by the unaided eye). In addition, the actual subject field recorded on the film is outlined by a brilliant reflected frame apparently suspended in space. Known variously as brilliant-frame, bright-line frame, or crystal-frame finders, these systems are more accurate than the simpler optical finders. The brilliant frame has two advantages. Firstly, the finder shows something of the surroundings outside the subject field itself—useful when dealing with moving subjects which can be observed before they actually enter the field of view of the camera. Secondly, the bright frame is only fully visible when the eye is correctly centred behind the finder eyepiece. Without such a frame, incorrect sighting can show an incorrect view; with the frame you are sure of correct viewing whenever you see the whole of the frame.

The brilliant-frame finder is a present-day version of the *Albada* view-finder.

With any form of view-finder, the question of parallax has to be considered. Put into plain English, this means the degree of error that exists between what the camera lens sees and what the finder shows. Because the finder may be placed at a distance of perhaps 1½ or 2 in. from

49

the centre of the taking lens, its view must somewhat differ from that seen by the camera itself. In many earlier miniature cameras, the danger of parallax is ignored by the finder built into the camera, and the user of one of these instruments will be well advised to remember this when taking pictures of *very* close-up objects—say between 3 and 5 ft. distant. If, for example, the head of a portrait is required to be large in the picture, allowance should be made for the fact that the finder is a trifle high and to the left in relation to the taking lens, and if it is desired to ensure the tip of the sitter's nose being absolutely central in the final picture it would be necessary to aim so as to have the sitter's right eye approximately in the centre of the finder of the horizontally held camera. This may sound complicated, but in actual practice one makes such trivial allowances almost automatically as soon as one is accustomed to the general handling of the camera itself.

Brilliant-frame view-finders often incorporate parallax correction marks. These may take the form of several short lines near the top of the reflected frame. To allow for near objects, you simply imagine a line joining these marks across the field of view. This imaginary line then marks the *upper* limit of the finder field for subjects 3 to 6 feet away.

Occasionally there may be parallax correction marks near one edge of the finder field as well; that will usually be the case where the finder is displaced *sideways* relative to the lens axis, as well as being above it.

A few miniature cameras feature automatic parallax correction. In this case the mask that produces the image of the brilliant frame is movable. Its movement is linked to the focusing mechanism of the lens, so that the brilliant frame automatically slides downwards as the lens focuses on near subjects. That eliminates all need for estimation and separate correction.

Directly the 5 cm. lens of the camera is removed and a wide-angle or long-focus lens substituted the normal camera view-finder ceases to have any useful function, and a separate view-finder has to be substituted. A number of such finders are available, some catering for certain specific focal lengths, and others for the whole range of lenses provided for a particular camera. The latter type is usually called a

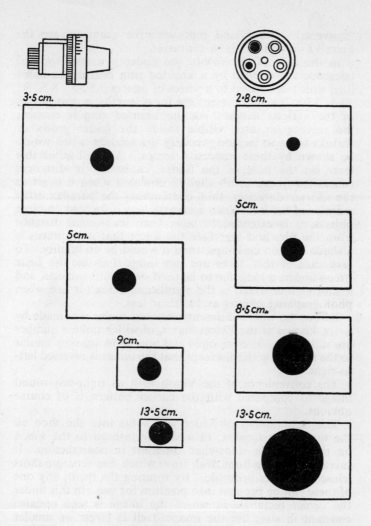

3·5 cm.

2·8 cm.

5 cm.

5cm.

9 cm.

8·5 cm.

13·5 cm.

13·5 cm.

Difference in view given by adjustable-frame (left) and adjustable-focus (right) variable view-finders. With the first, image size remains constant and field grows or shrinks to show what lens will include. With the second, field remains the same but image is large or small according to lens used.

"universal" finder, and representative examples are the Leitz *Viooh* and the Zeiss *Universal*.

In the case of the Viooh, the finder is a small optical telescope surrounded by a knurled ring bearing an index line, which can be set to a series of figures 3.5., 5., 8.5., 9., 10.5., 13.5. These represent the focal lengths in centimetres of the various lenses. As the knurled ring is rotated, the rectangular area visible inside the finder grows or shrinks so as to include precisely the amount which would be shown by these respective lenses. A small adjustable lever on the base of the finder, calibrated in distances causes the finder to tilt slightly downhill when it is set to the shorter distances, thus overcoming the parallax error mentioned before. When a camera lens is focused on close objects, it is extended to *more* than its normal distance from the film and therefore the angle that it embraces is a shade less, on close-ups, than it would be on infinity. To take care of this, there are *two* index lines on the Leitz *Viooh* finder, a long line to be used on distant subjects, and a shorter line which is the significant index for use when photographing objects at 13 ft. or less.

Before the war, a different universal finder was made by Leitz, known as the *Vidom* finder, of which quite a number are still about. The principle and operation are very similar to the modern version, except that the image is reversed left-to-right.

The convenience of the Viooh with its right-way-round image as compared with the earlier pattern is of course obvious.

The Zeiss *Universal* finder which fits into the shoe on the top of the Contax, in a similar fashion to the *Viooh* on the Leica, is somewhat different in construction. It carries a rotating front disc, from which five separate short telescopic lenses protrude. By rotating the front, any one of these can be brought into position for use. In this finder the *actual* rectangle in which the image is seen remains constant in size; but the image itself is larger or smaller according to which of the telescopes is brought into position; thus the *area* included varies with the setting of the finder, although the size of the aperture remains constant. Parallax figures are engraved on the rotating disc for each of these lenses. The standard focal lengths catered for by this finder are 2.8, 5, 8.5, 13.5 and 18 cm. (while a special finder has also been made with 3.5 cm. in place of 18). The Universal finder is necessarily more bulky than the Vidom, but it offers the considerable advantage that, with the size of the image varying while the aperture remains constant, the user gets a much larger and clearer idea of the picture.

Certain variable focus finders work on the *zoom* lens principle; movement of one of the lens elements along the lens axis changes the angle of view.

For general sports photography Leitz also produces a folding metal frame finder which by an ingenious and simple adjustment caters for 5, 9, and 13.5 cm. lenses. This particular pattern of finder has many adherents because it serves to bound one's vision only, and allows the user to look at the object *itself* rather than at a diminished reflection of it. Parallax adjustment is also provided.

On a number of modern cameras the built-in view-finder caters for several alternative lenses. In its simplest version such a multiple finder carries not one, but two or three reflected image frames for the standard, wide-angle, and long-focus lens respectively. Usually the alternative finder frames cover the most frequently used interchangeable lenses. With these lenses, therefore, no supplementary finder is required.

One or two other multi-lens miniature cameras, take this idea a step further. A selector or other control brings only *one* of the alternative finder frames into view. This avoids the confusion of having to watch the image through several frames at the same time. On the Leica M2 and M3 models this finder control is further linked mechanically to the lens mount, so that on insertion of the alternative lenses the correct finder frame automatically comes into view. In addition a finder frame selector can also be used to make any frame visible at will. This is useful for checking the field taken in by the different lenses, before you make up your mind which lens to use for a particular subject.

Naturally, the built-in multiple frame finder can only cover about three focal lengths at a time. With more frames, the view through the finder becomes really confusing. For the less frequently used lenses, separate finders are therefore generally available.

53

None of these view-finder problems arise, of course, with miniature single-lens reflex cameras. The screen image invariably shows the correct view—free from parallax—irrespective of the focal length of the lens or of the subject-distance. This is particularly practical with very long focal lengths, and several camera firms produce special reflex housings or attachments for range-finder miniatures. Such a reflex housing fits in front of the camera body in the same way as the lens, and in turn takes the lens itself. Examples are the Leitz *Visoflex* units and the Zeiss *Panphot*.

In addition to their use with long-focus lenses, these reflex housings are also a great boon for close-up photography with normal lenses. They are less suitable for photography at normal distances, since the depth of the reflex housing extends the standard lens too far. Even long-focus lenses often have to be fitted in special short barrels instead of their standard focusing barrel for rangefinder use.

SIMPLIFIED 35 mm. CAMERAS

SO FAR we have confined our remarks to 35 mm. cameras with interchangeable lenses and range-finder or reflex focusing.

The difference between top class and simplified 35 mm. cameras is primarily one of optical equipment. Simplification of the optical equipment quite naturally leads to applying less rigid standards to the construction of the camera. Consequently these cameras will have to be handled—if possible, even more carefully—as far as ensuring best definition, i.e. focusing, is concerned—provided that we aim at a similar quality.

These instruments fall into three main classes: those fitted with coupled range-finder; those focused by reflex methods; and those with focusing by scale (or with a separate range-finder used to measure the distance).

The manipulation of such models is in the main the same as that required with the instruments already described, except that, because the camera has only one lens, the user must necessarily devote more thought and perhaps skill to such matters as the ever-present need of making the picture fill the frame area so far as may be possible to avoid the need for excessive enlargement later on. There may be occasions when he will miss a picture that would be available to the owner of an extensive outfit; but the care that has to be exercised in making the single lens camera do the more difficult tasks has a very salutary effect on one's technical skill, and successful accomplishment of some of the more knotty problems produces a very satisfying sense of personal achievement. Because the user of such a camera has only one lens at his disposal, he generally becomes efficient in matters of manipulation more speedily than the owner of a more extensive kit, and for the same reason is frequently "quicker on the draw"— a matter of some importance to anybody desirous of making the most of his 35's potentialities.

With the more simple models focusing is usually accomplished by rotating the front lens cell, the periphery of which carries the usual engraved distances from infinity down to some 3 or $3\frac{1}{2}$ ft. or their metric equivalents. As we are dealing with a short focus lens—usually 2 in. (5 cm.)— the inherent depth of field (see p. 66) is very considerable and, even if focusing is carried out solely by estimation of distance, it usually will be found that the depth of good definition at moderate apertures is sufficient to cover up any slight inaccuracies on the part of the user. If, however, the lens is used at its full opening of e.g. $f\,3.5$ or $f\,2.8$, the use of a pocket range-finder will be well worth while, as at close distances, say under 10 ft., focusing does require some exactitude. At the risk of mentioning the obvious: it is desirable that the range-finder should be calibrated in the same system—feet or metres—as the camera itself, otherwise so much time will be wasted on the necessary conversion that the picture will probably be lost altogether by the time the camera is correctly set.

With an instrument of this type, time can profitably be spent in learning to estimate a series of set distances with something approaching accuracy. One cannot recommend actual distances as different models bear different scales, but 2, 3, 7 and 10 metres (or 5, 10, 20, 30 ft.) are convenient to take care of most subjects. A little practice—without a camera—will soon make the user considerably more certain of himself in this respect. Such practice can be carried out at any time and anywhere. Walking to the station in the morning, one can select a tree, a figure, or the edge of a building, and stop momentarily when at an estimated distance of, say, 20 ft. Then by pacing out the distance as one's journey is continued it is easy to see how near the estimate is to the measured distance. Similar tests can be carried out unobtrusively almost anywhere and with no danger of missing the train. By working with a few set distances in this way and really getting to know what they look like, one can become reasonably sure of one's ability to judge *these* distances, at least, with certainty; and by arranging to have the subject at one or other of the practised standards sharply defined pictures can be expected.

Most of these cameras are fitted with a depth of field scale (see p. 66). This should constantly be consulted, as by its aid one can ascertain the most suitable lens apertures and distances at which to focus so as to ensure adequately sharp definition over all the planes which are required to be sharp in the final result. Even if the estimate of distance is only approximately correct, the scale will show that there is appreciable latitude either side of the point of sharpest focus at any moderate lens aperture.

The better class single lens models are generally fitted with a coupled range-finder similar in type to that found on the more expensive cameras (p. 44). The actual *method* of focusing varies with different cameras, but is usually accomplished by turning a dial or knob on the camera body, or by a lever or other projection on the lens mount. All these range-finders employ the coincidence principle in one form or another—the images in some models being brought into alignment, while others require that the two images be superimposed.

The majority of these cameras are designed to accommodate 36-exposure cartridges of film (p. 60). Reloadable cassettes are not generally available. An exception is found in the old *Agfa Karat*, which used 12-exposure films marketed in a special cartridge, the film travelling from a supply cartridge into an empty one, where it is wound up by being pushed into the container. The more orthodox arrangement is for the film to be taken up on a spool (often an integral part of the camera); after exposure the complete film is rewound into the cartridge for removal from the camera. The *Robot* employs two reloadable chargers.

Almost all cameras of this class are fitted with the "Compur" type, or similar between-lens shutters, with speeds usually ranging from 1 to 1/500 second. Such shutters have the advantages of being extremely quiet and having a very good range of accurate slow speeds.

These comparatively simpler cameras, too, are involved to an increasing extent in the trend towards automation. But there is a subtle difference: with simple cameras exposure automation provides a means of making them even simpler—and, unhappily, less versatile.

In recent times, exposure automation of such cameras has followed two or three distinct lines. The first, at any rate chronologically, is the normal coupled exposure meter. Most exposure meters built into present-day cameras use a "setting-marker" system. The meter needle moves across a scale according to the light falling on the cell. Taking a reading then involves bringing a second movable pointer into alignment with the position of the meter needle. This movable pointer or setting marker is controlled by a ring or other device. With a coupled exposure meter this control is simply linked to the aperture and/or shutter speed setting ring. After pre-selecting a suitable shutter speed (according to the subject movement) the action of superimposing the setting marker with the meter needle automatically sets the correct aperture for the prevailing light conditions.

This system, identical with that found on many high-class cameras, was regarded as a little too confusing for the beginner. He still has to make up his mind as to the shutter speed to use, and he can select alternative aperture-speed combinations—being faced at the same time with the difficulty of making a choice.

So the first step of simplification was the scale-less shutter —a typical one being the Prontormat. Instead of carrying separate controls for the aperture and shutter speed adjustment, this shutter has a ring which selects *both* the aperture and the shutter speed. Movement of this ring alternately changes the aperture and the speed. The combination for the longest exposure might, for example, be 1/30 second at $f2.8$, then comes 1/30 second at $f4$, 1/60 second at $f4$, 1/60 second at $f5.6$, 1/125 second at $f5.6$, and so on up to 1/300 (or 1/500) second at $f22$. The ring is coupled to the setting pointer of the exposure meter as before; by taking a reading you simply set the aperture-speed combination provided for that particular exposure level.

This system is simple because the photographer does not have to worry about choosing a combination—in fact he has no choice. He cannot, for example, use an exposure of 1/125 second at $f2.8$. The slowest shutter speed is 1/30 second—enough for a sharp picture if the camera is steady.

The next step of automation concerned itself with eliminating the need for manipulating the setting ring at all. The setting operation was thus incorporated in the release button. On cameras of this type the meter needle often is not visible at all. The position of the meter needle instead serves as a mechanical stop for a programming mechanism inside the shutter. Taking a meter reading now only consists of pointing the camera with the meter at the subject, and pressing the release button. The latter locks the needle in position, releases the mechanism which selects the aperture-speed combination, and finally releases the shutter.

The moving force behind camera automation appears not so much to make life easier for the photographer who has been used to conventional camera systems of the previous generation, but to attract new enthusiasts. Such cameras are thus aimed at people who ten or twenty years ago might have bought a box camera, or no camera at all.

That is not to say that the simple 35 mm. camera is a toy. Today it has become a precision instrument almost equal in quality to much more expensive cameras of a generation ago. New types of optical glass have led to lenses that combine simple (and therefore low-price) design with quite adequate performance. And despite (or perhaps because of) modern mass-production methods the accuracy of such items as the film track and focusing movement is high enough to utilize the optical performance to the full.

HOLDING THE CAMERA

IF you are new to a 35 mm. camera you should spend the first few days of ownership handling it as much as you can, going over it in detail with the instruction book and familiarising yourself with every feature of its operation until you can manage the instrument literally blind-folded. Having acquired a new toy everyone experiences the natural desire to play with it immediately; but far better results will be more quickly obtained by the man who is patient enough to master the manipulation of his camera before even attempting to load it with film.

A point to bear in mind is that because a miniature camera *is* small, it is difficult to hold steady. According to the type of instrument chosen the best hold differs, but individual preference will naturally have some bearing on the matter. The crux of the problem is to adopt a hold which is perfectly firm, while at the same time the body and particularly the arms and hands are reasonably relaxed. In addition, when one is giving a relatively slow exposure—and in the case of miniature cameras anything under 1/50th or 1/60th of a second *is* slow—I always find that the camera can be held still more easily if the exposure takes place immediately *after* emptying the lungs of air.

With a Leica or Contax one can generally steady the camera by jamming the left hand corner of the instrument simultaneously against the side of the nose and the underneath of the bone at the base of the forehead. If the instrument is to be held for a vertical picture, one will have to choose whether to steady it against the forehead with the right hand end of the camera uppermost, working the shutter with the forefinger; or whether to hold the camera down the side of the face for support, in which case the shutter can be fired more easily with the thumb of the right-hand while the fingers of the same hand offer a supporting resistance on the base of the camera.

Latterly I have adopted a method of steadying the camera, which I think deserves publicity as it is so effective. The camera in its Ever-Ready case lies on my right side with the strap over my head and on my left shoulder. When taking a picture I grasp the rear part of the strap with my right hand and pull it forward from under the right arm until the camera is drawn up to my face by the pull of the strap over the left shoulder. When the camera (held in the left hand) is close to my face, I bring the right arm down close to my side, so as to hold the strap firmly between upper arm and body. Then, by leaning my *head* slightly forward I press the camera away from me until the resistance of the left-hand strap is felt. This strap supports the camera directly from the *shoulders*, and it is only necessary for the hands to *hold* the camera in position; there is no need to grasp the instrument tightly. It will be found that by this method relatively slow exposures can safely be given. (See p. 81.)

Although I have described this in relation to the Leica, the method applies to almost every camera in an Ever-Ready case.

A further point to bear in mind is that if the camera is in an Ever-Ready case one must adopt a hold which definitely ensures that the flap and the lid of the case are well out of the way; quite a number of vertical pictures have been spoiled by the securing flap being allowed to float round in front of the lens at the moment of exposure, without the photographer being in the least aware that this was happening. The lid and flap can generally be kept out of the way quite easily if they are put under the control of the little finger of the right or left hand.

If the lens is in a collapsible mount, make sure that this is pulled out and screwed to the right until it is not possible to pull or screw any further. A good many unsharp pictures have also resulted from inattention to this detail.

LOADING

SENSITIVE material for use in 35 mm. cameras is generally available in three forms.

Daylight loading cartridges of 36 exposures—suitable for all cameras, these are intended to be discarded once used, but with care they can be refilled if desired.

Darkroom loading refills of 36 exposures—already trimmed to shape at each end for attachment to the centre spools of the "reloadable cassettes" made by Leitz and Zeiss for their respective cameras. Replicas of these reloadable cassettes for the Leica and Contax are now made in Britain, as also is a reloadable, opening and closing cassette suitable for Retina and many similar cameras.

Bulk packings of 5, 10, 15 metres, etc.: from which any desired length can be cut and loaded into cassettes.

Daylight loading refills are lengths of 36-exposure film wound up on a spool, and sealed with black paper. These are ready to load into a cassette (not directly into the camera) in ordinary light. For loading, the paper seal is broken, the spool inserted into the cassette (taking care not to let the film unwind) with the paper leader protruding through the slit. After closing the cassette, the black paper can be pulled out until it brings the beginning of the film with it. The loaded cassette is then loaded into the camera in the normal way.

The daylight loading cartridges are most convenient, apart from the question of price. Refilling cassettes or cartridges from bulk film is, of course, cheaper though it means work. In this case the reloadable "cassettes" mentioned are to be preferred to the ordinary cartridge as they are designed so that they open when inside the camera, allowing film to pass in, or out, without risk of surface scratching.

In loading any container, in the darkroom, great care should be taken to avoid touching the surface of the film. Film is unbelievably sensitive to abrasion, and to fingerprints. *Handle it only by the edges.* Allow it to slide gently through the fingers, and while turning the spool see that the film winds firmly and evenly on it, so that there is no occasion to "cinch" the film to tighten it. This is the most common cause of scratches along the strip.

The end of the film has to be cut to a shape which will suit the spool—generally to a point, but the exact shape varies with different spools. Experiment with a scrap of waste film will indicate the best trim. If the spool is one where the film is clipped under a flat strap of metal, make a point of folding back the extreme tip of film that protrudes, and creasing it *flat* with the thumbnail, to prevent it pulling adrift if you inadvertently try to take more than 36 exposures on the strip.

The action of inserting the film into the camera varies in different models: but the basic principles are the same in all. The important things to observe are: that there is just enough film available to attach to the take-up spool and reach along the camera back without an excess of slack—that the perforated edge engages the sprocket that will propel it through the instrument—and that the film end is properly secured to the take-up spool and so aligned that it will wind up accurately thereon, without riding up either of the spool flanges when the spool is turned. Given these three essentials, there should be no trouble.

In the case of the Leica, I would mention one very important point; that is, that along the lower edge of the film, where it is cut away, *not more than two* perforations should be outside the film container at the moment when the film is being inserted into the camera. If more than two holes protrude, small pieces of film may break off and damage the shutter.

The user of any camera with a removable back should bear in mind that when the film has been loaded and the back of the instrument has to be replaced, this should be done by *placing* the back in position on top of the film in as near the closed position as it will go, and then sliding it gently home the necessary remaining distance; it should not be slid into position all the way from the edge of the camera, as by doing this the edge of the film itself is almost certain to be fouled and the film pushed out of place with possible subsequent complications.

In learning to load the camera, I would again stress the desirability of practising until this can be done in the dark. Get a length of waste film and load it into a cassette or cartridge of the type that will be used and load and unload the camera with it until familiar with everything that can possibly happen. Having then loaded the camera with a waste film, some time can profitably be spent in going through the motions of taking all sorts of imaginary pictures.

At the very outset a routine should be adopted and later followed, so that it becomes second nature.

SHOOTING

ALTHOUGH there is no special merit in doing the various preparatory jobs in any particular order, to follow a definite sequence is advisable, so that no detail is missed however unexpectedly the camera is called into use. My own routine is: (1) select subject, (2) examine it through view-finder to see whether normal lens is suitable or change of lens is desirable, (3) remove lens cap, and set lens to "infinity", (4) fit lens hood, (5) decide shutter speed and stop to be used, (6) wind shutter, set lens aperture, set (or verify) shutter speed, (7) focus, (8) compose picture in finder, (9) expose. It sounds a lot, but it takes less time to do than it does to read about it.

I generally carry my camera set at $f6.3$ and $1/100$ second, or at $f5.6$ and $1/125$ second; and I am thus ready for the majority of ordinary outdoor snapshots.

If the front of the Ever-Ready case is large enough, it sometimes is possible to carry the camera with the lens extended and pre-set (see p. 77). In this way the instrument is, literally, ready for instant use.

Pressing the button which seems the simplest of all tasks must, in fact, be learned. Anyone who has fired a rifle knows how essential it is to *squeeze* the trigger—and not to pull it. Similarly with any miniature it is vitally necessary to squeeze the release button, for the same reason. Most 35 mm. cameras can be held so that the soft fleshy part at the base of the thumb supports the camera body against the pressure of the forefinger on the release button.

On the Leica the finger should be lying across the winding knob, so that the first joint only flexes to press the button.

On other cameras the finger similarly can rest on the edge of the winding knob and rock over on to the release button.

To ensure satisfactory 35 mm. pictures one *must*, above all, hold the camera still at the moment of exposure—I make no apology for this reiteration—it is the groundwork of success.

Remember—it does *not* matter how slowly the button is pressed. The exposure is determined *solely* by the speed setting knob. Try to release the shutter slowly and gently using the hold described on page 59.

A LENS HOOD is perhaps our simplest and most essential accessory. It is a fitting which will always improve optical conditions and thus contribute to the betterment of the picture, but never the reverse. The hood, which may be of a circular and sometimes rectangular shape, clips on to the outside of the lens.

The first and principal use of a lens hood is that of a sunshade. How often have you noticed when driving a car into the sun that you can scarcely see the road and traffic through the glass of the windscreen? The film experiences just the same difficulty in seeing and recording the image, when the sun shines across the front glass surface of the lens. This is why beginners books used to say "Keep the sun behind you when exposing". To do this is, of course, to debar oneself from many of the most attractively lit subjects. But if one translates the instruction into "Make sure the sun does not shine *on* your lens by using a lens-hood", safe conditions will be achieved, and one can still work at a practically unlimited range of angles in relation to the sun.

A particular effect of the sun (or any bright light) shining on or across the lens, is to produce flare spots—those irregular, sometimes geometrically-shaped patches of light that appear now and again on pictures taken facing the source of light. These flare spots are the result of the splash of light on the outer element of the lens being reflected (often, several times) between the glass surfaces of the lens itself, until eventually an image of the light patch is thrown on to the film. Lenses vary in their susceptibility to flare, but it *can* occur with every compound lens under the conditions described. A lens hood, again, will minimise the chance of this fault. (See p. 261.)

Now let us consider, for a moment, what is going on inside the camera when an exposure is made. The lens, which has a circular aperture, is passing a circular cone of light into the camera body. A portion of that bright cone—that which forms the picture—is falling on to the front of the shutter blind, and will, as soon as the latter opens, impress itself, i.e. the image of the subject, on the film. In order that the rectangular piece of film shall receive practically the same amount of light all over, the cone of light must necessarily be larger in diameter than the diagonal measurement of this rectangle; and because of the optical difficulties of limiting the size of this cone, and at the same time providing the essentials of speed and superfine definition at the edges of the picture, the cone is usually considerably larger than that required to form the actual image. Now if the whole of this cone be allowed to enter the camera, quite an amount of the light which is not necessary for forming the image on the film will strike the internal surfaces of the camera body itself, and no matter how carefully the manufacturer has blackened the interior, much of this excess light will be diffused and reflected so that it will also reach the film the moment the shutter is opened. This will occur to some extent irrespective of whether the sun is shining or not, and whether the picture is taken facing the source of light or with the sun behind the camera. Any such incidental light reaching the film will fog or at the least degrade the resulting negative to some extent, usually causing it to produce a considerably less brilliant picture than would be the case if the excess light were eliminated. It is for this reason that some of the best lens hoods are made of rectangular shape or are fitted with a rectangular mask, so that the cone of light *entering* the lens is limited to just what is required to form the image and no more. Thus, after passing through the lens, the light cone is still more or less controlled in shape and thus does not reach surfaces from which it can scatter inside the camera body.

If you habitually use the maker's recommended lens hood, you will secure as much protection as is necessary, without the risk of cutting off some of the picture, which is bound to occur if too long a hood is used. The first sign of such cut-off is a darkening in the four corners of the print. To avoid this, care must be used with hoods of the extendable type, which must be set exactly as directed for the particular lens in use; while due allowance should be made for the thickness of a filter mount when used with an extensible hood.

ONE of the greatest advantages which the 35 mm. camera gives to its user is the possibility of using lens apertures of such size as would be unthinkable with larger instruments. The explanation of this can be found in the many favourable conditions created by the 35 mm. camera as far as depth of field (often known as depth of focus) is concerned.

Depth of field, i.e., the simultaneous definition of both comparatively near and distant objects with a sufficient degree of sharpness, is an optical function primarily dependent on the aperture of a lens and its focal length.

The shorter the focus of the lens, the greater will the depth be, at any given aperture; and the *smaller the aperture the greater will the depth be* for any given focal length.

Very broadly, the depth of field of any lens has a direct relation to the actual physical size of the stop or aperture used, so that a 4 in. lens used at f 8 (aperture diameter approximately $\frac{1}{2}$ in.) has the same depth as, say, an 8 in. lens used also with an aperture of $\frac{1}{2}$ in. diameter which would be f 16. Taking it a step further, our normal focus, 5 cm. (2 in.) lens, could be used at f 4 without sacrifice of the depth of field that the 8 in. lens would furnish at f 16.

Now, what is a *normal* focal length depends on the size of the negative. The larger its diagonal, the longer the focal length we need under average conditions. The miniature negative asks for a comparatively short focal length. This fact has made it possible to *use* apertures of f 2 and even f 1.5 on 35 mm. instruments while still securing sharpness over a series of planes adequate to ordinary needs.

There is, however, another side to this question. It must be borne in mind when comparing 35 mm. pictures with those taken with larger equipment that the negatives on 35 mm. film measure only $1\frac{1}{2} \times 1$ in., while the 8 in. lens mentioned is possibly being used with a $6\frac{1}{2}'' \times 4\frac{3}{4}''$ film. Thus for any given size of final enlargement the miniature negative will require to be enlarged rather *more than four times as much* to produce the same result, and in this extra degree of enlargement some of the depth of field will again disappear, as obviously by enlarging the picture we shall

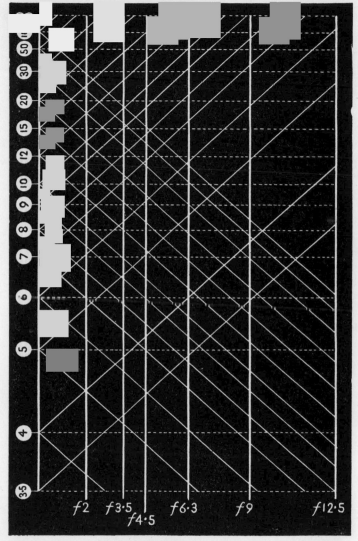

f2 f3·5 f6·3 f9 f12·5
f4·5

Depth of field chart in feet for all 28 mm. lenses. Find focused distance on left side. Follow along diagonal lines until they intersect vertical aperture (f) line. Read limits of depth on left-hand line opposite these points.

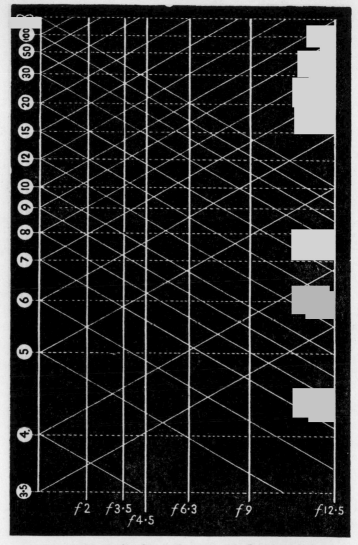

Depth of field chart in feet for all 35 mm. lenses. Find focused distance on left side. Follow along diagonal lines until they intersect vertical aperture (f) line. Read limits of depth on left-hand line opposite these points.

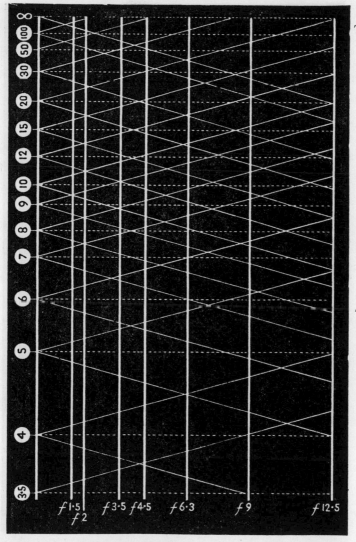

Depth of field chart in feet for all 50 mm. lenses. Find focused distance on left side. Follow along diagonal lines until they intersect vertical aperture (f) line. Read limits of depth on left-hand line opposite these points.

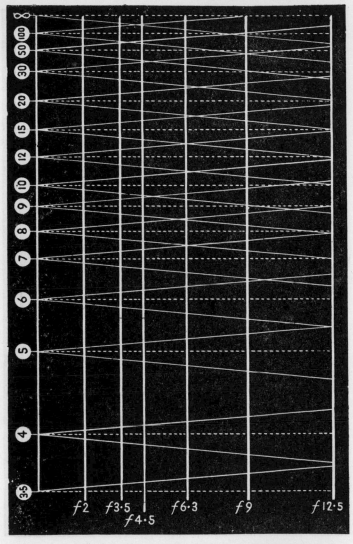

Depth of field chart in feet for all 90 mm. lenses. Find focused distance on left side. Follow along diagonal lines until they intersect vertical aperture (f) line. Read limits of depth on left-hand line opposite these points.

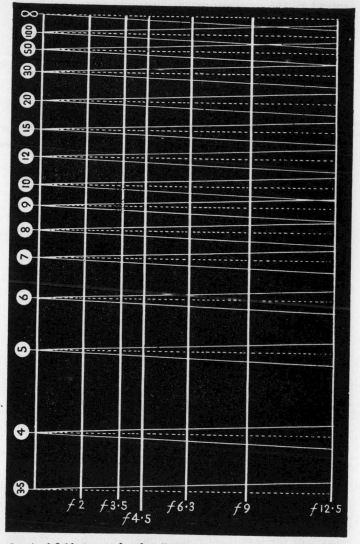

Depth of field chart in feet for all 135 mm. lenses. Find focused distance on left side. Follow along diagonal lines until they intersect vertical aperture (f) line. Read limits of depth on left-hand line opposite these points.

spread all the elements: details, lines and points—of which it consists.

What we call depth of field is, after all, really the extent of *satisfactory* definition. Now, every lens will yield an image of a point of light as a dot on the film when the lens is accurately focused on that point. If the light point be moved nearer to or farther away from, the camera, its image will cease to be a *sharp* dot, and will become gradually a larger spot (unless the focusing of the lens be altered to correspond). A purely arbitrary figure has been accepted by most manufacturers and photographers as to the maximum size that this spot may be in order to qualify for the term sharp. While in the case of really large cameras that spot or *circle of confusion*, as the technical term goes, can be accepted as sharp, provided that it does not exceed 1/100 in. diameter, most users of the more popular plate and film cameras have adopted 1/250 in. as a limit, while the 35 mm. camera makers had to set a *much* higher standard. So unless one point of light is recorded on the miniature film as a dot measuring less than 1/750 in. diameter, it is not accepted as sharp. Through adherence to this higher standard the miniature camera can compete on more or less level terms with its larger competitors, even after the pictures are enlarged.

DEPTH FOCUSING IN PRACTICE

IT IS worth bearing in mind that the depth of field at any given setting is always considerably greater *behind* the object focused on, than it is in front of it. For this reason it is a very safe rule to focus by range-finder on an object about one-third of the way through the depth of the subject, so as to ensure that the area of good definition is distributed more or less evenly over the whole. Reference to the "depth scale" of the lens is, of course, most advisable, if there is

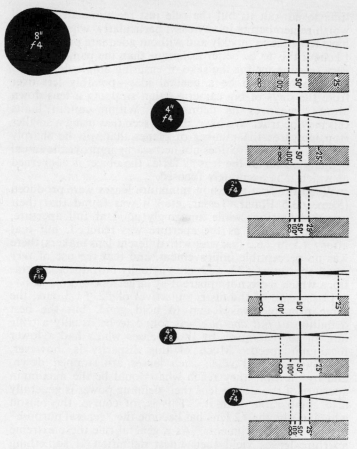

Extent of depth of field each side of focal plane is governed by diameter of "circle of confusion" (blunt end of black triangle). This covers very little in the case of an 8 in. lens, but a considerably greater range when a 2 in. lens is used at the same aperture. See respective focusing scales (upper group of diagrams).

It is necessary to stop down the long focus lens of a large camera to a considerable extent to secure the same depth of field as is available with a 2 in. standard lens of the miniature (lower group of diagrams). Therefore users of the 8 in. lens need to give 16 times the exposure of the 2 in. to secure the same depth.

35 mm.—E   73

time to consult it: but the rule just recommended is well worth remembering in any case; particularly, when pictures have to be taken quickly and without adequate preparation. I believe this to be better technique than the panicky use of very small stops for the sake of ensuring ample depth.

There seems to be a general idea—possibly left over from the days of big cameras—that stopping a lens down always improves its definition. Within certain limits this may be true. We have already seen that using a smaller stop increases the number of planes that will be sharply defined, but doing so does not necessarily improve the actual defining power of the lens as far as the object is concerned at which it is accurately focused.

When the first precision miniature lenses were produced (5 cm. f3.5 Elmar, Tessar, etc.) it was found that their actual definition, while amazingly good at full aperture, improved *slightly* as the aperture was reduced; but that after f4.5 or f6.3 (varying with different lens makers) there was no perceptible improvement, and that the use of *very* small apertures (f22, f32, etc.) actually introduced aberrations which were not apparent at larger openings.

In the case of the faster objectives of f2, f1.5, etc., the same principle was found to hold good, but the best definition *at full aperture* was found to be usually a trifle inferior to that given by those lenses which had a lower maximum speed. Much of this disparity is, however, quickly recovered when such lenses are stopped down, and by the time they reach what would be the maximum aperture of the slower lens their defining power is generally also comparable with it. This is, of course, the reason why, latterly, the f2 lens has become the "general purpose" lens on such instruments. As a general rule these extreme aperture lenses yield their finest definition at something between f4 and f6.3 according to type. If there *is* any drawback to a fast lens, I fancy that it lies rather in the fact that such objectives are a trifle more prone to flare (see p. 64, and picture p. 261) than those of more modest speed.

It has always been a source of wonderment to me that the *depth of field scale* with which almost every pedigree miniature camera lens is equipped, is not more generally and more intelligently used. The only criticism of the

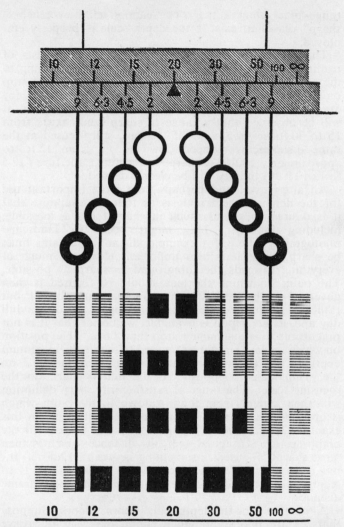

This is how the depth of field ring works. The smaller the stop left and right from the arrowhead (triangular mark) set against the focusing distance the larger the area which is sharply defined.

75

range-finder camera that "one cannot tell how much is sharp" ceases to exist if the depth scale is properly employed.

The basic use of the depth of field scale consists of reading off the extent of sharpness available according to the aperture used, opposite the figures denoting that stop on either side of the distance actually focused on. If, for example, the lens is focused on an object 20 ft. away, it will be observed that a range of sharp focus exists from 15 to 30 ft. at f 4.5, while if the lens, still focused at the same distance, is stopped down to f 9, from 12 ft. to approximately 100 ft. is sharp, and again at aperture f 12.5 from 10 ft. to infinity will be clearly defined.

An alternative, and perhaps even more important use for the depth of field scale is as follows. Suppose that it is desired to get as much in sharp focus as possible, including infinity. This might occur in landscape photography where, for example, distant mountains must be sharp, while it is also important to get as much of everything towards the foreground as sharp as possible. The point on which the lens should be focused is then governed not by the distance of any particular object, but rather by the practicable aperture. Suppose that it is a dull day and, as no tripod is available, we decide that it is not practicable to use a smaller stop than f 6.3. The position on which the lens should be focused to secure the maximum depth at this aperture is one in which the figure 6.3 on the *depth* scale is opposite to the infinity mark on the focusing scale. The range of satisfactorily sharp definition will then extend from infinity down to the point which is opposite the other 6.3 mark on the depth scale, in this example 20 ft., using a 5 cm. lens, as will be seen in the graph, p. 69. In actual fact, the distance which is then most sharply focused is something between 30 and 50 ft.; but this is of no consequence, as our only concern is to secure the greatest possible depth *including* the extreme distance.

Another use for the depth scale occurs indoors. Suppose that we are photographing a room and wish to secure sharp focus over all the furniture. The most distant object is, perhaps, 20 ft. away and the nearest perhaps 7 ft. The question is: on what point shall we focus? And then: what stop must we use? The answer to the first question is secured by setting the lens so that the focusing index points to a position midway between the 20 ft. and the 7 ft. marks on the scale itself: this is 10 ft. The stop to be used is the one which can be read opposite the 20 ft. and the 7 ft. respectively, in this case f 12.5.

Several modern cameras have an automatic depth of field indicator consisting of two pointers moving across the distance scale. Being coupled to the aperture control, the pointers automatically indicate the depth of the sharp zone at all stops.

Making use of the maximum depth offered by miniature lenses without sacrificing more of their exceptional speed than absolutely necessary, is one of the secrets of good photography with the range-finder camera. Exploiting the possibilities offered by a wide choice of focal length and thus influencing size and perspective is another, but first it seems necessary sufficiently to understand just what these possibilities are.

PERSPECTIVE, VIEWPOINT, IMAGE SIZE

MANY years ago, when I was struggling to get some of my more "pictorial" shots accepted and hung in local camera club exhibitions, more experienced workers, to whom I submitted them for criticism, often voiced the opinion that "the perspective was all wrong", because I had used a lens of too short a focus. At that time I used, mostly, a $3\frac{1}{4}$ x $4\frac{1}{4}$ camera with a 6 in. lens or a $3\frac{1}{2} \times 2\frac{1}{2}$ size with an objective of $4\frac{3}{4}$ in. focal length. Even now I frequently hear people suggesting that so and so's picture would have a better perspective "if taken with an 8.5 or 9 cm. lens" instead of the 5 cm. lens which we have come to accept as "normal" for a 35 mm. camera.

I think this subject warrants a certain amount of

consideration, and possibly, to use a well-worn expression, "de-bunking". I would like to make the point at the outset, that photographic perspective has in itself nothing whatever to do with the focal length of the lens with which the picture was taken, nor with the dimensions of the plate or film used.

The *perspective* of a picture is settled once for all by *the choice of the position from which the exposure is made*, and by nothing else. (See page 83.)

Every exposure of a given subject, from any given point, will yield identical perspective, whether you use a Leica or a whole-plate field camera, and irrespective of whether you employ a telephoto lens of astronomic dimensions, or the shortest focus wide angle ever made. I am repeating myself to emphasise this fact, because I am sure that far too few photographers appreciate it sufficiently. I can imagine someone asking, "If this is true, why do the makers provide such a galaxy of lenses of varying focal lengths?"

Suppose we lead up to the answer with another question: "What are the normal advantages of owning a battery of lenses?" I would say several! First, that, by the choice of a suitable lens I can include in my picture as much or as little as I want without changing my point of view. Secondly, that I can control the *size* of any chosen object in the picture within quite wide limits. Thirdly, that by choosing a suitable lens, *and viewpoint*, I can control the relative proportions of objects in the picture itself.

To deal with first things first. Let us try to visualise what the eye sees, and compare that with the view embraced by several lenses. Let us imagine that we are walking round the wall of a West Country fishing harbour. We are suddenly attracted by the play of light on the water between two of the floating craft. Our interest, *mine* anyway, will be almost solely given to that sparkle on the water, and the boats nearest to it—my interest will be so localised that I shall tend to ignore other objects in which I am less interested; although were I to allow my eyes to roam about, I should see many other craft afloat, the far side of the harbour and the houses and shops which surround it.

The camera unfortunately cannot readily enjoy that concentration of interest that presents itself to the eye. The limit of *its* field of vision is a hard and definite rectangle of film, the amount included in which is governed solely by the focal length of the lens in use. Let us imagine that we have taken a series of pictures of this subject with a fairly complete range of lenses. What do we secure? With our wide angle lens probably the whole harbour. The normal lens also includes more than we want. The 9 cm. perhaps secures a picture nearest to that which the eye first saw. The 13.5 cm. lens does not embrace sufficient to make a picture. Although no lens possesses the human gift of discrimination, a battery of lenses at least allows the user to select that one which most nearly includes only that part of the picture that excited his own admiration in the first place—while the *perspective* of our two boats remains unaltered, whichever lens is used. If, therefore, when composing your picture you find that you are too close to the subject to include all that you desire, you must use a wide angle lens. Similarly, if you are so far away that the standard lens embraces too much, your remedy is to employ one of longer focus, so as to include only what you require to make the picture *without leaving the viewpoint from which the perspective of the subject is agreeable.*

The ability to include a large or small portion of an object, at will, is only one of the advantages of a series of interchangeable lenses, and it must be admitted that—within limits—a similar effect could be achieved by enlarging only a portion of the negative. So perhaps a more important function of lenses of different focal length is that they provide the means of securing an object, of a given size, on the negative from a number of different distances. These distances are, incidentally, in exact proportion to the focal length of the lens. If, for example, a certain object, 5 ft. from the camera, gives an image exactly 1 in. high on the film when the normal 5 cm. lens is used, the same object will also yield a 1 in. image at $13\frac{1}{2}$ ft. with a 13.5 cm. lens, or at 2.8 ft. distance if we are using the 28 mm. wide angle lens.

To recapitulate; a lens of, say, three times normal focal

length will do two things: (*a*) it will embrace a smaller angle than the normal lens, but will give a negative in which any given object is three times as large (linear) as would the normal lens; and (*b*) it will give an image of any given object exactly the same size as that formed by the normal lens, but from a distance three times as great.

So it can be said, truly, that a long focus lens *influences* perspective—in the sense that its use will probably force the user back from his subject, and will prevent him exposing at such close range in his desire to secure a large scale picture, that the subject may become distorted or unpleasing. Obviously the same end can be achieved by retiring to a suitable distance, even when the normal lens is used, but as this necessarily involves enlarging only a portion of the negative, and this to a greater than normal extent, the final print is likely to be inferior in definition and grain, to one made through a more suitable lens.

Perhaps the greatest benefit that a choice of lenses offers lies, however, in the ability to control and vary the perspective of a composition within very wide limits. This power is, I think, the greatest reason for possessing a variety of lenses of varying focal length, and its capabilities are hardly ever fully exploited. *By the suitable choice of lens and position, objects can be made to appear large or small in relation to other objects in the same picture.* Emphasis can be placed on the principal object in a picture; undesirable features which would otherwise obtrude, can be minimised.

I have already stated that perspective depends solely on the viewpoint; but by choosing the appropriate position for the camera, it is possible to make foreground objects appear large or small in relation to their background, and—by the choice of a suitable lens—still to render the principal object on the scale desired.

The reason for all this is simple. When you are close to the foreground object, say, at 10 ft., the background, say, at 100 ft., is 10 times as far off, and an object actually the same size as the foreground object will appear only 1/10th of its size in the picture. But if you move back to a point, say 30 ft. from the foreground, you are still only 130 ft. from the background, and the *difference* in distance

Whatever miniature you use, you will get sharper pictures by adopting the short strap technique illustrated above, and described in detail on pages 62–63. Give it a trial— it saves many an unsharp negative!

Top Left: *Picture made with 2.8 cm. lens from position close to lamp post.* Right: *Reversal of apparent size of lamp and memorial resulting from a more distant viewpoint. Satisfactory size of objects secured by use of 9 cm. lens.*

Centre Left: *When the desired view is impossible with a normal lens because of some intervening object (e.g. the tree), the use of a wide angle lens from a closer viewpoint (right) may easily solve the difficulty.*

Bottom Left: *When the background is too insistent it can frequently be masked by the subject if the latter is closely approached and (right) a very wide angle lens employed.*

| 2.8 cm. | 3.5 cm. | 5 cm. | 9 cm. | 13.5 cm. |

Perspective—The above five pictures were made from the same view-point with lenses of the focus indicated. Note that, while the relative proportions of all objects remain the same throughout, the size of the object (e.g. memorial) varies in direct proportion to the focal length of the lens used.

| 2.8 cm. | 3.5 cm. | 5 cm. | 9 cm. | 13.5 cm. |

These five pictures were taken from varying distances, with the object of rendering the memorial on about the same scale in every case. The distance from camera to memorial was in each case proportionate to the focal length of lens used. Note that as the camera recedes from the memorial, the background (Buckingham Palace) is increased in apparent size with each successive move.

83

Focusing by rangefinder ensures that any one *object is sharp. The depth scale should be used for extended sharpness.*

Top.   SPRINGTIME—*Differential focusing concentrates interest on the blossom.*—Herm. Ebel.

Bottom.   DERWENT WATER IN AUTUMN MOOD—*Depth focusing to ensure full sharpness.*—W. A. Poucher.

between the camera and the foreground, and background, is now only in the proportion of (approximately) 4 to 1— and a picture taken from *this* position will show the foreground object only about 4 times as large as a similar object in the background. If the normal lens be used for both these pictures, the one from the second position would show all objects of such small (actual) size, that a considerable degree of extra enlargement would be necessary to produce a satisfactory picture; but substituting, say, a 13.5 cm. lens for the normal 5 cm. would restore the image size of the foreground object to what is desired.

The *first* basic rule, then, is: *To make distant objects appear larger in relation to the foreground object—use a long focus lens, and retire to a suitable distance to ensure that the foreground object is rendered in the desired size.*

Sometimes it may be found that the subject that you wish to photograph is marred by a large and unsuitable background. This case, too, can be dealt with in similar fashion, but applying the principle in reverse. By approaching considerably closer to the foreground object, you can increase the *proportionate* distance of the background, and by choosing a suitable short focus (wide-angle) lens you can still portray the foreground object in a satisfactory size, while the background becomes relatively small and unobtrusive.

The *second* basic rule, then, is: *To make the foreground object appear large in relation to the background, use a short focus lens, and approach the foreground object until its own size is satisfactory.*

A further way in which this second rule can be applied exists when a subject is marred by an overpowering background, which is relatively close to it. By employing the widest angle lens available, and approaching as close as may be possible to the subject, the unwanted background may be hidden by the subject itself. Choosing a really low viewpoint for the camera adds considerably to the efficiency of this expedient. (See page 82.)

By juggling with the wide range of lenses available, and employing variations of one or other of these two basic rules it is possible to depict objects of the same or different sizes on almost any desired scale and with a greater or lesser degree of actual truth. An object close to the camera can be made to look larger than a much bigger object at a short distance. A wide angle lens will allow you to get sufficiently close to the near object, and yet get it all in the picture. A picture of the same two objects taken from a greater distance with, say, the normal lens, will perhaps show them both of the same apparent size, while a third picture taken from a still more remote distance, with perhaps a 13.5 or 20 cm. lens, will depict the large (distant) object on a larger scale than the smaller and closer one.

When exploiting the capabilities of the longer focus lenses on work of this nature, it is most important to study carefully the depth of focus scale, as it will frequently be necessary to work at relatively small lens apertures if it is desired to secure adequate detail in both near and distant objects at the same time.

All the time do not forget: *perspective is governed by where you stand—object size and the angle of view included in the picture is determined by the focal length of the lens used.*

THE CHARACTERISTICS OF FILM

FILM, to many miniature camera users is just—film. Nevertheless, if we are to get the best out of a 35 mm. camera, it is a matter to which some thought must be given. All the makers supply several types and each of these is produced to fulfil certain very definite needs.

Of all the characteristics of films, the one of the greatest interest is *speed*. For years, makers have competed with each other to produce faster and yet faster emulsions and their advertising is often so worded as to suggest that this factor is by far the most important one to the user. Speed, as such, is undoubtedly desirable. It opens up fresh photographic fields indoors, when the light is poor, in the streets

86

at night, high speed subjects, and so on. But speed is obtainable only at the sacrifice of certain other qualities, which I suggest are at least of equal importance to the miniature worker. I would, therefore, advocate avoiding the fastest material for all normal purposes. I would reserve the very fastest films for use when their speed is so necessary that one is prepared to put up with the lack of definition and with the graininess which are inevitable with emulsions of the most rapid type.

The second factor that has to be considered is *colour sensitivity*. The films that we use nowadays are mostly *panchromatic*. That means that they are sensitive to all colours. Their relative sensitivity to the various colours is, however, not the same as that of the human eye, and it also differs a trifle between various films in their sensitivity to daylight as opposed to artificial light. As a rough guide, the faster films are likely to be somewhat more sensitive to the red rays that are so plentiful in the light produced by normal electric bulbs, and for this reason are preferred in connection with them. Still, if the camera is loaded with a medium speed panchromatic material, it will cope with almost anything that is likely to come along.

Third and, in fact, probably the most important question about *any* miniature film, is whether or not it will yield *fine grain*. The photographic image is composed of grains of metallic silver suspended in the gelatine emulsion— grains derived from the minute crystals of silver halide which become affected by exposure to light, and subsequently blackened, and thereby made visible, by the action of the developer. These individual grains are far too small to be seen even through a microscope, but under the action of development grains tend to clump together, and it is these clumps, large or small, that are visible and produce what we call "grain".

Slow films have less tendency to clump than fast films and, although various film makers have from time to time produced fast films for which they claimed comparatively fine grain, as a general rule grain size seems closely connected with speed.

Grain, however, can be influenced and modified very considerably by the nature of the developer in which the film is processed; by the degree of over- or under-development; and by errors in exposure. Any of the developers such as are commonly used for developing large films, plates and papers, may prove far too vigorous for satisfactory use with miniature materials. They will bring out everything possible in the way of film speed and detail, but they will also do the same to the grain and are thus not very suitable for our purposes.

A large number of formulæ have, however, been evolved which take better care of the particular needs of the 35 mm. user.

The emulsion on different films may differ somewhat in *thickness*. Slow films can be made thinner than those which are more rapid. There is a good deal of merit in a thin emulsion. When the light which forms the image strikes the surface of the film, it passes in through the emulsion itself; and, as that is a turgid medium, it becomes dispersed, and scattered so that it affects the sensitive substance all round the spot at which it first entered the film. It is easy to see that the thinner the film the less the light will be scattered, and the sharper will be the image of a point of light on development. Most slow films on the market are on the thin side—fast emulsions incline to be thicker. Therefore, even apart from grain itself, a slow emulsion may produce a sharper picture, i.e. one which is capable of greater enlargement, than will one of the more rapid materials. Or, as we say, the slow film is capable of greater *resolution* than the other.

When light enters the surface of a film, a relatively large amount passes straight through to the back of the emulsion. As it reaches the celluloid support, it is reflected back into the emulsion itself, thus affecting other emulsion points to the side of the ones forming the primary image. The resulting phenomenon, *halation*, is most easily seen where an unscreened light is photographed, say, in an interior.

To defeat this trouble most film makers use slightly coloured celluloid for the base itself.

Latitude—the ability to make a good picture out of both over- and under-exposures—provided no very disproportionate error occurred—is one of the most valuable characteristics that a film can possess, and, although all

88

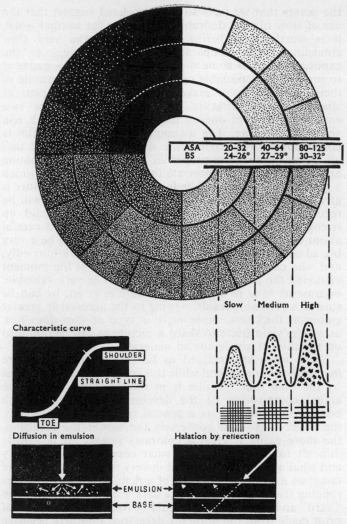

| ASA | 20–32 | 40–64 | 80–125 |
| BS | 24–26° | 27–29° | 30–32° |

Slow   Medium   High

Characteristic curve

SHOULDER
STRAIGHT LINE
TOE

Diffusion in emulsion

Halation by reflection

←EMULSION→
←BASE→

Film characteristics. Most slow films have fine grain, steep scale, good resolution. Rapid films are coarser grained, softer and cannot resolve such fine detail. (See pp. 86–91.)

the points that we have so far considered suggest that the use of slow films is desirable at all times for normal work, it is worth remembering that many of the very slow emulsions have comparatively little latitude, i.e. the exposure must be somewhere near right if the negative is to produce a respectable print. To increase the latitude of their products, some makers have adopted the plan of *double-coating*. That is to say, the film carries two emulsions; a rapid one on the outside, behind which is a very slow coating. The assumption is that if the film is considerably over-exposed the light will have "used up" all the image forming properties of the outer (fast) coating and will continue to penetrate the slow emulsion, in which a good strong image will be formed. If normal exposure is given, everything except the brightest highlights will be recorded on the outer layer, while these will build up strength on the inner emulsion. For the user who is careful about exact exposure the double coating may not be a very big advantage, but for the man who has to work hurriedly, and who cannot always check his exposure at the moment of taking the picture, double coating can be very valuable; because as long as *sufficient* exposure is given, he can be sure of a printable result. Owing to the necessarily greater emulsion thickness, however, this type of film does not, as a rule, yield quite so sharp a picture as can be obtained on the thinner single coated materials.

Some films are inclined to be *soft-working*, some are *inherently contrasty*, and while this can be largely controlled by the time that the film is in the developer, or by the actual composition of the developer itself, it is worth bearing in mind that as a general rule the faster the film, the softer it is—and conversely the slower the emulsion, the more easily it gives a contrasty image. It is a little difficult to describe exactly what constitutes a contrasty and what a soft emulsion. Put in very popular terms, if one imagines a subject composed of a definite number of tones ranging from a light grey to a dark grey photographed on "hard" and "soft" films, it would be found that in a normal print made from the normally developed *contrasty* negative the light tones are appreciably lighter than those of the original and the dark are a good deal blacker; while in a

90

normal print made from the normally developed *soft* negative, dark tones do not seem to be rendered as dark as they should be and the lighter tones seem to be lacking some of their brilliance.

This can be put to good account, by choosing the type of emulsion to suit the job in hand.

Acutance. In recent years new emulsions have appeared—often under old names—with what we have learned to call superior "acutance". This expression describes the ability of the film to record a sharp image produced by the lens as a sharp physical image in the emulsion. It is quite distinct from fineness of grain. Even a very fine grained emulsion will not necessarily yield the ultimate in image sharpness unless the emulsion structure minimises image dispersion resulting from light scatter between the particles in the sensitive layer itself.

Rapid emulsions usually (but not invariably) had a greater physical thickness than the slower materials. As internal scatter is largely related to the thickness of the film in which it takes place, the better image sharpness (resolution) on the slower materials was due to their thin coating, and not only their smaller grain size.

The emulsion coating of modern high-acutance films is considerably thinner than those to which we have been accustomed. This extra thin emulsion is no longer limited to the slow materials, although their naturally fine grain still gives them some advantages in terms of definition. Some of these new materials enjoy an emulsion thickness comparable with that of the thinnest of the older "micro" films, while still providing the speed and latitude of the more normal materials. In addition to the reduction in scatter by thinner layers, there is actually less light-scatter between the silver halide crystals themselves. Such emulsions are thus able to record the sharpest "edge" where two dissimilar tones meet. This superior "edge-defining-ability" is, of course, of the utmost value to miniature camera users who have long been blessed with lenses capable of recording finer detail than normally could be resolved on the majority of film emulsions.

The relatively thin layers also develop, fix, wash and dry far more rapidly. The use of P.P.D. and other specially fine grain developers is no longer desirable; adequately fine grain *plus* superior definition being more easily obtained with normal fine grain solutions.

This revolutionary improvement means, in practice, that when speed is required some of the more rapid emulsions can now safely be used without having to put up with an inevitable loss of definition.

TYPES OF 35 mm. FILM

THE characteristics of the slow, medium and fast films of *all* makers are so fundamentally similar that the various materials can easily be divided up into *five basic types*.

FILMS CLASSIFIED

GROUP AA
Adox KB14
Agfa Isopan F.F.
Ilford Pan F.
Kodak Panatomic X
Perutz Pergrano 14

GROUP A
Adox KB17
Agfa Isopan F.
Ferrania P.3
Gevaert Gevapan 27
Perutz Perpantic 17

GROUP B
Gevaert Gevapan 30
Ilford F.P.3
Kodak Plus X

GROUP C
Adox KB21
Agfa Isopan I.S.S.
Agfa Isopan Ultra
Ferrania S.2
Gevaert Gevapan 33
Ilford H.P.3
Kodak Tri-X
Perutz Peromnia 21

GROUP D
Adox KB25 and KB27
Agfa Isopan Record
Ansco Super Hypan
Gevaert Gevapan 36
Ilford H.P.S.
Perutz Peromnia 25

(AA) *Very slow films* (23°–25° BS, 16–25 ASA) of exceptionally fine grain and high contrast.
(A) *Slow Films* (26°–28° BS, 32–50 ASA) of fine grain and moderate contrast.
(B) *Medium Speed Films* (29°–30° BS, 64–80 ASA) of reasonably fine grain and moderate contrast.
(C) *Fast Films* (31°–34° BS, 100–200 ASA) inclined to be of coarser grain and softer contrast.
(D) *Extreme Speed Films* (35 BS or 250 ASA and faster), rather grainy and soft contrast.

The films in Group AA have mostly what is known as a steep tone gradation, i.e. they are contrasty; and, in the majority of cases, have a thin and almost grainless emulsion which is capable of resolving the finest possible details.

Group A films also yield images of fine grain, and will produce negatives from which enlargements can be made to twenty or more diameters without definition suffering or grain becoming too apparent in the print. These two films should be chosen for technical work or for anything where the best definition is required and where their relatively slow speed does not matter.

The films in Group B are those which will best meet the needs of nine out of every ten miniature camera users. Their speed is mostly adequate, and their inherent contrast is less than is that of those in the foregoing groups. While they have not *quite* so fine a grain as the slower films, they are still sufficiently good in this respect to allow of very considerable enlargement. They also have considerable exposure latitude.

The films in Group C have the high speed emulsions usually called "Super—something or other". These films are considerably faster than those previously mentioned, particularly when used in artificial light; they are therefore not to be recommended for general use, but rather to be kept in reserve for employment when speed is the really vital factor.

The films in Group D are recent additions—they are fantastically rapid emulsions with speeds up to *three times* those of Group C. These films are comparatively grainy, as one would expect: but they open up a completely fresh field in "available light" photography and permit of snapshots, in the true sense of the term, in the street at night, or indoors.

The fact that speed means grain must be kept in mind constantly, as the whole crux of 35 mm. work is the ability to produce grainless enlargements: just how far, and in what way this requirement is influenced by processing is considered later.

For the moment the essential facts are that slow emulsions are virtually grain-free, and that, as their speed rises, so does the probability of coarser grain increase. (But see also p. 91.)

FILTERS—THEIR USE AND MIS-USE

AS LONG as manufacturers list a round dozen or so different coloured filters, so long will the photographer become a collector of vari-coloured pieces of glass or gelatine, often without knowing *why* he has so many, or how they should all be employed to the best effect. I have passed through this phase myself, and now have reduced my stock of these attractively coloured circles to what I consider the sensible *maximum*.

Filters are required for two specific purposes—either to "correct" inaccuracies in the translation of colour into black and white as offered by the emulsion—or to modify some particular colour so that it will photograph lighter or darker than it would otherwise do in comparison with other colours in the same picture.

Let us deal with correction first. Suppose we are using a panchromatic film and that our subject is a normal summer landscape—green trees, white clouds, blue sky and perhaps golden flowers in the foreground. Even without a filter we shall secure a pleasing picture, but, because our film is still over-sensitive to blue, the blue sky will photograph lighter in tone than it appears to the eye. The yellow flowers may appear a trifle too dark, and the trees probably about right. Now if we retake the same scene through a medium density yellow filter—the blue sky will be rendered appreciably darker than before and the white clouds will stand out clearly in contrast with it; the trees will not be very different from before, but the yellow flowers will appear somewhat lighter.

What the filter is doing is to *hold back* some of the coloured rays to which the film is over-sensitive, meanwhile giving the other colours, as it were, a chance to make their impression on the film. There is a basic rule underlying the use of *all* filters: *any coloured filter will make objects of its own colour, photograph lighter, and at the same time render objects of the complementary colour in a darker tone* than would otherwise be the case.

Now for the second purpose for which we use filters. Let us imagine that we have a coloured diagram: a circle divided into segments coloured respectively red, orange,

RELATIVE BRIGHTNESS AS SEEN BY	INFRA RED		RED	ORANGE	YELLOW	YELLOW-GREEN	GREEN	BLUE-GREEN	BLUE	VIOLET	ULTRA VIOLET
Human Eye											
Ortho Film											
Pan Film											

AS REPRODUCED BY **PAN** FILM WITH VARIOUS FILTERS

Pan and Yellow											
Pan and Green											
Pan and Orange											
Pan and Red											
Pan and Blue											

The response of film compared with that of the eye in respect of various colours and showing how certain colours can be emphasized or repressed by the use of pan film with various colour filters. (This must be accepted as approximate only, as different makes of film vary to some extent in their response to colour.)

95

yellow, green, blue and violet. Suppose we take a picture of this chart through a *red* filter: the red segment will now photograph very light, the green (its complement) very dark; almost black if the colours are pure. The other colours will also be affected, but to a lesser degree: the orange will be rather lighter than before; the blue and violet somewhat darker. This general principle holds good all the time.

Through a *green* filter green becomes light and red is rendered much darker. A yellow filter darkens blue and violet and tends to make green, yellow and orange register as lighter tones than they otherwise would. Once this basic principle is grasped a filter can be used intelligently. There should be a definite *reason* for wanting to use it every time any filter is extracted from its case.

A green car standing in front of a red brick wall may quite easily photograph very much the same tone as its background. Here one has the choice of making the wall dark and the car light (green filter), or rendering the car dark against a light wall (red filter). Almost every combination of colours can be modified to some degree by the choice and use of a suitable filter.

I do, however, suggest that many filters are so similar that anything like a "complete" set of all that one filter maker produces is quite unnecessary. The difference in result obtained between No. 1 and No. 2 Yellows of the same make, for example, is so slight as to be almost unnoticeable; and for outdoor work at least I recommend the purchase of one each yellow, green and red filters, as all that are ever likely to be used. The two latter will in any event only be needed relatively infrequently in comparison with the yellow.

For general correction the medium yellow will do all that will be required, and will secure landscapes which appear natural and pleasing with almost all present-day films.

To emphasize the contrast between white sails, white buildings, or white clouds and a blue sky, use yellow. Grossly to exaggerate the difference, use a red filter. Green will produce a little less effect in this respect than yellow.

Because the green filter darkens the black-and-white

version of red colour, it is valuable for male portrait work where it is desired to retain some tone in the skin—particularly in the case of sunburned subjects, where this characteristic is to be emphasized.

Yellow, orange and red filters have another useful property. With pan films they have the power of penetrating haze to some extent, the red giving the greatest degree of penetration. For this reason such filters can usefully be employed in the photography of distant landscapes where the utmost clarity is desired. The red filter will necessarily falsify the tone rendering of all colours to some extent, but it will help to clarify the distant details.

No filter will, however, penetrate heavy water vapour (fog), haze resulting from suspended dust particles, or the air vibrations which we commonly call heat haze.

There is no gain in mounting two filters one on top of the other, e.g. yellow and orange, or yellow and red. The two will produce no better result than the dark one alone. Remember, too, that a filter will strengthen a blue sky so that white clouds show up against it, but it can have no effect if the general sky tone is grey.

When a filter is used, it prevents some of the light rays from reaching the film. For this reason, the use of *any* filter involves increasing the exposure, to an extent depending on the density of the filter, and the colour sensitivity of the film. Approximate *and adequately accurate* factors for this increase are given in the appended table. The makers' practice of quoting filter factors to decimal places is unnecessarily exacting. No one, even using a photo-electric exposure meter of the most expensive type, can determine the "correct" exposure with sufficient accuracy for it to matter whether the filter factor is rated at 1.3 × or 1.4 ×, even if it were possible to set the shutter speed and stop with the requisite accuracy (and, as will be seen presently, there is always the question of what *is* "correct" exposure, as it is not always necessarily right for all parts of the subject at once!).

An entirely different type of filter that has come into prominence in recent years is the *polarising screen*.

When a ray of light strikes a surface, some of it is

		PAN FILMS	
		Groups AA, A, B, C	Group D
ILFORD	Alpha. Yellow	1½ ×	1½ ×
	Beta. Yellow-Green	2 ×	2½ ×
	Gamma. Green	4 ×	4 ×
	Delta. Dark Yellow	2½ ×	2½ ×
	Iso. Yellow	2 ×	2 ×
	Aviol. Yellow	1½ ×	1½ ×
	H.W. Green	4 ×	4 ×
	Micro 5. Orange	5 ×	4 ×
	Tri-colour Red	6–8 ×	5–7 ×
KODAK	K.2. Yellow	2 ×	2 ×
	K.3. Yellow	2 ×	2 ×
	Wratten G. Orange	2½ ×	2 ×
	Wratten A. Red	8 ×	7 ×
	Wratten F. Strong Red	16 ×	16 ×
	Wratten XI. Green	4 ×	4 ×
LEITZ	U.V. Almost colourless	—	—
	No. 0. Yellow. Very light	1½ ×	1½ ×
	No. I. Yellow. Light	2 ×	2 ×
	No. 2. Yellow. Strong	2½ ×	2½ ×
	Green	3 ×	3 ×
	Red. (Hell) Medium dark	8–10 ×	8–10 ×
	Red. (Dunkel) Very dark	40 ×	40 ×
ZEISS IKON	G.0. Very light Yellow	1½ ×	1½ ×
	G.I. Light Yellow	2 ×	2 ×
	G.2. Medium Yellow	3 ×	3 ×
	G.3. Dark Yellow	4 ×	4 ×
	G.4. Orange	5 ×	5 ×
	G.R.55. Yellow-Green	2 ×	2 ×
	G.R.5. Green	3 ×	3 ×
	R.10. Red	10–12 ×	8–10 ×

For use in average weather by daylight on the majority of 35mm. films. The figures quoted are given to the nearest convenient multiple. Small fractions and decimals have been ignored as they are of no importance (see text). When alternative factors are quoted, the higher figure should be used when the light is inclined to be bluish in colour. The lower figure applies when the sun is shining, particularly early and late in the day.

Filter	Advertising	Architecture	Clinical	General	Industrial	Landscape	Mountaineering	Nature Study	Portraits	Press Work	Record,Copying	Sailing, Marine	Sports
1. U.V.							A						
2. Very light yellow	F						B					D	C
3. Light yellow	A			A		A		A	A	A		A	A
4. Med. yellow			A			B							D
5. Deep yellow	E	A		C	B					C	C		
6. Yellow-green		C	B			D	C						B
7. Green	C		D	D	A				B		A	C	
8. Blue-green									C				
9. Blue	G										D		
10. Orange	D	D			D	C	D	B	D	B		D	
11. Bright red	B	B	C	B	C	E	E						
12. Deep red							F				B		

Examples of actual filters coming under the above types are as follows :

1. Ilford Q; Leitz U.V.
2. Ilford Aviol; Leitz No. 0 ; Zeiss Ikon G.0
3. Ilford Alpha; Kodak K.2; Leitz No. 1; Zeiss Ikon G.1
4. Ilford Iso; Kodak K.3; Leitz No. 2; Zeiss Ikon G.2
5. Ilford Delta; Kodak G; Zeiss Ikon G.3
6. Ilford Beta; Leitz Yellow Green; Zeiss Ikon GR. 55
7. Ilford Gamma; Kodak X. 1; Leitz Green; Zeiss Ikon GR.5
8. Ilford H.W.
9. Ilford Tricolour Blue; Kodak C.5; Leitz Blue; Zeiss Ikon Blue
10. Ilford Micro 5; Kodak 23A; Leitz Salmon; Zeiss Ikon G.4
11. Ilford Tricolour Red; Kodak A; Leitz Red (Hell); Zeiss Ikon R.10
12. Ilford Narrow Cut Red; Kodak F; Leitz Red (Dunkel); Zeiss Ikon R.20

Letters indicate in alphabetical sequence the order of usefulness for the subjects listed.

99

absorbed while the remainder is reflected. Any such ray of light is composed of vibrations in every direction, and in the course of being reflected from the surface (glass, enamel, leather, plant life—in fact most surfaces with the exception of bare metal) it undergoes change invisible to the human eye. On striking a reflecting surface at a moderate angle (not 90°) some of the vibrations are absorbed, or damped out; while the remainder which were vibrating in the other directions are reflected—still vibrating. This phenomenon is called polarisation. A polarising screen can be likened to an opaque disc, pierced by countless straight and parallel slits. If this be placed over the camera lens so that its slits are in the same plane as the light vibrations reflected from the subject, they will be able to pass almost unhindered and do their job of forming an image on the film. If, however, the slotted disc be turned so that its slits are at a right angle to the reflected light vibrations, hardly any of them will be able to get through and the lens and film will not see or record light rays which are clearly visible to the human eye. In other words some of the reflections will be cut out and so the general glare reduced.

The purpose of such a filter is to eliminate *unwanted* reflections, e.g. in shop windows, eyeglasses (in the case of a portrait) or perhaps on furniture. Its effect is clearly visible to the eye when looking through it—and as it varies according to the angle of the filter in relation to the angle of vibration of the reflection, the degree of correction required can be assessed by revolving the filter while studying the subject through it. When the correct angle has been chosen, the filter should be fitted to the camera lens at *exactly* the same angle. It is not always desirable entirely to eliminate the reflections, as this may kill the quality or "feel" particular to that subject, but, as the effect of the filter is progressive as it is turned round, the setting which will give the most satisfactory result can easily be identified.

Because a polarising filter—which usually takes the form of a glass disc, somewhat streaky in appearance and greenish grey in colour—obstructs some of the light rays as described above, it requires an increase of exposure so

Filters are generally used to provide a means of controlling the tone of the sky in relation to the remainder of the picture. They should not *be used unless there is a definite reason for so doing.*

Page 101. REX—*This picture owes much to the use of a dark yellow filter which has lowered the tone of the sky against which the liner's white painted bows are shown to the best possible advantage.*—G. Schuh.

Above. THE ROAD TO TYROL—*A medium yellow filter provides the truest tone rendering at normal altitudes on both pan and ortho materials. This picture also emphasizes the value of a wide angle lens for mountain landscapes in that it includes something of the* surroundings *and not only what is* immediately in front of *the camera.*—H. S. Newcombe.

102

At higher altitudes filters have a stronger than normal effect, and the use of a dark yellow filter will usually render the blue sky over-dark.

Above. THE ICEFIELD—*An example of the degree to which the lightest yellow filter (Leitz No. 0) will tone down the sky at about 8,000 feet elevation. A stronger filter would have made it unnaturally dark.*—H. S. Newcombe.

Page 104. SKYE LANDSCAPE—*In northern latitudes a* dark *blue sky is a rarity, but even a pale blue can frequently be darkened by the use of a strong orange or red filter. In this instance the effect is emphasized by deliberately under-exposing so as to secure the foreground in silhouette.*—H. S. Newcombe.

103

that the remaining rays may have time to form the image. This factor is usually $3 \times$ to $4 \times$.

An additional use for this filter lies in its ability to control, to some extent, the tone of a blue sky without affecting the colour rendering of any other blue or other coloured object in the picture. This effect is most noticeable in that part of the sky which is about 90° from the sun's position. That is, if the sun is exactly behind you, you will get the greatest effect on the part of the sky lying directly to your right or left side. There will be no effect on the tone of the sky in front, nor on the scene facing the source of light. This phenomenon exists *only* when the sun is shining; and again it can be assessed by the eye—through the filter.

THE NEED FOR CORRECT EXPOSURE

THE latitude of films to-day (p. 88) is one of their most valuable features, but it should not be over-stressed and 35 mm. workers in particular are advised to estimate their exposure with all accuracy reasonably possible, as only by so doing will the best quality print result.

On page 89 is shown a representative graph of sensitivity of a typical modern single coated film. At what is called the "toe" of the curve, the gradient is very gentle, higher up it is relatively steep and becomes a fairly straight line, while eventually the bend gradually flattens out to the end where, if continued, it would be practically horizontal. If this, then, is a film which has received *normal* exposure and development, and records the image of a subject of not too contrasty a nature, the tones forming the lights and darks of the image will be spaced more or less over the whole of the straight region of the "curve". The shadow parts fall in the vicinity of the lower, and the highlights in the region of the upper end and beyond, in which circumstances all the tones corresponding to the bulk of the

105

original will be nicely spaced out and they will be adequately separated in a print made from this negative.

If, however, we *under*-expose, the probability is that the brightest lights (the densest part of the negative) will not extend much into the straight portion of the curve, with the result that only the highlights will be properly separated, and all of the other detail that is recorded will be down on the gradually flattening part of the toe: thus shadow detail will be lacking, or will be so inadequately split up into different tones that the shadows will print as a more or less uniform black mass.

Over-exposure, on the contrary, will result in the shadows being set high up on the straight portion of the curve, which will, of course, ensure good separation of the shadows, and very good shadow detail; but the bright tones will be pushed up into the gradually flattening upper part of the curve and will be apt to print as a uniformly chalky white entirely devoid of well-separated detail or modelling.

Thus camera exposure has a considerable effect on the resulting print, beyond the elementary need of securing all the necessary detail. If the interest is confined to the shadows, a "more than minimum" exposure will ensure that they fall on the straight line portion of the curve where they will be better separated than if only a normal exposure had been given. Similarly, in the case of a picture in which the whole interest lies in the highlights and lighter tones and where it is of no importance if the shadows show little or no detail, the best tone separation and most satisfying rendering will be secured by cutting down the exposure to the point where the highlights are adequately spaced out over the straight line of the curve, although of necessity the shadows will then be crowded together in the toe.

It must be borne in mind that the above explanation relates only to single coated films. A few emulsions are double coated; and these are actually able to record an infinitely longer scale of tones. As, however, their extreme highlights become almost unprintably dense and as our printing paper has so limited a scale (see page 284) the advice given for these single coated films also applies to those which are double coated.

THE USE OF EXPOSURE METERS

IF the characteristics of any miniature film are to be exploited to the best advantage, it is essential that it be correctly exposed, and I would urge the consistent employment of a dependable photo-electric meter. The exact make chosen is not so important as that one should learn how to use it and how to interpret its readings. For this reason a few experiments should be made with every new meter before implicit reliance is placed on its accuracy. As the way in which a photo-electric meter is handled can seriously influence its readings, it is worth considering the construction and use of such instruments so as to adopt a method which will ensure that they are used to the best possible effect in producing perfect negatives.

The photo-electric meter itself is basically a device in which the light directed on to or reflected by the subject is allowed to reach the surface of a photo-electric cell. The action of light falling on this cell generates electric current, the strength of which varies in proportion to the intensity of the light itself. This current in turn causes a needle to move—according to the intensity of the light—over a numbered scale, which is calibrated to indicate the exposure required for given stops, film speeds, etc.

This, then, is the general principle on which such meters work, and it might reasonably be thought that the use of one of the more expensive (and accurate) meters might take *all* the guesswork out of photography and ensure perfectly exposed negatives every time. Whatever may be the theory, it does not work out quite so simply in practice.

Consider for a moment what happens when the meter is allowed to look at the subject. Suppose, for example, that the subject is a black motor car standing in front of a white stone house, in direct sunshine. Exposure meters, of the type under discussion, have, like lenses, a definite angle of view, called here "angle of acceptance"—in some cases possibly as large as 90° or 100°, in others as little as 50° or 60°. According to this angle the amount of subject seen by the meter will vary. If the meter is one embracing a very wide field, it will see a great deal of the surrounding white house in proportion to the motor car, and will be unduly influenced by its brightness, which will result in the indication of a much shorter exposure than would produce a satisfactory picture of the car itself. So if we are to use a meter successfully, we must approach the subject until the meter cannot see more of the subject than that part in which we desire to secure correct exposure. The *Weston Master* meter covers 50° with the grid closed, 80° with the grid open.

With the majority of meters, a fairly safe rule is to *approach the subject (or that part of it which is to form the picture) until the distance from meter to subject does not exceed the width of the subject itself.*

But what *is* the subject? That is not always easy to answer. If you are taking a landscape of normally open character with the horizon about midway up the picture space, it will probably be a mistake to allow the meter to view the whole of the picture; as, like the white house and the black car, the overwhelming brightness of the sky will make the meter indicate far too short an exposure to be adequate for the darker foreground. In this case, the meter should be tilted *down* so as to include the landscape only; you will thus ensure giving this the correct exposure, and the latitude of the film will probably take care of the sky. If your subject is 90 per cent. sky or clouds with only a narrow strip of land at the base, *and if you are content to show this strip in silhouette*, then it is correct to point the meter at the sky, and to expose accordingly.

If the subject is of a very contrasty nature—open sunlit landscape seen through a dark archway or its equivalent, which will probably tax the latitude of the film to its limit— the best plan is to take *two* separate readings: one of the distant landscape unobscured, and the other of the dark foreground close up. The most useful exposure that one can give in such circumstances will probably be the mean of the two indicated. For example, if the meter indicates that $1/100$ second at $f\,11$ is correct for the distance, while say $\frac{1}{4}$ second at $f\,11$ is required for the foreground, you will probably get the most useful negative by giving an exposure at this stop of $1/20$ to $1/25$ second, trusting in the latitude of the film to take care of some of the detail in both the over- and under-exposed parts of the negative.

The *S.E.I. Photometer* provides an entirely different

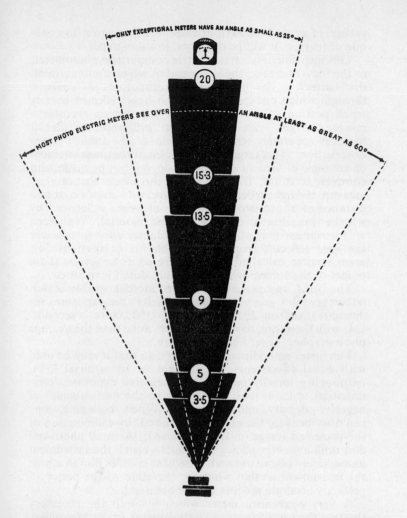

Why it is so necessary to approach the subject closely before taking a reading with a photo-electric meter. Some meters have a wider field than even a wide angle lens, and when long focus lenses are used (as shown by the gradual narrowing of the black angles) the discrepancy becomes greater and still more dangerous.

system of exposure determination. As it is so far the only one of its type, it will be discussed in more detail.

This instrument is a true electric comparison photometer, in the form of a tube, the lower end of which houses a small dry battery. The photometer incorporates a telescope through which one can examine the light reflected by any small portion of the subject. By adjusting a rheostat a minute "target" can be varied in brilliance, so that it matches accurately with the portion of the subject under observation. This target area is so small that measurement of an angle of view of only half a degree can be made with complete accuracy. In other words, this means that one can measure the light reflected by a button on a man's coat at a distance of about two yards, without being influenced by whether his jacket is of light or dark material. With such an instrument it is of course abundantly easy to measure the light reflected from small highlights or deep shadow areas, and to calculate the exposure so as to favour those points of the subject where maximum detail is required.

The *S.E.I.* instrument has three interchangeable scales, which give it a great recording capacity; the exposures indicated range from $2\frac{3}{4}$ hours down to 1/500,000 of a second!

It will, therefore, cover a far wider range than the average photographer is ever likely to require.

The meter embodies special filters, so that it may be used with equal effectiveness in daylight or in artificial light. Although primarily intended for negative exposure determination, it lends itself very easily to the measurement of negative density and contrast. When enlarging, one can also measure the exposure required, by examination of the projected image on the baseboard. A small photo-cell and milli-ammeter allows the user to check the instrument immediately before use and a rheostat enables him to adjust the instrument so that whatever the state of the battery a perfectly accurate reading can be obtained.

A very convenient meter which fits into the accessory shoe on the top of most modern cameras is the *Metraphot*. Different models are available, including one specially designed for the Leica M.3 and M.2, which couples with the shutter speed setting knob for semi-automatic operation.

110

THE CONFUSION ABOUT FILM SPEEDS

WE are faced always with another problem set by the impossibility of accurately reconciling the various film speeds claimed by the makers with the considerable range of exposure meters and calculators on the market. A variety of film speed indicating methods is still employed in different countries; and different exposure meter manufacturers calibrate their instruments according to one or other of these systems suited to their own views. It is impossible to specify any strict correlation between all the different systems, but the following table will fill practical needs.

APPROXIMATE COMPARISON TABLE OF FILM SPEEDS

BS & ASA Index (Old Arith.) & Weston III	BS Index (Logar)	ASA Arith. Index (Post-1960)	ASA Log Index (Post-1960)	Original Weston (I, II)*	European Scheiner	DIN
10	21°	20	2.5°	8	22°	11°
16	23°	32	3–3.5°	12	24°	13°
25	25°	50	4ª	20	26°	15°
40	27°	80	4.5°	32	28°	17°
64	29°	125	5–5.5°	50	30°	19°
100	31°	200	6°	80	32°	21°
160	33°	320	6.5°	125	34°	23°
250	35°	500	7–7.5°	200	36°	25°
400	37°	800	8°	320	38°	27°
640	39°	1250	8.5°	500	40°	29°

*The current Weston ratings (Weston Master III meter) are identical with pre-1960 BS and ASA arithmetical index numbers.

With some systems (Scheiner, BS Log. Index, DIN) speed doubling corresponds to an increase of 3°, while in others the speed is itself proportional to the speed number (BS Arith. Index, Weston) and therefore inversely proportional to the exposure needed. The latest ASA Log Index uses an increase of 1° to signify a doubling of the speed; this links up conveniently with the exposure value scale on many camera shutters where each increase of 1 value corresponds to a doubling of the effective exposure.

As different exposure meters also have their own vagaries

in scaling, it is not always possible to "convert" one system into another by the above table with anything like a positive assurance that the figure will be satisfactory with the particular meter to be used. The only way to be really certain is to find out by a series of test exposures exactly what is the correct speed rating to use *on your meter*.

This involves sacrificing one film of 36 exposures, which conveniently accommodates five 7-exposure tests. Start with a straightforward subject, say an average landscape, and take a meter reading with the meter set to the film speed recommended by the film maker. This might for instance be 80 ASA. Expose the first frame accordingly at a medium aperture of (say) *f* 5.6. Next, make a series of exposures based on meter readings obtained with the meter set to 40 ASA, half-way between 50 and 64 ASA, half-way between 100 and 125 ASA, 160 ASA, half-way between 200 and 250 ASA, and 320 ASA. This gives a series of exposures, at half-stop intervals, from twice the correct exposure to one-quarter the correct figure. Repeat this with a few other subjects. After development of the film check which frame in each series appears best exposed with the minimum exposure—the speed figure chosen for that exposure is the one to use on the meter.

You may notice that the minimum correct exposure is in fact often obtained with a film speed figure around twice that suggested by the makers. This is because the ASA exposure index numbers in use until 1960 incorporate a safety factor against under-exposure as an insurance against errors. With modern films, especially high-speed ones, even slight overexposure leads to a definite deterioration of negative quality, in particular increased grain. For that reason some manufacturers started to recommend two speed index numbers, the official one, and a second figure for minimum exposure. Then, in 1960, the ASA speed system was revised with the result that the official figures are now twice as high as before—*without any change in the films themselves*. The post-1960 figures are thus speed settings for minimum correct exposure.

Colour film speeds are not subject to this duality; there you just use the maker's recommended figure. A test may suggest slight amendment, but it will not be much.

112

Exposure is all important. If it is more than adequate, tone separation is frequently poor; if insufficient, there are invariably large areas of detailless black. The rule is to expose accurately for those parts of the picture where satisfactory tone rendering and detail are required.

Above. LIONS—*A picture where exposure had to be estimated carefully. It required to be adequate to secure satisfactory texture and detail in the darker parts of the animals' fur, but any serious over-exposure would have resulted in lack of highlight detail. —* K. Hubschmann.

Page 114. BLACK FOREST VILLAGE—*Adequate exposure for the shadows, coupled with moderate development to avoid "blocking up" the highlights, has retained detail in the light and dark parts of the picture.*—H. S. Newcombe.

113

Exposure at night out of doors is almost invariably a compromise. It usually involves giving as long as one dare, without seriously over-exposing the bright lights, in order to secure as much shadow detail as may be possible.

Page 115. CHRISTMAS EVE—*Well illustrates the difficulties that the night photographer has to face. The lighted windows are already over-exposed, while there is only just enough detail in the surroundings. A subject of this nature can frequently be improved by the use of a surface developer.*—Paul Damm.

Above. STREET LAMPS—*Halation is the greatest enemy of night pictures. The use of a really good anti-halo film is imperative, and the inherently soft character of the very fast pan films is an advantage, even apart from their speed.*—H. S. Newcombe.

116

Indoors at night, particularly if moving figures are involved, the problem is usually one of securing sufficient exposure without risk of subject movement, and for this reason the most rapid films are essential.

Above. GROSVENOR HOUSE CABARET—*With a subject of this nature in rapid movement, fairly high shutter speeds are required, together with a really fast lens. Even then much depends on the skill of the photographer in catching a moment when the movement is less rapid than usual and in exploiting the available lighting to its best advantage.*—L. Vining.

117

In the snow, exposure requires to be estimated with care. If the motif is the sunlit snow itself, the exposure must be based on this, even if other darker objects, figures, etc., are rendered in silhouette. Remember, the shadows on snow are blue—*a yellow filter is usually desirable.*

Page 118. SNOW BLOSSOM—*A subject where the exposure has to be kept short, to make the most of the limited contrasts in the snow.*— H. S. Newcombe.

Page 119. STARTING BACK—*Facing the source of light, this picture preserves the texture of the snow with all its subtle inequalities which would be invisible if the sun were behind the camera. Again short exposure was used to bring detail into the light halftones while letting the shadows go. The light natural sky tone proves that it was not over-filtered.*— Paul Wolff.

Above. ALPINE VILLAGE—*An easy subject for exposure: no serious contrasts, no large areas of deep shadow. Focusing accomplished by depth scale so as to secure sharp detail in foreground and distance. Yellow filter used to preserve cloud forms against the blue sky.*— H. S. Newcombe.

120

HANDLING THE FILM

35 mm. film, because of its small size and the extent to which it must be enlarged, requires more than ordinarily careful handling. Scratches and minute flaws that might pass unnoticed in prints made from larger films are apt to appear as giant scars across the face of an enlargement made from the smaller negative. Flaws of this type can be caused at almost any stage of the proceedings.

Handle film by the edges only—even then, if your hands are not always bone dry and free from grease, wear a thin pair of cotton gloves whenever you are holding film, either in loading cassettes, cutting up or cleaning negatives or putting the film into the enlarger. I know it is a bit more trouble, but believe me it is worth while if you value your negatives.

If the film is bought in daylight loading cartridges, one may be sure that the maker has taken all possible precautions to ensure that it reaches the customer in a state of mechanical perfection; but it is not impossible for there to be some small hard fragment of adhesive or other substance in the velvet or felt with which the container is light trapped, and if you are so unfortunate as to secure a film container with this trouble it may quite easily show itself in the form of dead straight scratches, parallel to the edge of the film itself.

Fortunately such a mishap is rare in fresh films inserted into the camera as soon as they are unpacked; but it is rather more frequent in cartridges of film which have been carried about loose in camera case or pocket, where dust may have found its way into the mouth of the trap itself, and the trouble is infinitely more prevalent in cartridges which have been reloaded with film after previous use.

The makers' reloadable cassettes for Leica and Contax are not subject to this dust pest in the same way, as the aperture is open while the film is being used and rewound, but it is desirable to see that even these are not stored where dust can enter the container, as it will in all probability cause similar, but more intermittent, scratches on the celluloid back of the film, where it makes contact with the shell; or, by getting between the layers of film, may cause similar marks on the emulsion surface. The "cure" is prevention—ensuring that cassettes are free from dust when loaded, and that they are not exposed to dust prior to use.

Longitudinal scratches on the celluloid back of the film— if dead straight and very uniform or continuous, are almost always caused by the camera itself—possibly by a scratch on the pressure plate. This should be examined, and if it bears any mark that corresponds to that on the negative it should be referred to the maker's agent for correction.

HANDLING SHORT ENDS

THERE can be little excuse for producing scratched negatives when dealing with full camera loads of film. Admittedly it is somewhat more tricky to remove part of an exposed film for development.

If one has access to a dark room it is fairly straightforward to cut off any desired number of exposures provided that the camera has a removable back, as in the case of the Contax and others; and provided, of course, that you remember which *side* of the frame aperture you should make the cut. In the dark, it is not so obvious as it would seem to be when discussed in daylight. Remember the film lying across the "gate" is the one you have last exposed— better wind one more on for safety, and then cut through the film strip at the side of the gate *most distant* from the knob by which you have just wound on the film.

Leitz—realising that it is not quite so easy for the Leica user—make a special V-shaped knife which can be inserted into the camera, as soon as the cover plate is removed. The "V" catches the edge of the film, and cuts it through in the correct place, as the knife is thrust home. Again, it is necessary to wind on the film to clear it from the "gate" before cutting.

I do not consider this knife one of Leitz's most satisfactory accessories. I have known it break off fragments of film which have gone adrift inside the camera body where they have come to light by causing unexpected

122

trouble at a later date. My own method—primitive, but safe—when I wish to remove a portion of an exposed film from the Leica is: (*a*) Take one "waste" shot. (*b*) Remove the lens entirely. (*c*) Set shutter on "T" (or "B" if model I or II). (*d*) Open shutter—and while it is open— (*e*) Score a line across the film with the point of a penknife (do *not* cut *through* the film—only the emulsion surface). (*f*) Close shutter—replace lens. (*g*) Rewind film in normal manner as though removing a completely exposed roll. (*h*) (In the darkroom.) Pull film out of cassette, allowing the back of it to pass lightly over a finger tip as you do so. The faint "score" made by the knife will be clearly distinguished by touch and the film is cut at this point.

The remainder of the film is then trimmed to shape, and later re-inserted in the camera. It takes far less time to *do* all this than it takes to describe!

THE VARIABLE INFLUENCE OF DEVELOPMENT

DEVELOPING miniature films differs in no fundamental respect from processing larger materials, but there are certain differences which have to be kept in mind if the *best* results are to be obtained from 35 mm. negatives. These differences relate both to the developing formulæ and the developing methods which we employ.

There are four basic types of developers in use to-day. We can classify the three most generally used as *semi-fine grain, normal fine grain* and *ultra fine grain*. (See also pages 133 to 137 and 156.)

The *semi-fine grain developers* are those which exert considerable effect on the exposed film. They are generally used in the trade for amateur miniature film processing. (These should not be confused with the regular metol-hydroquinone developers used for processing large-sized films—which in any case would be *far* too vigorous for satisfactory use with miniature films. The types I have in mind are those in which the reducing agent is usually of the metol hydroquinone type, but used with a much milder alkali.)

123

Normal fine grain developers are usually to be found among those which employ a less vigorous reducing agent— possibly one of the "diamines" in conjunction with metol or glycin, or both; and which usually have a larger than normal proportion of sodium sulphite. With films in Class B, my own preference is for developers of this type. The only possible objection to their use is that they require a slightly more generous exposure than is necessary when using the semi-fine grain type of developer. As a rule an increase of 50–100 per cent is desirable, but this differs with different films and developers. Generally the slower films require less proportionate increase.

Ultra fine grain developers again make use of a very gentle developing agent. Paraphenylene-diamine, ortho-phenylene-diamine or the British proprietary chemical Meritol, all have this character, and they are for the most part used without alkali or with the very mildest alkali as an "accelerator". For this reason such developers do not build up excessive contrast very easily, and in almost every case require a considerably longer developing time than those previously mentioned. These developers require an even more fully exposed film than those handled in the normal fine grain developers. An increase in exposure time two to four times may be necessary.

Another type of developer, which is not so commonly used in this country, is what could be called a *surface developer*; this description exactly fits. The most generally used agent for such developers is *pyrocatechin*. While it does not form a particularly fine grain image it tends (in suitable formulæ) to confine its image-producing energies to the surface of the film. As has been said (p. 88), when pictures are taken in artificial light, more particularly where the actual light source is visible in the picture, the strong light impresses itself strongly on the film and penetrates to a considerable extent, thereby laying the foundation for trouble through halation. If, however, such a film be developed in a solution which acts mainly on the surface, a great deal of the reflected and scattered light which has affected the silver grains in the body of the emulsion will not be developed, and much of the potential halation will therefore never become visible.

124

Some of the fine grain producing qualities of these ultra fine grain developers are attributable to the amount of sodium sulphite which they contain. This has a solvent action on the silver halide grains, dissolving parts of them away during development. The dissolved silver halides are reduced to metallic silver in the developing solution and may be deposited on the surface of the emulsion during the process, and, if this is found to occur, it is desirable to remove it by gently swabbing the film with a tuft of the softest cotton-wool—under running water, between fixing and the final wash. Considerable care should be exercised in doing this to avoid physical damage to the very tender surface of the emulsion, but such treatment will prevent the formation of *dichroic fog*, as this deposit is called (it appears reddish when examined by transmitted light, and greenish when examined by reflected light).

DEVELOPER CLASSIFICATIONS

Semi-Fine Grain Developers requiring *normal* minimum exposure.

> Agfa Final
> Ansco 17
> Dupont N.D.2
> Edwal 10
> Ilford I.D. 11
> Johnson's Fine Grain
> Johnson's Unitol
> Kodak D.23, D.76
> Promicrol
> Tetenal Neofin Red
> Tetenal Neofin Blue
> Two-Bath   (Has special qualities—see p. 154.)

Normal Fine Grain Developers requiring generous exposure.

> Agfa Atomal
> Edwal 12
> Edwal 20
> Edwal, Minicol
> Focal Super Fine Grain
> Ilford I.D. 48
> Ilford Microphen
> Johnson's Meritol-Metol
> Kodak D.25
> Kodak Microdol
> M.C.M. 100
> Paraphenylene Diamine-Metol-Glycin (Dr. Sease)
> Tetenal Ultrafin
> X.33 Fink-Roselieve

Johnson's Meritol Super Fine Grain (increase 4×)
Sease III and N.D.3 (increase 2×)
Windisch W.665 Orthophenylene-diamine (increase 2–3×)

Because paraphenylene-diamine figures so largely in published ultra-fine grain formulae, it is desirable to record that this particular chemical has certain demerits. It is toxic and produces severe skin irritation in people who are susceptible to developer poisoning, and it also stains very badly. There are certain alternatives to paraphenylene-diamine, notably orthophenylene-diamine and the chemical Meritol.

Although very popular at one time, ultra fine grain developers have greatly declined in importance with the advent of fine grain and ultra fine grain films of reasonable speed. For finest grain and definition it is thus more sensible to use an ultra-fine grain film in conjunction with a high-definition developer (pp. 136–137). Even with a medium-speed fine grain film the results are often better on development in a normal fine grain developer than with a high-speed film developed in an ultra fine grain developer. Ultra-speed films should never be developed in a developer requiring any exposure increase; the whole point of such films is to make the most of speed. Under light conditions where no other film would yield an acceptable picture at all, a grainy negative is still better than an unprintably thin one.

When an exposed film is put into one of the light-tight tanks, used for 35 mm. processing (p. 140), and the developer poured in, all that is taking place is hidden from the photographer. In a way, the old-fashioned worker who developed his less colour sensitive plates in an open dish by a fairly bright red light had much more fun. He had the immense thrill of watching a smooth creamy surface as it gradually darkened under the influence of the developer. He saw faint signs of blackening after the first minute or two; he watched until he was able to recognise them as the shapes of the brightest parts of the subject—perhaps the sky—if he were developing a landscape. As these traces of tone gradually grew in strength, he watched other less brightly lit parts of the subject appear in order of their

126

brilliance, until at last he saw that all the available details had been recorded on the plate.

While this process had been taking place, the first parts to darken had grown gradually in density, and all other parts of the image had followed the same plan. If he had removed the plate too early—i.e. before development was "complete"—and fixed the *under*-developed negative, he would have been disappointed to find that it was lacking in contrast, and that the details in the shadow parts were missing altogether. By continuing development until he saw that all the necessary detail was on the plate, he also ensured that there was adequate contrast between the light and the dark parts of the subject. If he *over*-developed his plate, he was faced with a negative which would only make a very harsh print, in which, by the time he had printed it sufficiently to secure detail in the high lights, the shadows would be almost black and devoid of detail.

The old-fashioned worker had, then, certain advantages over the present-day camera user. He could, at least, see *when* he had secured the best result. We have to rely on developing according to time table. Fortunately the film and developer makers have provided us with fairly accurate information on this point, and I think it is safe to say that a far higher percentage of satisfactory results is probably to be had when tables are used than when the matter was left to the judgment of the operator.

Temperature, however, influences development time. A cold developer acts slowly and its energy increases fairly regularly with increases of temperature until a point is reached where it is unsafe to develop because of the risk of the relatively hot solution softening, or even dissolving, the gelatine of the film itself. The makers' instructions or the particulars of time and temperature given with the various published formulæ should be carefully studied in this connection.

In my own experience, however, some of the developer manufacturers quote a developing time which, irrespective of temperature, gives a somewhat more contrasty negative than that which I find best for miniature work. I have heard many other people offer the same criticism, and I believe that the explanation is that most of the

127

developer manufacturers realise that films frequently are going to be exposed with an implicit acceptance of their makers' estimate of the film speed, the exposure possibly being assessed by means of a photo-electric meter used in the ordinary "aggregate" way (see p. 108). The result of this is that the film to my mind is a shade under-exposed, and that much of the image is being formed on what we have already learned to call the "toe" of the curve (p. 105). In such cases a fairly prolonged development time is necessary to secure adequate tone separation so that the negative itself will print satisfactorily.

The majority of popular miniature film developers, particularly those which are packed ready to make up into convenient quantities of 20, 30 or 35 oz. can be used more than once and, although one cannot lay down a hard and fast rule, the majority can be returned to the stock bottle (preferably filtering the solution) and used again for anything up to 3 or 4 reels of film. Almost all the developers with which we are concerned have some degree of solvent action on the silver halides in the emulsion of the film itself and it is not uncommon for them to become cloudy after the first or second time of usage. This cloudiness does not necessarily disappear entirely with filtering, and it seems that it can be ignored as it has no apparent effect on the performance of the developer itself. Each time a developer is used, however, it loses something of its strength and, although different developers vary to a trifling extent in this particular, it is a fairly safe rule to increase the development time by about 5 to 10 per cent. for each successive film that has been put through it. Some makers give definite information in this respect, and when such guidance is explicitly given it can be safely followed. One or two developers appear to be a little erratic in this respect and are unsafe to use after perhaps three times, but this seems to vary in different districts and it is probable that such vagaries can be attributed to the differences in the chemical content of the local water supply. During the past few years the use of replenishers has found wide acceptance. The addition of a prescribed quantity of replenisher after each development makes it possible to maintain the original developer strength throughout the useful life of the solutions.

NO CHAPTER on making miniature negatives would be regarded as adequate without some reference to "gamma". I have the feeling that there has been more careless talk about this word than about anything else in photography. Film makers, and technical writers on miniature processing are probably originally responsible for the way in which it has slipped into the ordinary photographer's vocabulary, as in describing the action of materials and solutions they have frequently adopted the course of stating that development of so many minutes duration produces a gamma of ".7" and so many more minutes of ".8" and so on.

Now "gamma" is something which the ordinary camera user cannot easily measure; it needs instruments and procedures of a sensitometric laboratory.

"Gamma" (indicated by the symbol γ) is the scientific term describing the degree of contrast in a negative; and a negative in which the contrasts of the original subject are *exactly* reproduced (black reversed to white, etc.) is said to possess a γ of 1.0. Consequently a negative in which the contrasts between the various tones are *less* than the contrasts between the same tones in the original itself is said to have a γ of "0-point-something", while one which shows an *increase* of contrast in comparison with the original will have a γ of "1-point-something". This "contrast", as compared to that of the original subject, is *primarily* governed by the length of time the film is left in the developer.

When an exposed film is immersed in the developing solution, those parts which have been affected by light gradually darken in proportion to the extent to which they have been exposed. At first there is very little difference between the "steps" of the tones, but as development proceeds the contrast steadily grows, until after a predetermined time, according to the developer used, the contrast is sufficient for our purposes, and for the requirements of the particular printing process to be employed. The film is then rinsed, fixed and dried.

Any degree of under-development will produce a negative which, while full of detail, is deficient in contrast between the various tones, i.e. is of "too low a gamma".

129

Similarly, too long an immersion in the developer will result in an unwanted increase in the degree of contrast.

For moderate degrees of under- and over-development, a good remedy lies in the right choice of printing paper (p. 281). (Intensification and reduction are also correctives of under- and over-development—within limits.)

In describing the films that we use 1 have referred to films which are "inherently contrasty"—or, as the scientist would say, films which "readily yield a high gamma". This must be understood to mean that such films *can* produce a contrasty image, rather than to infer that they *must* do so. *With suitable development* even those films that are described as contrasty will produce soft, well-graded negatives.

I suggest that, when starting with an entirely new developer, a piece of film should be used up in making a really informative test. My own method is to select a subject in which there is a long range of tones, and to ascertain the *correct exposure by meter* (CEM). I then make a series of exposures, at ¼CEM, ½CEM, CEM, 2CEM, and 4 CEM. Then, after one blank frame, I scratch the film as described on p. 123, and expose a further blank frame. This procedure is repeated twice more. After that the film is then cut into its three sections, one being developed for the time recommended by the maker, and, after this has been examined, the second and third strips are developed for longer or, more probably, for shorter times. Whichever of the three results turns out to be satisfactory will supply my basic developing time for future films of that make with this particular developer and temperature. In general I have found that most of the developer makers' times can be cut by 10 or even 20 per cent, *provided that the film has been adequately exposed*. If a film is known to be under-exposed, as may happen through force of circumstances, then the full recommended time should be given.

One of the soundest basic rules ever offered to the miniature camera user is attributable to that famous Leica pioneer *Dr. Paul Wolff*. His recipe for securing fine grain was given as: "Expose generously—develop moderately". I mention this now because the rule can still safely be followed *with films of moderate speed*.

SUITING THE FILM TO THE DEVELOPER

WE HAVE already considered our films as coming under five headings, and we have seen our more popular developers similarly grouped. It will have occurred to the reader that, apart from Groups AA and D, we have three types of films which have a speed ratio of about 1: 2: 4. Also that we have three developer classes which have what we can call an "image-producing potential" in the proportion of 4: 2: 1, and which consequently call for overexposure in the reverse proportion. We can say that if the three main types of films have the same exposure (which should be that which is correct for the slowest) and are then developed in the three appropriate developers— we shall get something like the same result (in grain size and effective speed) from:—

normal exposure on slow (A) film if developed in semi-fine grain developer;

twice the normal exposure on medium fast (B) film if developed in a normal fine grain developer;

three or four times normal exposure on very fast (C) film if developed in ultra fine grain developer.

Casting the mind back to the individual characteristics of the films and the developers, it will be apparent that while the grain size and the ultimate net speed exploited will be similar, there are other features that will make for considerable differences in the results. The slow film is so fine grained that it will stand semi-fine grain developer without the grain size becoming unduly enlarged; the medium film will yield a smooth and grain-free image with the normal fine grain developer; and the inherently large grain of the rapid film will be minimised by the ultra-fine grain treatment it receives. One point, however, in which these three films may differ considerably is in contrast or brightness. Slow film is itself of a fundamentally contrasty nature, and the energetic development to which we have subjected it is likely to maintain this characteristic; the intermediate film and developer will be somewhat softer in character and probably better suited to most enlarging needs, while the fast film with its gradation will be kept still softer by the super-fine grain development.

Ultra fine grain developers should never be used with *ultra*-fast films; the latter are designed primarily for specially difficult light conditions, and not for fine grain techniques.

A subject which is in itself of soft and gentle contrast can be made crisp and bright by using the slow film semifine grain developer combination; and similarly, a subject in which there are wide extremes of contrast can be softened by a combination of fast film and ultra fine grain developer.

Both combinations have some advantages—both have drawbacks—and I suggest that the needs of the majority of miniature workers will best be met by the remaining combination—that is, to employ a film of medium speed, processed in a *normal fine grain* developer. The makes favoured do not matter a great deal, but, whatever pair is selected, stick to them until the peculiarities of both film and developer are fully mastered. *Nothing is so likely to produce consistently bad results as to keep changing from one make of developer or film to another.*

To make the most of the speed potentialities of a fast film, the method of development recommended above is of course no good. If you want speed you can have it—at the expense of grain. For pictures of subjects where you know that your fastest films are likely to be underexposed, you must choose your developer from the *semifine grain* list, or, if the degree of under-exposure is severe, from the developers recommended on p. 156. If the results are a little granular and if you cannot enlarge them as much as you would wish, you must be satisfied that you have got some sort of result after all. No matter what makers suggest in their advertisements, *high speed means coarser grain*—to some extent at least. Some makes of film may be better than others. The basic fact remains: if you choose speed you must sacrifice something.

If you want the finest possible grain, then select one of the slower type films and develop it in a developer from the normal fine grain list. The normal fine grain developers seem to give almost as fine a grain on the very slow films as do those from the ultra fine grain group. As already mentioned, these slower films do not require proportionately as much over-exposure as the fastest films.

With the very slow films of the AA class, the grain is inherently very fine. It is therefore quite satisfactory to employ developers of the D76 or I D.11 type, which bring out full film speed and still secure fine grain negatives. *But:* exposure must be right, and development carefully controlled; the slightest over-development will produce a negative which is extremely difficult to print satisfactorily.

For the worker who has difficulty in accurately determining the exposure required, or who wants to record a variety of subjects of widely differing contrast ranges, the use of an A or B film, and the development advocated on page 124 is, probably, still the best compromise.

The secret of successful 35 mm. work is very largely covered by the word *moderation*. Avoidance of extremes, in film speed, exposure and development, makes possible the production of a negative in which the range of tones from highlight to shadow is well recorded, and in such form as to be printable. The perfect miniature negative yields its best print on a medium grade of paper (see p. 282). If the negative be placed face down over a page of printed matter we should be able clearly to distinguish the shape of bold type through even the densest part of the film, except in the case of some films on a deeply tinted base. This thin, detailed type of negative is desirable for miniature work, as it is usually more grain-free than one with a heavier deposit; and in addition it is considerably easier to focus in the enlarger, while requiring shorter enlarging exposures.

FINE GRAIN V. GOOD DEFINITION

AMONG the film types we have discussed, the "AA" group deserves some further note. These films are fundamentally of the finest practicable *grain* structure. Their emulsions are very thin; and—this is the really important part—they are capable of recording infinitely finer *detail* than any of the other emulsions. But they must receive the correct treatment for this purpose.

Hitherto we have discussed methods of procuring the

Type of Film	Type of developer	Makers' Film Speed rating ° BS (ASA)	Degree of over-exposure required	Actual Net Film Speed	Grain characteristics
Slow (A or AA) Fine grain Panchromatic	Semi-Fine grain	23° (16) to 25° (25)	None	23° (16) to 25° (25)	Very fine grain
Slow (A or AA) Fine grain Panchromatic	Normal Fine grain	23° (16) to 25° (25)	1½ × to 2 ×	20° (8) to 23° (16)	Exceptionally fine
Slow (A or AA) Fine grain Panchromatic	Ultra Fine grain	23° (16) to 25° (25)	2 × to 3×	20° (8) to 22° (12)	Grainless
Medium Speed (B) Panchromatic	Semi-Fine grain	27° (40) to 30° (80)	None	27° (40) to 30° (80)	Reasonably fine
Medium Speed (B) Panchromatic	Normal Fine grain	27° (40) to 30° (80)	2×	24° (20) to 27° (40)	Very fine
Medium Speed (B) Panchromatic	Ultra Fine grain	27° (40) to 30° (80)	3× to 4×	21° (10) to 24° (20)	Exceptionally fine
Super Speed (C) Panchromatic	Semi-Fine grain	31° (100) to 34° (200)	None	31° (100) to 34° (200)	Rather coarse
Super Speed (C) Panchromatic	Normal Fine grain	31° (100) to 34° (200)	2×	28° (50) to 31° (100)	Moderate grain
Super Speed (C) Panchromatic	Ultra Fine grain	31° (100) to 34° (200)	3× to 4×	25° (25) to 28° (50)	Reasonably fine
Extreme Speed (D) Panchromatic	Semi-Fine grain	35° (250) and over	None	35° (250) and over	Coarse

Gradation or contrast	Resolution or definition	Purpose for which combination is best suited
Rather contrasty	Exceptionally good (See also p. 138)	Suitable for subjects which are lacking in contrast, e.g. on a dull day—or by very flat lighting.
Bright and "crisp"	Very good indeed	A good combination where a considerable degree of enlargement is required: particularly for soft contrast subjects.
Moderate contrast	Very good	Produces grainless enlargement to a considerable size.
Bright and "crisp"	Very good indeed	Suitable combination for all average work and for reasonable degree of enlargement.
Ideal for big enlargements	Very good indeed	*The best combination for all general outdoor work. Enlarges exceptionally well.*
Gentle but adequate contrast	Quite adequate	A good combination for all subjects which will require *considerable* enlargement ($15 \times$ or more).
Average to soft contrast	Reasonably good	The best choice for poorly lit subjects and where maximum speed is required.
Soft contrast	Moderately good	A good combination for contrasty subjects—or where the photographer must be prepared to tackle any type of event by day or night.
Very soft	Only fair	Useful to reduce the contrasts of *very* hard subjects to produce a harmonious negative.
Moderately soft	Fair	For pictures under "impossible" conditions. Do *not* use other developer types.

finest *grain*, but this does not necessarily mean the best *definition*. The methods by which we obtain finely divided silver grains—the use of " gentle" reducing agents or developers with silver solvent, coupled with a degree of over-exposure—do undoubtedly produce negatives in which the grain structure is smooth and unobjectionable. But the result of the generous exposure is a certain degree of "spreading" of the light forming the image, so that the resulting negative, while commendably grainless, may lack the ultimate crispness of definition.

I am not condemning the methods so far recommended, which are completely satisfactory with the more commonly used films. But for maximum resolution of fine detail, films from the "AA" group—despite their low speed, high contrast, and limited latitude—seem to offer the best solution when treated as recommended below.

For the finest detail we need a comparatively vigorous developer, and minimum exposures for the rated speed. Except with subjects of extremely rapid movement, the large apertures of our lenses will overcome the drawback of a relatively slow emulsion. The lack of latitude can only be dealt with by the careful use of an exposure meter, and by avoiding subjects of excessive contrast (for which films from the "A" or preferably the "B" group should be chosen). Careful timing in development, and standardised agitation will keep the contrast of the image within reasonable bounds.

Under these conditions, it is possible—in fact *desirable*—to use developers which, in the ordinary way, are considered as unsuitable for successful miniature work.

With films which are so inherently fine grained, we have no need to try to improve this characteristic. We can confine our attention to securing the sharpest possible detail, and this will be produced by developers which have no excess of silver solvent in their make-up. Because the films with which we are concerned are fundamentally contrasty, we must select a developer which is soft-working.

For our immediate purpose, a formula containing Metol and sodium carbonate (with only sufficient sulphite as a preservative against oxidation) is likely to prove most suitable. Other developers which are to be recommended for this work are the commercially prepared single solution

136

(para-aminophenol) types, e.g. *Rodinal, Perinal, Azol,* etc., all of which have the desired property of making the most of under exposure, and building up density gradually. This method—in my experience—gives better *definition* than I can obtain by any other means.

Exceptionally good proprietary solutions designed to produce the maximum resolution with these slow, grainless films are represented by *Kodak "High Definition" developer, Neofin Blue (Tetenal)* and *Adox E.* 10 (*Dr. Schleussner*).

These developers yield the finest resolution without building up excessive contrast; and with them *minimum* exposures must be given. In fact it is generally necessary to rate the film slightly *above* its normal speed to secure the best results.

Neofin Blue is appreciably different in its behaviour from most other developers. Although it yields detail in the shadows very readily, it does not seem able to produce harsh contrast, even on slow and inherently contrasty emulsions— unless, of course, development is prolonged far beyond the recommended time. Because of this *Neofin Blue* should only be used with films in the "AA" and "A" classes; with softer emulsions it does not produce negatives of sufficiently high gamma for normal printing. For such films the makers produce *Neofin Red* which has a rather more vigorous action. Its performance—at least to my mind—is, however, not greatly different from some of the other fine grain types already listed, and I would advise readers seeking the finest technical quality to experiment along the lines mentioned with the "AA" materials and the appropriate processing.

Nowadays, except when my films contain negatives of subjects of widely varying contrast, I have adopted the "AA" film with this form of development as my standard practice. I find that it is producing perceptibly sharper results, on average, than I can obtain by any other combination of materials and processing procedure.

Where the absolute ultimate in resolution is not vitally necessary, a useful compromise that I have used over thousands of exposures is a combination of Pan F with D.76 or D.23, and normal exposures. This is simple, the developer is inexpensive and reliable, and keeps well for intermittent use.

SUCCESSFUL miniature processing depends on attention to detail. For the 35 mm. negative adequately to compete with its bigger brothers, processing must be carried out with care. Surface marks on the negative, due to scratches or dust, are fatal. Our place of work must be as dust-free as possible. Tanks and other utensils should be clean, chemically as well as physically. In short, the worker should secure the nearest approach to "laboratory"—as distinct from ordinary "darkroom"—conditions.

In domestic surroundings the dust menace can never entirely be overcome, but much can be done by keeping the darkroom, whether it be temporary or permanent, free from unnecessary furniture and other articles that can harbour dust. A vacuum cleaner should frequently be employed all over the room, including walls, shelves, etc. This should not be done, however, immediately before commencing work as, while the vacuum cleaner will remove much of the trouble-causing fragments, it will also stir up those that it does not collect. If a ventilating system is employed, one with an extractor fan is to be preferred, and this should be placed—adequately light trapped—high up on a suitable wall. An air inlet, low down on the opposite wall is desirable; and if a moistened cloth is lightly draped over this—inside—it will do much to trap the dust particles that are in the air drawn in. Further, I would like to stress the desirability of moving about as little as possible when preparing for a session of developing or enlarging.

Some form of heating is desirable. Nothing is so conducive to bad work as cold working conditions, even disregarding the necessity for maintaining the proper temperatures of solutions. In my own darkroom I have a 1,000 watt workshop heater permanently installed on a shelf under my "wet" work bench. As it can be enclosed or open at will it serves to heat the room and/or to keep the top of the work bench at a temperature of 70° to 75° F. when required.

The positioning of one's processing equipment naturally is dependent on the shape and dimensions of the darkroom; but it is well to divide this into *wet* and *dry* processes, and to arrange benches for these on opposite sides as far as possible. The wet bench is used for all film and paper processing operations and for preparing solutions. A sink with hot and cold running water can usefully be built in at one end of it. A rubber connection from the cold tap to a large developing dish via an *Eastman* washing syphon is adequate to take care of print washing—at least on a non-professional scale.

In my own darkroom, chemicals are stored in wall cupboards and on shelves over this bench—which, incidentally, is 3 ft. 6 in. high so as to avoid the necessity for stooping to examine prints, etc. Under the bench, shelves are provided for the storage of developing tanks, dishes, etc.

On the dry side of the room is found the enlarger, together with shelves and cupboards for the safe storage of bromide paper, cans of film and other perishables. Print trimming and mounting are dealt with here or elsewhere in the house as convenience dictates.

Because it is called a darkroom, many people seem to think that its walls should be painted a sombre colour. Never was there a greater mistake. My walls are covered with washable cream and white paint and, although my only illumination (when working) comes from a 12×10 in. safelight lamp hanging over the developing dishes, the light walls reflect enough light to ensure comfortable working conditions anywhere in the room. If the original light *is* "safe" for the material used—as it will be if the appropriate screen is chosen from the manufacturer's range—there is no added risk in reflecting this light all over the room, while the gain in comfort is very considerable. My workroom has a 60-watt lamp for general illumination; and in addition a 40-watt "Daylight Blue" lamp mounted over the fixing bath. I find this invaluable when examining a print to ensure that it is of good colour. The yellower tint of the ordinary gas-filled lamp does not so readily show subtle tone or colour variations; nor does it reveal the—mercifully rare—lemon yellow stains which occasionally result from prolonged print development.

35 MM. FILM development is usually carried out in circular tanks made of moulded composition material or in some cases stainless steel. Two principles are employed.

In one (*Correx*) the tank contains a plain spool, on which is wound a transparent celluloid apron 35 mm. wide which is somewhat longer than the film. This apron has indentations and projections alternating along each edge where the perforation of the film runs and is plain in the larger centre area, corresponding to that part of the film on which the picture lies. In use, the end of the apron is secured under a spring clip on the core of the spool and the end of the film is similarly attached with its emulsion inwards. To load such a tank the film is removed from its cartridge or cassette, and attached to the core as just described. The tank spool is then held so that the apron hangs down by its own weight and the spool rotated so as to wind the film and apron on it simultaneously. The indentations in the edge of the apron prevent adjacent layers of film and apron from touching each other, except on the perforated edges. The film is guided into its proper position by allowing it to pass between finger and thumb resting lightly on its edges only. When all the film is wound on to the spool it is detached from its own core and the apron securing clip fastened over the edges of the reel.

The other type of tank, of which there are many makes, has no apron. Instead, the film is fed into a spiral groove moulded on the inner faces of the spool flanges. The majority of these tanks are loaded by feeding the free end of the film into the outside groove and coaxing it in until the spiral is filled tight to the centre. Some grooved tanks, however (e.g. *Leitz* and *Agfa*), are so designed that the film is first attached to the *centre* of the spool, and the film (which has to be bent concave to clear the edges of the spiral grooves) is then allowed to expand to fill the grooves as the spool is slowly turned with the hand. Some modern spiral groove tanks have a top section which rotates to and fro. With each half of the spool alternately gripping one side of the film, this to-and-fro movement automatically feeds the whole film into the groove without any trouble.

Most tanks have some provision for the developer to be poured in after the film is inside and the lid attached, but I much prefer to have the tank already filled with developer and then to plunge the spool in, so as to ensure wetting the whole film surface at once. After a few brisk movements—vertically, and by rotating the spool—to ensure that any trapped air bubbles are broken, I put the lid on the tank and switch on the light.

To ensure regular and uniform development the film should be moved in the developer at intervals during development. If a film is allowed to remain stationary in stagnant developer for the whole of the developing time it will in almost all cases show dark lines running vertically down it; lines corresponding in position to the perforations along the edge of the film.

Standard agitation is, however, important as the difference in development time between stagnant development and development in which the film is agitated continuously may be as great as two to one.

This agitation business deserves considerable attention. If it is inadequate the film will be unevenly developed, probably blotchy, and of insufficient contrast.

If, however, it is overdone there will be even greater troubles: in addition to excessive contrast, the local turbulence effects of too much "knob-twiddling" will probably produce negatives in which the edges are perceptibly denser than the centre of the film.

The old agitation method—gently turning the spiral, and *gently* raising and lowering it—is usually completely satisfactory with a processing time of some 15–20 minutes. But with modern slow films and development of 5 to 10 minutes, agitation by these methods may not produce completely even negatives. In such cases the increasingly current "watertight" tanks are to be recommended, as with these agitation is secured by *inverting* the tank, thus moving the developer in relation to the stationary film and spool, rather than the reverse. I can vouch for the efficiency of this method: the only one that I now use.

It would seem that there is precious little new under the sun—thirty years ago I used a Kodak developing box and tank for rollfilms which employed precisely this method!

141

WHEN a miniature film has been developed it should be rinsed for a few minutes by allowing water to run through the tank prior to filling the tank with the fixing solution, temperature 65° to 70° F. An alternative to this is to pour out the developer and pour in an acid stop bath:

Water	500 c.cm.	or 16 oz.
Chrome alum.	10 grm.	or 145 gr.
Sodium bisulphite (anhydrous)	10 grm.	or 145 gr.

Dissolve in order stated *and filter*. This solution will not keep.

THIS solution should go straight into the tank as soon as the developer is emptied out; no intermediate rinse is necessary. The film should be allowed to remain in the stop bath with slight agitation for five minutes, after which this should be discarded and the normal acid fixing bath poured in. This stop bath is sufficiently acid to arrest development immediately, and it exerts a hardening effect on the gelatine emulsion which protects the film from mechanical injury in subsequent operations, encourages it to dry more rapidly, and at the same time kills any excessive alkalinity in the film itself prior to its immersion in the acid fixing bath.

Another excellent stop bath which *will* keep in solution—is:—

Water	1000	c.cm.	32 ozs
Chrome Alum	30	grm.	1 oz.

The function of the fixing bath (hypo) is to remove from the film all the silver salts that have not been "reduced" to metallic silver during the process of development; and it is necessary, in order to avoid stains and to secure permanence, that fixation be *complete*. Most recommended fixing baths are acid in character, and thus, by neutralising the alkaline developer, also arrest development almost immediately.

If the film were to be examined at this stage (this should, of course, *not* be done) it would present itself as an opaque creamy coloured strip on which the negative image appeared in various shades of grey. Fixation disposes of this creamy deposit of unused silver salt, and leaves behind the developed silver forming the image. Unfortunately there is no hard or fast rule as to the exact length of time required for complete fixation, but it is safe to remove the tank lid and examine the back of a film after it has had—with intermittent agitation—about 5 minutes in any freshly made acid fixer. Fixation may be considered complete when the film has been in the bath *at least twice* as long as is necessary for the last traces of the creaminess to disappear. Films should not be allowed to remain unnecessarily long in the fixer, as it may dissolve some of the more delicate shadow details. The period suggested above will be perfectly safe.

Thin, slow and single coated films invariably fix more speedily than rapid or double coated emulsions.

Cold fixing baths work slowly. So keep the temperature up to 65°–70° F.

Make a practice of using fresh solutions and filter them immediately before use. This is particularly important with acid fixers and acid stop baths.

When fixation is complete, rinse the film in the tank and put it under running water, so that the stream from the tap falls into the hollow top of the spool centre. This encourages the water to flow down the core, and spread upwards through the film.

Once the film has been adequately washed—which means at least 20 minutes in running water—it should be hung up to dry. Some workers make a practice of swabbing it down with a tuft of cotton wool, very soft chamois leather or a viscose sponge. I have tried all these methods, but now prefer to hang the film up and let it drain naturally. The drying marks on the surface of the emulsion which are supposed to be removed by wiping the film down, do not seem to occur with modern films and I am convinced that, by avoiding touching the surface of the film while it is wet, the majority of scratches found on miniature films are also avoided. The surface of a film immediately after development is unbelievably tender. The only advantage that I can see in wiping a film down is that the drying time is appreciably lessened, and the only *safe* wiper that I have discovered is one with two soft rubber blades—something like those of a windscreen wiper.

Parallel but "wavy" scratches down the surface of the emulsion almost always owe their origin to wiping down the film after development and washing. As I have just said, I find no drawback to hanging up the strip just as it comes from the final wash and allowing it to drain off without touching it until it is dry. If I had trouble with drying marks on the surface, I would try the use of a *wetting agent*, of which several are now on the market. Wetting agents reduce the "surface tension" of the film and allow water to drain more rapidly along and through the emulsion, which also promotes rapid drying. Bathing the film in a dilute (about 2 per cent) solution of Hydrochloric or Citric Acid dissolves any scum due to chalk or lime, leaves a very clean film, but tends to soften the emulsion.

I find it unwise to use acid bath and a wetting agent on the same film. It sometimes causes trouble through scum and/or reticulation. Results vary however and some workers use both without trouble. If I may repeat the warning—*if possible avoid wiping wet films*. I have seen more scratches from this cause than from any other.

Drying must be carried out in a dust-free atmosphere. The wet film is a trap for any fragments of matter suspended in the air and, once dust has dried on to the emulsion, nothing will remove it. Choose a suitable room that is free from dust, suspend the film from a line or pin it to the picture rail (emulsion outwards) with a weighted clip on the lower end to ensure that it dries flat. Avoid using the room while the film is drying. Avoid draughty places— draught usually means dust as well. This is, I think, the only advice that I can give to the "domestic" worker. The professional will doubtless have a dust-free and possibly heated drying cupboard for the purpose.

When a film has been drained and dried naturally, as I advocate, the emulsion will almost always be flawless, but the *celluloid back* will usually show a variety of drop shaped drying marks. These are easily removable. As soon as the film is perfectly dry place it face down on a *clean* piece of smooth paper, and, *holding it so that it cannot possibly slip*, which might cause emulsion surface scratches, wipe the back with a slightly moist soft rag (an *old* handkerchief is ideal). Do this with a very light circular movement and then polish off the film with a piece of similar material which is bone dry. The celluloid should

144

now look like polished glass and be free from all marks.

Chemical cleanliness is highly desirable at all times. Dishes, measures, etc., should be periodically treated. Developing tanks of the spiral groove type will prove easier to load if they are cleaned regularly by immersion in one of the solutions given below. Only a small quantity need be poured in the tank, which can be tilted so that the fluid has access to all parts. Spiral reels can best be dealt with in two separate halves, as then less solution is required to cover them. After allowing the cleanser to act for about one minute, the article must be *thoroughly* washed under running water. Tank spirals *must* be bone dry before attempting to load, so cleansing should take place *after* use rather than just before it is intended to develop.

CLEANSING	Potassium bichromate	90 grm.	7 oz.
DISHES	Sulphuric acid	96 c.cm.	8 oz.
	Water	1000 c.cm.	80 oz.

Always add acid to water—*not* the reverse, and do it *slowly*—while stirring.

| *Alternatively* | Hydrochloric acid | 200 c.cm. | 16 oz. |
| | Water | 1000 c.cm. | 80 oz. |

HOW DO YOU STORE YOUR FILMS?

I HOPE that you take them down after drying and cut them up *at once* into strips of 3, 4 or 6 frames. Some misguided manufacturers used to make boxes with many small circular holes, expressly for storing 35 mm. films in rolls. Nothing will ruin your negatives more quickly than rolling and unrolling them whenever you are searching for a particular subject. If you *do* keep your films this way, I feel fairly sure that at some time you have found the roll just too big to fit the hole in the box, and the natural action— to decrease its diameter—is to hold the roll in one hand and to pull the free end with the other, cinching it into a tighter spool. Examination of a film after this treatment will reveal a host of "tramlines" on both front and back, where the two surfaces have been pulled over each other.

No! Please cut your films up as soon as they are dry and store them in one of the many filing systems which are on the market. If you use one in which the negatives are contained in semi-transparent paper containers, and if, as I do, you make contact prints of your film strips for reference, I suggest that you file the strip of prints with the film strip, in the same pocket. If you do this so that the film lies emulsion *up*, and then place the print strip, picture side *up*, on top of it, you can then slide both *together* into the container and thus eliminate even the risk of surface scratch to the film against the paper or Cellophane container. You can usually see the prints quite well enough to identify what is in the pocket, and can remove both for closer examination at any time it is desired.

If by any mischance a strip of negatives becomes dusty, tap its edge smartly on the table to dislodge the dust and remove any that still adheres with a *soft* camel hair brush, kept for the purpose. *Do not wipe* it off with a cloth— or the fingers!

35 mm. film receives the most incredible care in manufacture—and by attention to a few details in the subsequent handling such as are suggested above, there is no reason why this same physical perfection should not be retained so that the production of flawless enlargements of considerable size can be looked for, almost as a matter of course.

Never handle films—even by their edges—if your hands are moist; and in the darkroom *never* dry your hands on a towel after they have become wet with developer or hypo. Go out and wash them thoroughly with soap and water and dry them on a clean towel before touching any film or printing paper. In fact—to be *really* safe—*never* allow developer or hypo to touch your skin. Use vulcanite or stainless steel tweezers all the time when enlarging, and make a point of keeping one pair for developing and another of different type for the hypo so as to avoid mistakes.

146

RECOMMENDED DEVELOPER FORMULAE

In the formulæ which follow, the metric quantities do not *necessarily* correspond with the avoirdupois, owing to the different volumes of developer. The actual composition of the solution is of course the same whichever system of measurement is adopted.

SEMI-FINE GRAIN DEVELOPERS

ANSCO	Metol	1.5	grm.			23	gr.
17	Sodium sulphite (anhydrous)	80	grm.	2 oz.	360		gr.
	Hydroquinone	3	grm.			46	gr.
	Borax crystals	3	grm.			46	gr.
	Potassium bromide	0.5	grm.			7.5	gr.
	Water to make	1000	c.cm.			35	oz.

EDWAL	Metol	5	grm.			77	gr.
10	Sodium sulphite (anhydrous)	100	grm.	3 oz.	230		gr.
	Borax crystals	10	grm.			154	gr.
	Potassium bromide	5	grm.			77	gr.
	Water to make	1000	c.cm.			35	oz.

DUPONT	Metol	2.5	grm.			38	gr.
N.D.2	Sodium sulphite (anhydrous)	75	grm.	2 oz.	280		gr.
	Hydroquinone	3	grm.			46	gr.
	Borax (granulated)	5	grm.			77	gr.
	Water to make	1000	c.cm.			35	oz.

KODAK	Elon (metol)	2	grm.			31	gr.
D.76	Sodium sulphite (anhydrous)	100	grm.	3 oz.	230		gr.
(ILFORD	Hydroquinone	5	grm.			77	gr.
ID.11)	Borax crystals	2	grm.			31	gr.
	Water to make	1000	c.cm.			35	oz.

A recently introduced formula producing about the same film speed and grain as *D*.76 is

KODAK	Elon (metol)	7.5	grm.			115	gr.
D.23	Sodium sulphite (anhydrous)	100	grm.	3 oz.	230		gr.
	Water to make	1000	c.cm.			35	oz.

Designed to serve as an ordinary developer for use at 68° F. (20° C.), when it requires an average developing time of 20 minutes, this formula is particularly recommended for tropical use as it may safely be employed at temperatures up to 85° F. without fear of chemical fogging or other troubles, provided a chrome alum stop bath (p. 142) is used between development and fixation. The time of development is likely to be 4 to 7 minutes at this temperature for most films.

Other well-known developers in this class, with fundamentally the same characteristics, include *Agfa Final, Buffered Borax, Burroughs-Wellcome Fine Grain, Gevaert G. 203. Johnson's Fine Grain, Unitol, Metol Sulphite, Piramid.*

NORMAL FINE GRAIN DEVELOPERS

CHAMPLIN	Sodium sulphite (anhydrous)	100	grm.	3 oz.	230	gr.
16	Chlorquinol	50	grm.	1 oz.	280	gr.
	Tironamin "C"	60	c.cm.	2 oz.	2	dr.
	or Kodalk	21	grm.		320	gr.
	Water to make	1000	c.cm.		35	oz.

EDWAL	Gradol (or Para-aminophenol)	5	grm.		77	gr.
20	Sodium sulphite (anhydrous)	90	grm.	3 oz.	80	gr.
	Paraphenylene diamine	10	grm.		154	gr.
	Glycin	5	grm.		77	gr.
	Water to make	1000	c.cm.		35	oz.

FOCAL	Metol	3	grm.		60	gr.
SUPER FINE	Sodium sulphite (anhydrous)	90	grm.		3½	oz.
	Borax (crystal)	1	grm.		20	gr.
	Sodium carbonate (anhydrous)	1	grm.		20	gr.
	Glycin	5	grm.		100	gr.
	Potassium sulphocyanide	1	grm.		20	gr.
	Potassium bromide	0.5	grm.		10	gr.
	Water to make	1000	c.cm.		40	oz.

KODAK	Elon (metol)	5	grm.		77	gr.
DK.20	Sodium sulphite (anhydrous)	100	grm.	3 oz.	230	gr.
	Kodalk	2	grm.		31	gr.
	Potassium thiocyanate	1	grm.		15.5	gr.
	Potassium bromide	0.5	grm.		7.5	gr.
	Water to make	1000	c.cm.		35	oz.

M.C.M.	Sodium sulphite (anhydrous)	88	grm.		1¾	oz.
100	Meritol (Johnson's)	16	grm.		140	gr.
	Borax crystals	2.3	grm.		20	gr.
	Tri-basic sod. phos. recryst	6.9	grm.		60	gr.
	Potassium bromide (10% soln.)	2	c.cm.		20	min.
	Water to make	1000	c.cm.		20	oz.

SEASE	Water (about 125°F.)	750	cm.		26	oz.
P.D.M.G.	Paraphenylene diamine	10	grm.		154	gr.
	Glycin	5	grm.		77	gr.
	Metol	6	grm.		92	gr.
	Sodium sulphite (anhydrous)	90	grm.	3 oz.	80	gr.
	Cold water to make	1000	c.cm.		35	oz.

148

SEYEWETZ	Metol	5	grm.		72	gr.
	Sodium sulphite (anhydrous)	60	grm.		880	gr.
	Paraphenylene diamine	10	grm.		146	gr.
	Tri-basic sodium phosphate	3.5	grm.		50	gr.
	Potass bromide	1	grm.		14	gr.
	Water to make	1000	c.cm.		32	oz.
FINK-	Ortho-phenylene diamine	8	grm.		123	gr.
ROSELIEVE	Metol	5.5	grm.		85	gr.
X.33	Sodium sulphite (anhydrous)	82	grm.	2 oz.	396	gr.
	Glycin	1.5	grm.		23	gr.
	Tri-basic sodium phosphate	3	grm.		46	gr.
	Potassium bromide	.25	grm.		4	gr.
	Water to make	1000	c.cm.		35	oz.

An interesting formula of similar type is:

KODAK	Elon (metol)	7.5	grm.		$\frac{1}{4}$	oz.
D.25	Sodium sulphite (anhydrous)	100	grm.	3 oz.	145	gr.
	Sodium bisulphite	15	grm.		$\frac{1}{2}$	oz.
	Water to make	1000	c.cm.		35	oz.

This developer can be recommended for tropical use, as its *best* performance is secured at a temperature of 77° F. (25° C.) when development of most films ranges between 12 to 25 minutes. It can, however, also be employed at normal temperatures (68° F.), but in this event requires 20 to 40 minutes according to the film used.

Proprietary developers and other well-known formulæ of basically similar type to the foregoing include: *Agfa Atomal, Kodak Microdol, Ilford ID.48, Hauff Atofin, Minicol, M.P.G., Panthermic 777, Ultrafin 55, Promicrol,* etc.

Normal fine grain developers particularly recommended for subjects embracing *extreme* contrasts, e.g. artificial light pictures in which the source of light is visible:

WINDISCH	A. Sodium sulphite (anhydrous)	1.25	grm.	60	gr.
"SURFACE"	Pyrocatechin	8	grm.	360	gr.
	Water to make	100	c.cm.	10	oz.
	B. Sodium hydroxide	10	grm.	450	gr.
	Water to make	100	c.cm.	10	oz.

For use, take 12 parts A, 7 parts B, 500 parts water, developing time 15 to 20 minutes at 65° F. for medium speed films. For use with *extremely* contrasty subjects take 20 parts A, 5 parts B, 500 parts water, developing time 18 to 20 minutes at 65° F. *Note*: These solutions can be used only once.

149

WALLACH	Metol	6	grm.	180	gr.
W.80	Sodium sulphite (anhydrous)	75	grm.	5	oz.
	Paraphenylene-diamine				
	hydrochloride	10	grm.	300	gr.
	Glycin	5	grm.	150	gr.
	Pyro	1	grm.	30	gr.
	Tri-basic sodium phosphate	2	grm.	60	gr.
	Water to make	600	c.cm.	40	oz.

ULTRA FINE GRAIN DEVELOPERS

SEASE	Water (about 135° F.)	750	c.cm.	24	oz.
III	Sodium sulphite (anhydrous)	90	grm.	3	oz.
	Paraphenylene diamine	10	grm.	146	gr.
	Glycin	6	grm.	88	gr.
	Cold water to make	1000	c.cm	32	oz.

SEASE	Sodium sulphite (anhydrous)	90	grm.	3	oz.
N.D.3	Paraphenylene diamine	10	grm.	146	gr.
	Glycin	2	grm.	29	gr.
	Water to make	1000	c.cm.	32	oz.

WINDISCH	Sod. sulphite (anyhdrous)	91.5	grm.	3 oz. 85	gr.
665	Orthophenylene diamine	11.6	grm.	180	gr.
	Metol	11.6	grm.	180	gr.
	Pot. metabisulphite	10	grm.	154	gr.
	Water (boiled) to make	1000	c.cm.	35	oz.

Suggested development times for use with the foregoing formulae are given on p. 151. These times are based on average requirements as regards negative quality and are given on the assumption of "moderate agitation" at a temperature of 68° F. (20° C.) except where otherwise stated.

Although films can be segregated into three basic groups, different *makes* may require slightly different treatment in development (for instance the latest Kodak and Adox films do not require as great a variation in development times as other makes). The table on p. 151 provides guidance as to the probable times of development required to produce the type of negative we need. It should be considered only as a guide, as different workers' preferences, the type of paper, or the enlarger used and of course, the actual nature and contrast of the subjects most usually photographed, also have some influence on the time required.

Developer	Effective Film Speed	Time in Minutes at 68°F. for Films in Groups				
		AA	A	B	C	D
SEMI-FINE GRAIN	%					
Agfa Final	100	5– 6	8–10	12–15	14–20	15–23
Ansco 17	100	5– 7	8–11	11–14	15–18	N.R.
Edwal 10	100	6– 8	10–13	13–18	17–22	N.R.
Ilford ID11	100	5– 6	7–10	10–15	14–20	15–24
Johnsons Fine Grain	100	5– 6	6– 7	8–10	12–14	14–18
Johnsons Azol (1 : 50)	100	8– 9	10–11	12–14	N.R.	N.R.
Johnsons Unitol (1 : 16)	100	6– 9	10–12	15–19	18–24	20–27
*Kodak D 23	100	5– 7	8–10	12–16	16–20	N.R.
Kodak D 76	100	5– 6	7–10	10–15	14–20	15–24
M. & B. Promicrol	150	5– 7	6– 8	7–11	10–12	12–14
Rodinal (1 : 100)	100	14–18	16–20	12–16 (1:75)	N.R.	N.R.
NORMAL FINE GRAIN						
Agfa Atomal	70	6– 7	7– 9	9–12	12–15	N.R.
Edwal Minicol	75	6– 7	7– 8	8–10	10–12	N.R.
Focal Super F.G.	70	6– 7	7– 9	11–13	15–18	N.R.
Ilford ID 48	50	5– 6	7– 8	9–11	12–15	N.R.
Ilford Microphen	80	5– 6	7– 8	9–10	10–12	14–16
Kodak Microdol	75	5– 6	7– 9	9–12	12–14	N.R.
Kodak D 25 (at 77°F.)	100	5– 7	8–10	10–13	16–18	20–24
Meritol-Metol	50	5– 6	6– 7	8–11	13–16	N.R.
Sease P.D.M.G.	75	5– 6	7– 8	10–12	14–16	N.R.
Tetenal Ultrafin 55	75	7– 8	9–10	11–12	13–15	N.R.
ULTRA FINE GRAIN						
Sease III	50	N.R.	N.R.	10–14	18–22	N.R.
Windish 665	70	N.R.	N.R.	10–13	16–20	N.R.
VARIOUS						
†*Agfa Isonal (1 : 20)	200	11–12	13–14	15–20	N.R.	N.R.
†Kodak High Definition	150–200	10–12	12–14	16–19	N.R.	N.R.
†*Neofin Blue	200	12–15	15–30	20–35	N.R.	N.R.
†Neofin Red	150	N.R.	N.R.	14–16	16–20	N.R.
Windish "Surface"	100	5– 7	8–10	13–17	18–22	N.R.

*These developers are particularly soft-working. †Developers designed to secure utmost resolution. N.R. = not recommended.

151

The changes of development time for different temperatures are tabulated below. Page 153 shows the increases in development time if the developer is used more than once.

DEVELOPMENT TIMES AT VARYING TEMPERATURES

Normal Time in Minutes at 68°F. (20°C.)	*Approximate Time at Other Temperatures* 62°F. (16.5°C.)	65°F. (18.5°C.)	71°F. (22°C.)	73°F. (24°C.)
4	5½	4¾	3½	2¾
5	8½	7¼	5	4¼
6	8½	7¼	5¼	4½
7	10	8½	6	5
8	11	9½	6¾	5½
9	12½	11	7½	6¼
10	14	12	8½	7
11	15½	13	9½	7¾
12	17	14½	10	8½
13	18	15½	11	9
14	19½	17	12	10
15	21	18	12½	10½
16	22½	19	14½	11¼
18	25	22	15	12½
20	28	24	17	14
22	31	26	19	15½
24	34	29	20½	17
26	36½	31	22	18½
28	39	33½	24	19½
30	42	36	25½	21
32	45	38	27	22½
34	48	41	29	24
36	50½	43½	31	25½

Note.—Not all developers have the same time/temperature reaction. These figures are therefore necessarily approximate.

APPROXIMATE INCREASES IN DEVELOPMENT TIME WHEN 1,000 c.cs. ARE USED FOR MORE THAN ONE FILM

	Time in minutes				
Original Film	*Film 2*	*Film 3*	*Film 4*	*Film 5*	*Film 6*
4	4½	4¾	5¼	5¾	6
5	5½	6	6½	7	7½
6	6½	7¼	7¾	8¼	9
6½	7½	8	8½	9¼	10
7	7¾	8½	9½	10	10½
7½	8	9	9¾	10½	11¼
8	8¾	9½	10½	11¼	12¼
9	10	10¾	11¾	12¾	13½
10	11	12	13	14	15
11	12	13¼	14¼	15½	16½
12	13¼	14½	15¾	17	18
13	14¼	15½	17	18¼	19½
14	15½	17	18¼	19¾	21
15	16½	18	19½	21	22½
16	17½	19	20¾	22½	24
18	19¾	21½	23½	25	27
20	22	24	26	28	30
22	24¼	26½	28¾	31	33
24	26½	29	31¼	33¾	36
26	28½	31	34	36½	39
28	30¾	33½	36½	39	42
30	33	36	39	42	45
32	35	38½	41½	45	48
34	37½	40½	44	47½	51
36	39½	43	47	50½	54
38	41½	45½	49½	53	57
40	44	48	52	56	60
45	49½	54	58	63	67
50	55	60	65	70	75
55	60	66	72	77	83

Note.—Exhaustion factors of different developers vary. These figures are therefore approximate and subject to test.

"Compensating" development, particularly useful for subjects having a considerable contrast range, consists of a system by which the film is first immersed in a developing bath composed of the *reducing agent* and a *preservative* for a short period, after which it is removed and inserted in another bath containing the *accelerator* part of the developer, where it remains for a further short time.

The advantage claimed for this system is that the developer absorbed by the film in its first bath is caused to function during its second immersion; but as developer rapidly becomes exhausted by the task of converting the exposed salts into the visible silver image, the parts of the film which are very fully exposed can never attain an unprintable opacity—while the developer in the less fully exposed parts of the emulsion reaches exhaustion point more slowly, and thus has the chance to coax out all available detail in the shadow areas. The method undoubtedly works according to plan; but in my experience the grain does not seem to be quite as fine as by normal methods.

The first formula of this type to enjoy a considerable popularity was published about 20 years ago:

LEITZ	A.	Metol	5	grm.		77 gr.
		Sod. sulphite (anhyd.)	50	grm.	1½ oz.	115 gr.
		Water	1000	c.cm.		35 oz.
	B.	Sod. carbonate (anhyd.)	14.8	grm.		230 gr.
		Sod. sulphite (anhyd.)	5.7	grm.		88 gr.
		Water	1000	c.cm.		35 oz.

Films: according to type require an immersion in A of from 4 to 10 minutes, followed by immersion in B (without rinsing) of 3 minutes. The times recommended for bath A are:

Agfa Isopan F.F.	4	minutes
Ilford Pan F.	4	„
Adox KB 14	4	„
Adox KB17	5	„
Agfa Isopan F.	6	„
Ilford F.P.3	8	„
Kodak Panatomic	6	„
Adox KB21	7	„
Agfa Isopan I.S.S.	8	„
Ilford H.P. 3	8	„
Kodak Tri. X	10	„

This formula used at 68° F. (20° C.) produces excellent results.

For the press photographer, to whom speed of processing is of paramount importance, there are several variants of the two-bath method available employing a strongly alkaline "B" solution. Although old, one of the best of these is:

STOECKLER	A. Metol	2 grm.		31 gr.
HIGH-SPEED	Sodium sulphite (anhyd.)	100 grm.	3 oz.	230 gr.
	Hydroquinone	5 grm.		77 gr.
	Borax	2 grm.		31 gr.
	Water	1000 c.cm.		35 oz.
	B. 10% Sol. caustic soda	50 c.cm.		2 oz.
	10% Sol. pot. bromide	50 c.cm.		2 oz.
	Water	400 c.cm.		16 oz.

Development time varies slightly with different films; but the majority of medium-speed emulsions will produce satisfactory results with 1½ minutes immersion in Sol. A followed by 30 seconds in Sol. B. Two tanks must be used, so that the film can *immediately* be transferred to Sol. B without loss of time. Development is checked by a short immersion in a 5 per cent. Glacial Acetic Acid stop bath, after which the film is fixed.

A more recent variant of the two-bath system is the popular Meritol-caustic formula advocated by Messrs. *Johnson and Sons.*

MERITOL	Meritol	16 grm.		140 gr.
CAUSTIC	Sodium sulphite (cryst.)	180 grm.	3 oz.	260 gr.
	Water to make	1000 c.cm.		20 oz.

This is diluted for use as follows:

	Stock Meritol sol.	125 c.cm.	40 dr.
	Water to make	500 c.cm.	20 oz.

The film is developed with usual agitation for 3 minutes at 65° F. and the developer discarded and (without rinsing) the following poured in.

	Caustic soda 10% sol.	25 c.cm.	8 dr.
	Water to make	500 c.cm.	20 oz.

This should be allowed to act, with agitation, at 65° F. for 3 minutes after which (again without rinsing) the film is placed in a hardening fixing bath for at least 5 minutes.

FIXING	Hypo.	250 grm.	5 oz.
BATH	Sodium bisulphite	25 grm.	½ oz.
	Water to make	1000 c.cm.	20 oz.

to which is added *immediately before use:*

	Saturated sol. of chrome alum 6 c.cm.	1 dr.

Note to preserve a constant time of 3 minutes in the Meritol solution, the strength should be adjusted to suit the film used—the following is *suggested* as a basis for further experiment:

155

	Meritol Sol.		Water	
Ilford Pan. F.	100 c.cm.	32 dr.	500 c.cm.	20 oz.
Ilford F.P.3	125 c.cm.	40 dr.	500 c.cm.	20 oz.
Kodak Panatomic X	112 c.cm.	36 dr.	500 c.cm.	20 oz.
Kodak Plus X	125 c.cm.	40 dr.	500 c.cm.	20 oz.
Ilford H.P.3	125 c.cm.	40 dr.	500 c.cm.	20 oz.
Kodak Tri X	138 c.cm.	44 dr.	500 c.cm.	20 oz.

This developer is still undergoing trial at the hands of interested workers, and a number of variations have been advocated. The formula given above is dependable and has its maker's endorsement.

The benefits claimed for this system are:— a *considerable* increase in emulsion speed; excellent gradation without the somewhat flattened highlights sometimes produced by "two-bath" treatment; and of course improvement in shadow and highlight detail as compared with normal "straight" development, without any sacrifice in grain size.

MAXIMUM ENERGY DEVELOPERS

During the past few years there have been several developers, or substances to be added to existing developers, for which very remarkable claims have been made.

As the formulae of these " special " agents are not generally disclosed, I cannot compare them in detail, nor suggest why they should have the power of producing satisfactorily printable negatives from films which have had a bare fraction of the exposure that is normally considered essential to success. The experiments that I have so far carried out with the " additions ", however, tend to confirm the views expressed in the American Press. Certainly, in my hands, these chemicals made very little difference to the results.

The continued increase in film speeds seems to offer more promise for the man who must get pictures under "nearly impossible" conditions, than does the addition of some accelerating substance to the developer. The unbelievable of yesterday is today commonplace: and the recent introduction of Agfa Isopan Record and of Kodak's Royal X pan film (unfortunately not yet available in 35 mm.) is a pointer that we soon may have almost unlimited speed at our disposal.

These particular materials (Royal X pan in roll film form)

have proved to be most effective rated at 1600 A.S.A.—
with the maker's normal recommended development. With
these materials, the day of "developer additives" and the
like will be over.

Even now one can do some very wonderful things with
emulsions such as Ilford H.P.S.—one of the fastest 35 mm.
materials that I have ever tested—even with normal development.

But—as I have said elsewhere—these films are *not* for
general use. They should be reserved for the pictures that
cannot be made on the slower materials.

POST-DEVELOPMENT FORMULAE

WITH care and attention to all the necessary details of
exposure and development, negatives should maintain a
gratifyingly high average quality; but accidents and mistakes
do happen, and we may find that an otherwise excellent
film suffers from the effects of either under- or over-
exposure, or under- or over-development, or even a combination of any two of these. Fortunately, the majority of
such errors can easily be remedied.

For *severe* under-exposure there is no cure. If the detail
is not visible on the negative, nothing in the world can put
it there; so negatives of this type may as well be discarded
at the outset. Now for the remainder. The first thing is to
identify the exact fault or faults.

Here are safe rules by which you can be sure exactly what
is wrong. They apply to all types of film and all types of
subject.

Under-exposure: the basic characteristic is absence of
detail in what should be fully detailed shadow areas. If the
lighter tones in the subject (which of course will be the
darker parts of the negative), are clearly defined, but there
are large areas devoid of detail elsewhere, this is almost
certain to be the fault.

Over-exposure is generally evidenced by the negative being
very "thick" in appearance. The shadow areas will almost
certainly have a fairly heavy silver deposit and the denser
parts of the negative will be so dense and "clogged up" that

157

you will have difficulty in examining the details unless you hold the negative against a strong light.

In both these cases I have assumed that the film has been normally and properly developed.

Under-development manifests itself by the film lacking contrast, although there is a fair amount of detail everywhere. The darker parts of the negative—the sky, or a white collar in the case of a portrait—will be only a medium grey tone instead of a dark grey, approaching black.

Over-development is recognisable by an excess of contrast. The thin (shadow) areas will be full of well defined details— the half-tones will be strongly rendered—while the dark (highlight) parts of the negative will be so opaque and harsh as to be practically unprintable unless the softest grade of printing paper be used (see page 281).

In these two examples, I have assumed that the film was correctly exposed.

Let me now describe the combinations of errors that can arise.

Under-exposure and under-development will produce a thin ghost-like negative in which there will be no shadow detail at all (under-exposure) and in which the darkest silver deposit will be only a light grey (under-development). Not much can be done with *this* negative.

Over-exposure and under-development give us a negative in which all the available details are visible, but in which the darkest deposit is still only of a light colour. In consequence this type of negative appears to be unbelievably "flat" and devoid of contrast, and, although not lacking in actual detail, it is at present quite unprintable. There is, however, hope for this one.

Under-exposure and over-development usually result in a negative which appears very "brilliant" to the eye. (If the fault is not severe the negative will appear "pretty" and promising, but will produce a disappointing print.) This negative will have very little detail in the deeper shadows; but the less intense shadow areas will be full of good strong contrasts, the half tones will be strong to brilliant and the highlight areas well defined and rather "hard".

Over-exposure and over-development: the last one of the series is easily recognised by its thick muddy "dense-

158

all-over" appearance. A good image is undoubtedly there, but, because of the excessive exposure, it is buried underneath a good deal of unwanted silver. Because the film has been over-developed the contrasts between the tones (which would otherwise have been somewhat flat) are quite adequate; and the negative is capable of yielding a passably good print provided a long enough exposure be given.

Now for the Remedies. Fortunately almost everything except severe *under*-exposure can be cured. Negatives which are too thin and lacking in contrast can be intensified. Those which are over-dense or of too severe a contrast can be reduced. I append three formulæ. Formula A is the intensifier that I recommend. Formula B is a reducer which seems to attack the shadow areas proportionately more than the highlights and thus apparently *increases* contrast. Formula C is a reducer which attacks the highlights much more vigorously than the shadow areas and thus *decreases* contrast. The following table indicates which remedy or combination of remedies is most likely to prove effective for the faults already enumerated.

Nature of fault	First treatment	Second treatment
Under exposure and under development	Very bad case Try intensifying in A.	Wash *thoroughly* and repeat again in A.
Under exposure and normal development	Intensify in A.	
Under exposure and over development	Reduce in C.	Wash thoroughly and intensify in A.
Normal exposure and under development	Intensify in A.	
Normal exposure and over development	Reduce in C.	
Over exposure and under development	Reduce a little in B.	Wash thoroughly and intensify in A.
Over exposure and normal development	Reduce a little in B.	
Over exposure and over development	Reduce in B.	

INTENSIFIER A

Stock Sol. I	Potassium bichromate	50 grm.	2 oz.
	Water to make	1000 c.cm.	40 oz.
Stock Sol. II	Hydrochloric acid	100 c.cm.	4 oz.
	Water	900 c.cm.	36 oz.

For use the negative must be *thoroughly* washed, and is then bleached in a solution of:

Stock Sol. I	I part
Stock Sol. II	I part
Water	5 parts

The bleaching proceeds quickly and is carried out until there is no visible *black* in the negative, which should now appear a yellowy cream in colour. When the bleaching is complete the film must be washed in running water until the whole of the *yellow* stain is discharged. It is then re-developed in any good non-staining developer (e.g., M.Q. as used for bromide printing). This *should* be carried out in bright light. If the degree of intensification is insufficient the process can be repeated after *very* thorough washing, but one application should be sufficient for all except very bad cases. Fine grain developers are not advisable because of their solvent action.

REDUCER B.

Stock Sol. I	Hypo Crystals (*not* acid fixing)	125 grm.	5 oz.
	Water to	1000 c.cm.	40 oz.
Stock Sol II	Potassium ferricyanide	100 grm.	4 oz.
	Water	1000 c.cm.	40 oz.

For use—the negative is immersed in a solution composed of:

Stock Sol. I	10 parts
Stock Sol. II	I part

Note. The mixed solutions decompose quite rapidly, so the reducer should be prepared as required: the stock solutions keep well.

The film *must* be kept on the move the whole time that it is in the reducer. It should be inspected at frequent intervals, and removed just *before* it is thin enough, when it should be promptly and thoroughly washed for 15 mins. in running water.

160

REDUCER C.   Stock Sol.
    Ammonium persulphate   30 grm.   1¼ oz.
    Water to   1000 c.cm.   40 oz.

The negative must be very thoroughly washed before reduction. Just before use add 1 c.cm. of a 5 per cent. solution of pure Sulphuric Acid to every 50 c.cm. of working solution. Immerse the negative and keep it constantly moving all the time it is in the reducer. The appearance of a certain cloudiness on the surface of the film shows that the solution is acting properly—this should become visible in ½ to ¾ of a minute. When the degree of reduction is sufficient the action of the reducer is checked by immersing the film for 10 minutes in a 5 per cent. solution of soda sulphite, after which it is washed and dried in the usual way.

Failure to secure satisfactory results from these after-processes can almost invariably be traced to lack of chemical cleanliness or to insufficient washing prior to the intensification or reduction.

Because the human skin gives off a minute trace of grease, it is most important that the surface of films destined for further treatment should *never* be touched, otherwise stains or irregular chemical action are almost a foregone conclusion. In any case, this is a very good rule to which to adhere where *all* negatives are concerned.

Ammonium persulphate is not always dependable in its action; and *Farmer's* reducer, while entirely satisfactory for use on negatives which are over-dense but without excessive contrast, is not so suitable for negatives which are suffering from the result of over-development, as it appears to attack the thin shadow areas proportionately more than the denser parts.

A very dependable reducer, the action of which is about midway between that of B and C, is the following:

TWO-SOLUTION Sol. A. Potassium ferricyanide 12.5 grm.   ½ oz.
REDUCER   Water   500 c.cm.   20 oz.

              Sol. B. Hypo crystals (Not
                       Acid Fixing Salt)   100 grm.   4 oz.
                       Water   1000 c.cm.   40 oz.

For a moderate degree of reduction immerse the negative, which must be well washed in Sol. A, and agitate gently. Watch the *surface* of the emulsion which will gradually assume a slightly milky appearance (in about 60 to 120 seconds with a negative which has previously been dried). Allow the solution to act for about *double* the time required to reach this point, then briefly rinse the negative and immerse in Sol. B (full strength). The negative will clear in about 2 to 3 minutes. The process is then completed by thorough washing for at least 15 minutes. This method of reduction is particularly suited to miniature work, as it tends to reduce grain. It is also perfectly controllable, the time of immersion in Sol. A governing the extent of the action. If the degree of reduction proves to be insufficient, the complete process can be repeated, provided that the negative has had *thorough* washing. Brief experiment on some valueless negatives on the film normally used will give an indication of the time likely to be required. The solutions keep well. "A" (which should be stored in the dark) can be returned to the bottle after use. "B" should be discarded as used.

TOURING WITH A CAMERA

DURING the period in which the miniature camera has grown to its present degree of perfection, the holiday habits of the country as a whole have turned more and more to open air pursuits—in particular touring—at home and abroad. This parallel development is fortunate, as 35 mm. equipment is undoubtedly the most suitable and convenient for the traveller, whatever his means of locomotion.

Ignoring the possibilities and requirements of air travel, and, for the moment, water, we are left with four general touring methods, each of which has its devotees, and for each of which there are certain definite advantages. Having had considerable experience of miniature camera work on tour in this country and the Continent, as a pedestrian, cyclist, motor cyclist and motorist, I feel encouraged to offer a few recommendations as to what to carry and how to carry it, as well as some observations on how to use it.

The problems of the pedestrian are very much the same as those that confront the cyclist. For those who provide their own motive power, weight and bulk are the two

162

principal considerations. As most of their exposures are likely to be made out of doors, I question whether an $f2$ or $f1.5$ lens is worth carrying; and would choose the $f2.8$ *Elmar* for my Leica or the $f3.5$ or $f2.8$ *Tessar* if carrying the Contax. Both these lenses when collapsed result in a conveniently "thin" camera, which, at a pinch, can be taken along in the pocket; whereas the more speedy lenses almost invariably increase the overall thickness of the camera considerably, and, in addition, provide it with an awkward hump which makes it rather more difficult to pack, and also somewhat vulnerable.

For the pedestrian who confines his activities to roads and footpaths, the camera can be carried in any convenient way; but for the more hardened rambler, who includes fell walking and scrambling, a camera in an ever-ready case is a source of danger. It will, sooner or later, entangle itself on a rock at a time when both hands and feet are wanted to ensure the security of its owner; or its continued antics will take the climber's mind off more important matters, causing him to expose himself to unnecessary risks. If these do not occur, the camera itself will, in all probability, become damaged. Because of this latter danger, pockets are not to be recommended either. If there is no choice, then an inside breast pocket is the best one to use, with the jacket buttoned right up; but if a rucksack is worn, the right place for the camera is an ever-ready case, wrapped in something soft, just inside the neck of the bag, on top of all one's other belongings. The foregoing applies to the rough country scrambler, rather than to the man who specialises in rock climbs. He will naturally be encumbered with the minimum of personal gear and will find the best way to transport his camera is in an ever-ready case on a very short strap, so that, when not in use, the camera lies snugly beneath his coat underneath his armpit. A second, clip on, strap surrounding the body is sometimes an advantage to keep the instrument in this position. Such a strap can be unfastened whenever the camera is brought into use.

The cyclist carries the bulk of his touring requisites in a large bag suspended behind the saddle, and often supported from beneath by a small metal carrier which takes some of the weight and prevents the bag swaying unduly. These touring bags are frequently fitted with outer side pockets of convenient size and shape to accommodate a camera, but I do not think that such pockets are suitable for expensive miniature equipment. The ideal way to carry a camera is one which keeps it supported and insulated by one's own body. If simply suspended round the neck or shoulders, however, it is apt to be a source of considerable irritation to the wearer after a short time. Should this method be chosen, again, a great improvement in personal comfort results from an extra strap round the waist, attached to each side of the ever-ready case, which will then lie in reasonable comfort, just above the hip. My own preference, when cycling, is to avoid loading myself with apparatus and to let the bicycle support the weight. On top of my touring bag, supported by a *strong* strap surrounding the saddle, I carry an old leather case, which once housed a folding plate camera: it measures about $7 \times 6 \times 3$ in. The inside of this I have lined with pads of soft rubber of the *Sorbo* or *Dunlopillo* type, and a plywood division splits the container into two parts: one takes the camera, complete in its ever-ready case, while the smaller space provides snug storage for two extra lenses, view-finder, lens hood, wire release and one spare film. This case does *not* rest on the carrier, but is held down behind the touring bag by a strap surrounding both. Most of my own wanderings by bicycle have included considerable sections of exceedingly rough roads and tracks, but, so far, no camera that I have ever carried in this way has suffered in the least; and it cannot strike anything hard, even if the machine falls over!

The motor cycle, due to its considerably greater speed, provides a problem which cannot be solved in the way suggested above. With any ordinary machine (without rear springing) it is impossible to insulate a camera from vibration sufficiently well by packing it with one's personal luggage or attaching it to any part of the machine itself. The top of the petrol tank immediately in front of the saddle is, without question, the point where vibration is least apparent, and for some time I carried various cameras in a *Sorbo* lined case in that position, secured by metal

164

brackets and straps under the tank. Even in spite of these precautions, screws gradually worked loose, and the case could never be kept entirely free from dust, so that I was finally forced to the conclusion that wearing an ever-ready case was the only safe method. My present practice is to sling the strap over the left shoulder and to let the camera lie on the right side at the front. It is kept in position by slipping the case underneath the belt of my leather coat. The weight of the camera, which is partly supported by the upper part of the right leg, is barely noticed. While vibration is effectively overcome by this method, the camera is still too exposed to weather conditions, and I lately devised an oilskin cover to the case, with openings for the supporting strap, which seems to have got over most of the difficulties; even so, on Austrian and Italian byways, in the summer months, thick white dust was to be found inside the case whenever the camera was removed. Fortunately, none ever found its way into the camera itself, which is a tribute to the way these instruments are made.

For these first three classes of road users we have considered something of *how* to carry the equipment. There now remains *what* to carry. The answer is the same (although for slightly different reasons): "No more than you need."

I have already suggested one of the more compact normal lenses. I would add, first of all, a 35 mm. wide angle lens; as second choice, an 85 or 90 mm. long focus lens; with, of course, the appropriate finder and lens hoods. For filters: at home, a light or medium yellow, and a salmon or red. For an Alpine tour, I would add an "ultraviolet" or the lightest of yellow filters.

I think that this outfit will meet all normal touring needs. Additional luxuries to consider are: a neck support, which I find a considerable aid to securing sharp pictures when one's hands are a shade unsteady as the result of exertion or vibration; a self timer if your camera does not include this feature; and an exposure meter. If one is doing colour work, or if in a strange country, the last item is indispensable.

For all travellers, other than motorists, lenses, spare films, filters, meters, camera supports, view-finders, etc., have to be carried more or less as they best can. If suitable cases are available for the filters, I see no objection to using one's pockets.

On my own ever-ready case I had a "false lid" fitted: the false top was stitched on to the top of the normal lid, and is divided into three partitions, each with a separate press stud fastening. This provides me with convenient space to carry the three filters that I use most. If no filter is used the case is opened normally, while the increase in the weight of the lid itself serves a useful purpose in keeping it hanging down so that the fastening tab is less likely to intrude in front of the lens; at least when held in the horizontal position.

As for the other things, I would mention that the exposure meter *must* be carried on the person, for cyclist and motor cyclist; possibly in the rucksack for the walker.

Telephoto lenses, well padded and not able to rattle, should be safe in the rucksack, or even in the cyclist's touring bag, but the motor cyclist will do well to use his pockets or, more conveniently, a separate leather case holding lens, lens hood and finder, slung over the shoulder, or even a small leather case attached to his belt well out of the way.

A tripod or unipod is not likely to come to harm if carried where one would carry clothes, maps and other kit. The same thing applies to lens hoods, spare films and other non-optical accessories. As far as cassettes or cartridges of film are concerned, it is a good plan to wrap the protruding tail of the film tightly round its container, and to secure it thus with that permanently "tacky" Cellophane tape or surgical plaster. This stops the end disappearing into the cassette, as it sometimes will if subjected to vibration or movement in its normal non-secured state. If you can then find room to wrap each cassette in paper or lead foil, before putting it away in its metal box, you may feel fairly sure that its contents will not suffer as the result of road dust entering, or of vibration (which also causes dust by chafing the film itself).

Keep an eye on your lenses and filters for dust—remove it if it appears—but please dust it off lightly with a soft, clean camel hair brush kept for the purpose. *Don't* rub it off—or in—with a handkerchief. Good lenses are really very soft, and are easily abraded.

If there is rainwater or mist on the lens or filter, it will have to be wiped, and one must be as careful and gentle about it as possible. In rainy weather one can always use a very light filter to protect the lens. Little or nothing will be gained from it in the way of colour correction on a dull day, and it will of course increase exposure; but at least you will feel happier if you have to be continually wiping dry a filter worth a few shillings, instead of a lens costing as many pounds. Also always use a lens hood in the rain. If you are unlucky enough to get salt spray or sea water on your lens, wipe it off at once; and take the first possible opportunity to wipe it off again with a suitably soft cloth moistened in *fresh* water. Then dry it thoroughly. This advice also applies to *any metal* parts of your camera.

The tourist who takes his car has none of the transport worries. For the most part he will carry his equipment as he does at home, probably in a complete padded outfit case, which will travel safely and comfortably on one of the rear seats, and from which he will select just that part of his possibly extensive outfit that is necessary for the job in hand. This, of course, presupposes that the car is a saloon or drophead and that it can be securely locked whenever it is left unattended. I know, only too well, the uncomfortable necessity of carrying a bulky and heavy outfit case round continental show places because I dare not leave the unwanted part of it behind in a sports car with no better protection than was afforded by a tonneau cover. Unless he is prepared to devise a stout lock-up camera container properly secured to the inside of the body, the owner of an open sports car is advised to limit his photographic equipment to that which he is willing to carry on his person whenever he leaves the vehicle, and to see that it is in such cases or containers as will make this comfortable and convenient.

Abroad, or where conditions are appreciably different from those in which one normally works, it is definitely reassuring to develop an occasional film *en route*, to ensure that exposures are reasonably correct. I prefer to leave most of my processing until I am in my own darkroom; but unless impracticable on the score of bulk, a spiral groove tank, a thermometer, one or two 20 oz. packets of a well-tried developer, and a ½ lb. tin of acid fixing salt, could with advantage find space in the car.

Darkroom facilities, on tour, will almost certainly have to be improvised, but as the majority of continental hotel bedrooms are blessed with running water, such improvisation, after dark, is not usually difficult. The tank may have to be loaded in a wardrobe or closet, or even, at the worst, under the bedclothes if there are street lights near by and the window coverings are not opaque, but this is not a particularly difficult task, and after development and washing the film can usually be hung in a cupboard or doorway to dry overnight, while the room is in occupation, so that there need be little fear of it being meddled with or damaged by members of the hotel staff.

The slight inconvenience of doing such trial processing away from home is more than outweighed by the knowledge that there is still time to adjust one's ideas of exposure to suit local conditions if necessary, and the comforting certainty of satisfactory results on one's return home.

Abroad, or in any new districts for that matter, one is all too easily overcome by the novelty of the surroundings, so that there is a tendency to make all sorts of exposures on subjects of a type which would excite no attention from the photographer at home. For this reason it is necessary to hold oneself somewhat in check, and to assess the possible value of a picture before pressing the button.

I am not thinking of the obviously strange sights that one comes across everywhere. I would cheerfully make an exposure on, say, a Belgian street car—because it is different, and therefore interesting. But I feel that one is apt to be too easily satisfied (at the time of exposure) by strange sights and places and to devote less attention to matters of subject selection and composition than is really necessary.

Everywhere one goes there are picture post cards. Make use of them. Study them—and then try to avoid duplicating them. The average commercial view card is very unimaginative and banal. It has to be to meet a general and widely diffused demand. We, however, are out to make

Photography on tour demands an observant eye which will select those things most typical of the district and most likely to be of interest to others on one's return home. Picture postcards should be studied and their all too obvious viewpoints religiously avoided.

Page 169. THE FOUNTAIN—*By concentrating interest on the fountain and the sky, its author has produced a picture very different from any postcard showing the Place de la Concorde.*—G. Schuh.

Above. A FRENCH ROAD—*The author was attracted to this scene as one which typified northern France as seen by the touring motorist. Other exposures made at the same time, showing the road disappearing into the distance, draw the attention to the road rather than to the country alongside.*—H. S. Newcombe.

Page 171. THE BAY—*A Mediterranean composition in which the white of the surf is emphasized by the absence of sky.*—H. S. Newcombe.

170

172

Page 172. THE MOUSKY, CAIRO—*Markets and shopping areas in the Near East can provide the observant traveller with unlimited material for pictures. Extremes of contrast and the ever-present risk of under-exposure require to be guarded against. A wide angle lens can be very valuable in such confined surroundings.*—J. Allan Cash.

Page 173. EVENING—*The best time for depicting lighted streets is the last half-hour before it gets dark. There is still a sufficiency of general illumination to make it possible to record detail everywhere with snapshot exposures, while the street lights can be got without risk of serious over-exposure.*—E. Loose.

Page 174. THE NIGHT TRAVELLER—*With reasonably light surroundings even a car's headlamps can be pressed into service to provide a pictorial record of one's travels.*—G. Schuh.

174

Page 175. TWO REFLECTIONS—*Even the back panel of an auto-mobile can produce a picture in certain circumstances. The "hand of the master" is very apparent in the arrangement and composition of this very simple subject.*—Paul Wolff.

Above. THE BARTENDER'S VIEW—*A novel and very informal shot in a country hostelry. The great depth of focus of the miniature is here exploited to advantage.*—K. Hubschmann.

176

individual pictures wherever possible; and frequently this can best be done by concentrating on a bit, rather than on the general view beloved by the guide-book and post card publisher.

The nature of the district in which one is working necessarily has considerable influence on the type of subject to be sought. The attractive shapes of domestic architecture in the narrow streets of mountain villages—where incidentally exposures will need to be generous in comparison with those adequate to the open country through which one has just passed—close-ups of Alpine flowers in the meadows or of mountain cattle with their melancholy sounding bells. The store of winter fuel neatly stacked against the walls of the upland farmstead and of course the natural beauties of the countryside itself, all these lend themselves to the production of *pictures* as distinct from the more ordinary *views* of the place.

In foreign lands it is desirable to remember that *you* are the foreigner. Never use your camera in such a way as to give offence to those whose home it is. Excluding parts of Holland and a few other countries, where the people have commercialised their local mode of dress to the extent of encouraging you to photograph them—for a consideration—try always to be discreet in securing your records of "what the natives look like".

Open street markets offer unlimited opportunity for this type of "genre" figure study. In the absence of an *angular finder*, by means of which one can take pictures at right angles to the direction in which one appears to be interested, it is a good plan to disregard the range-finder entirely and to rely implicitly on estimated distance, aided by the depth of focus scale; and to learn to shoot from the hip, or chest, by merely turning in the desired direction without making any attempt to employ the view-finder. This method is naturally somewhat approximate, but one quickly learns to estimate roughly how much will be in the picture, and the natural and unposed results make such an expedient well worth while.

For this kind of work there is much to be said for a 3.5 cm. lens instead of that of normal focal length of 5 cm. The wider angle that the shorter lens opens up makes it easy to include all of the subject, while at the same time one is assured of such a great depth of sharpness even at moderately large apertures that the camera can easily be pre-set to a convenient focusing point.

Every now and again pictures present themselves while one is travelling by train or other vehicle. Provided that the camera is kept ready for immediate use there is no reason why such subjects should not satisfactorily be tackled. Because the camera is in motion a short exposure will be necessary, even for a distant view, and I have found 1/200 second about the minimum safe speed that can be employed. Care should be taken to avoid any close objects like hedges and telegraph poles. Being quite near to the camera their "apparent speed" is so considerable that they cannot but be recorded very blurred. The camera should be held firmly but easily, and the body flexed as much as possible so as to insulate the instrument from vibration. On no account should the arms be steadied against any part of the vehicle itself—that will have just the opposite effect to that expected. Given attention to these details, the percentage of good results should be surprisingly high.

The camera user in the tropics has much to contend with. The heat, or heat and moisture combined, has a considerable effect on the keeping properties of sensitive emulsion of film and paper. For this reason it behoves one to secure the freshest supplies available, and if possible to ensure that they are tropically packed, i.e. in a really airtight, sealed container. The conditions mentioned manifest themselves in the speedy generation of an all-over "fogging", which reduces the contrast of the negative and makes it difficult to secure clean bright prints or enlargements. Even the relatively short time that a film is exposed to air while it is in the camera is sufficient for it to absorb moisture; and, as the effect of the moisture becomes greater the longer the film remains in that condition, it is most desirable that it should be developed as quickly after exposure as is practicable. On no account should a film be packed away in an air-tight box *after* exposure. The moisture that it has absorbed will cause more trouble by "sweating" than will arise through normal storage even under bad con-

178

ditions. If for any reason it is impracticable to develop promptly after exposure, the best plan is to wrap the film up in some material—cloth, newspaper, etc.—which will absorb any fresh moisture to which the package may be exposed while permitting the film itself a chance to breathe.

The high temperature at which processing has to be carried out is also conducive to further trouble through chemical fogging or even frilling (emulsion separating from celluloid at the edges). In the absence of any means of keeping the solutions down to normal temperatures, the use of a developer such as *Kodak D*.25 (p. 149) is advocated. This formula should not be used below 77° F. for the best results, and, as will be seen, can satisfactorily be used at even higher temperatures.

Although the normal acid-hardening fixing bath is generally satisfactory, if temperatures are really high, it will probably be worth adding 1 grm. of chrome alum to every 100 c.c. of the normal fixing solution (approximately 100 gr. to 1 pint in avoirdupois measure).

When such films have been washed, surplus water should be removed as far as possible by means of a viscose sponge (unless the emulsion is very soft) so as to expedite drying. Insects and bacteria are apt to cause trouble in the soft emulsion by consuming parts of it, leaving unpleasant pinholes in the process.

Once the hardened film is dry, it is fairly immune; but care should be taken that it is not stored in an enclosed moist place which will probably give growth to mould.

PANORAMS

PANORAM pictures, taken as a series and joined up after printing, are perhaps easier with 35 mm. equipment than with any other camera. Leitz used to supply a special

179

metal tripod head, the upper part of which (carrying the camera) rotates on the lower which is secured to the tripod. A set of interchangeable rings is available, each calibrated to suit a particular lens, 35, 50, 90, 135, etc. These rings engage with a spring which clicks into position when the camera has been turned the requisite amount so that the second picture will mate up accurately with the first, and so on. The amount that it has to be turned is, of course, governed by the lens used, which in turn is the reason for the variety of suitably calibrated rings.

Obviously any lens can be used for panoram work, as the amount included laterally is governed only by the number of exposures made as the camera is turned round on the tripod; but if the *vertical* area which one wishes to include is large, it will probably be desirable to employ a wide angle lens (say 35 mm.) so as to secure all the subject required. If on the other hand the whole of the interest is confined to a relatively narrow strip along a distant horizon—as is so often the case in such pictures—then a longer focus lens, 9 or 13.5 cm. will be superior in performance, as it will render distant detail more clearly and on a larger scale at the expense of a few more frames of film as the camera is turned through a smaller angle between each individual exposure.

The head just described carries a second set of markings, usable if it is desired to carry the camera in a vertical position, which expedient, of course, also increases (by 50 per cent.) the vertical height included. As all the rings are so marked, this method can be applied to any lens.

The one essential for panoram work is that the tripod be absolutely level, so that the horizon does not wander up and down as the camera is rotated on the stand. I advise securing this visually, by inspecting the image through the view-finder as the camera is turned through the full 360°. Spirit levels can obviously also be used, but where the horizon is in itself fairly level, I suggest that my method secures greater accuracy, and it is a good deal quicker. I have said the stand must be absolutely level; so must the camera, *laterally*—but if the camera position is high or low in relation to all the surroundings, it is permissible to tilt it downhill or uphill in a fore and aft direction, so long as

180

the degree of tilt is small. If the camera is tilted up or down too much there will be difficulty in making the adjoining picture "mate up" when printed.

When using a device such as has been described, panoram work is virtually foolproof. The tripod head ensures that the camera is turned each time just enough so that each successive picture will join up accurately with its neighbour. I have, however, frequently found myself in a situation where I required a panoram picture, at a time when the head was at home, and have now become so accustomed to panorams without such aid that I think my improvised method may be interesting to others as well.

The essential difference between the two methods is that, with the system described above, mechanical means are taken to ensure that the camera is moved precisely the correct amount. To do the same thing with the camera held in the hand would be impossible, but by taking picture No. 1 (preferably commencing at the *left* hand end of the required view) and taking particular note of the last object (tree, etc.) that appears completely in the *right hand* side of the picture, as visible in the view-finder, the camera can be carefully swung to the right until the same object is only just completely in the *left* hand side of picture No. 2. The right hand end of No. 2 now becomes the mark point for the left end of No. 3 and the process is repeated until the whole of the desired panoram has been included. When using this method particular care should be taken to ensure that the horizon is in about the same vertical position, except where it may rise or fall by virtue of some alteration in the landscape itself. If the latter is very rugged, it is necessary to imagine an artificial horizon, and to try to adhere to this, otherwise it will be found that so much of the tops and bottoms of the various prints have to be cut away when piecing the individual prints together that what is left, common to all the negatives, is only a narrow strip across the centre.

I have mentioned the desirability of having the horizon (true or imagined) as near the vertical centre as possible. This again is to avoid distortion. If the camera is tilted so that the horizon is close to the upper or lower edge of the picture, it may appear in a series of very slight curves, which when joined up look, at least, a trifle odd. This phenomenon is more apparent when wide angle lenses are used, while the warning can safely be ignored where pictures with long focus lenses are concerned.

When exposing panorams, all negatives must have the same exposure; and similarly, in making the prints, it is not enough to ensure that they all have identical printing exposure—they should all be developed for *precisely* the same length of time (preferably all together in a large dish); otherwise, when they are dry, they will exhibit trifling differences of colour, density or tone which will prevent their being joined up into what we always hope will be one long and apparently unbroken strip.

In joining up hand held panorams there will obviously always be some overlap between the individual exposures, and to secure the best join, and the neatest finished result, the same amount should be trimmed *from each* of any pair of adjacent prints. If one is to be cut at the end only, and the next print cut where it would be necessary to fit, it will be found that the two are not quite an accurate match and that it is impossible to join them so that *all* lines mate up properly. This is, of course, due to the trifling distortion that occurs towards the ends of almost every photograph.

WATERSIDE AND MARINE PICTURES

BECAUSE, in this country, one can hardly live more than one hundred miles from the sea, or ten miles from some sizable stretch of water, the photography of aquatic subjects will always be one of the most popular phases of miniature camera work.

To get the best out of subjects of this type, panchromatic film should always be employed. Much of the beauty of sailing pictures lies in the contrast between the white sails (and their reflections) and the blue sky. Because

182

the water reflects and is coloured by the sky above it, the rich blue sea of a summer's day is, like the sky, controllable in tone to a large extent by the use of colour-sensitive film and a suitable yellow or even light red filter.

On a grey day, however, or if the clouds are overhead, much of the colour in the water disappears, and it is well to remember that in such conditions the scene will photograph more or less as the eye sees, and filters will cease to exercise any appreciable control on the respective tones.

One of the most frequent causes of ultimate dissatisfaction in river pictures is the presence of the opposite bank —or, in pictures taken on a wider expanse of water, the hard line of the horizon. If the camera is held normally, this line tends to lie across the centre of the picture space, bisecting it and giving almost equal value to the upper and lower halves. Although the camera must always be held level laterally—for a sloping horizon is anathema—I would recommend the choice of a higher, or lower, than normal viewpoint, so as to place the horizon line off centre —or even tilting the camera up or downhill to some extent with the same object. This can be done quite freely, without fear of betraying the tilt in the finished picture, as there is usually little or nothing in the subject to give away, by converging verticals, the fact that the camera was not quite level.

In composing marine pictures, make a point of arranging things so that the subject is sailing *into* the picture space— so that there is more space in front of the boat than behind it. Avoid, as far as possible, direct broadside views; they seldom show a ship to the best advantage.

Exposures require to be chosen with care. A dependable meter should be used if possible, and readings taken in such a way that the meter is not unduly influenced by the intensely brilliant splashes of sunshine on the water, which would otherwise cause it to suggest far too high values with the result of considerable under-exposure. On the open sea, where everything is relatively light in tone and there are no large areas of dense shadow, exposures should be cut to the minimum in order to preserve adequate contrast.

Such negatives should be thin and detailed, and should not have large areas of great density, which always indicates too generous an exposure. The direction of the light influences exposures afloat in a rather different way from those inland. Facing *into* the light, one is usually concerned with securing the best possible rendering of the effect of the sun on the water and is consequently prepared to accept darker objects as more or less silhouetted against their background. In such cases the necessity for ample exposure to secure shadow detail does not exist, and for such scenes—if it is difficult to secure a satisfactory meter reading—I suggest an exposure of 1/200 second at f 8 on medium-speed (Group B) films when using a normal fine grain developer. This will generally secure the desired result.

The most suitable lens equipment depends largely on what one wishes to do. For river pictures from the bank my shots are made about equally with 5 cm. and 9 cm. lenses. On board one's own little ship, however, conditions are different; and then I find that I do not use the 5 cm. lens a great deal but am continually changing between the 3.5 cm. and the 9 cm. according to whether I am taking pictures in which the happenings on my own craft are the principal motif, or securing relatively long shots of passing vessels. Even in the second case the wide angle lens can be useful on many occasions, because it allows me to include a sufficiency of my own boat to form an attractive foreground, the standing rigging and gunwale, or perhaps the boom and main sheet, forming an interesting frame pattern for the more distant subject proper. In such cases the considerable depth of focus of the wide angle lens is invaluable; and incidentally the depth of focus scale will probably prove far more useful than the range-finder.

The one accessory that must *never* be omitted in marine

Page 185. WAITING FOR THE TIDE.—H. S. Newcombe.

Page 186. IN HARBOUR.—C. Croeber.

Page 187. FITTING OUT.—H. S. Newcombe.

Page 188. THE SMALL CLASS.—C. Croeber.

work is the lens hood: without it, irrespective of the sun's position, pictures will be flat and degraded. The hood also helps to protect the lens from splashes. Salt water is injurious to cameras and lenses—even in the form of the finest spray. The camera should be shielded as far as possible at all times, and the lens cap kept in place whenever the camera is not actually in use. If salt spray does reach the instrument, it should be removed—as mentioned before—with a soft cloth just moistened in *fresh* water, and then thoroughly dried. Extreme care should be exercised in cleaning the lens in this way, but do not at any cost allow the salt water to dry on: it may cause marks which are irremovable.

A regatta affords endless picture-making opportunities. To make the most of these the photographer should be afloat, preferably in a fairly speedy launch skippered by someone who knows the competing craft and, more important, who understands the technique of racing under sail. This is essential, as, while his task will be to put the camera in positions where good pictures will be available, he must at the same time *ensure* that he does not in any way incommode the competing craft. Given this approach, the photographer will be welcomed by the competitors, many of whom will be glad to see and perhaps acquire pictures of their yachts under way: but on no account should the photographer venture among the fleet without skilled guidance, as it is fatally easy to be in the wrong place at the wrong moment.

For racing pictures one can usually work without the range-finder, as even at shutter speeds of 1/200 to 1/500 second—which may be necessary to combat the movement of one's own boat—the light is generally good enough to permit of lens apertures ranging from $f\,8$ to $f\,4.5$, and at the distance at which one is usually working these should allow sufficient depth for scale focusing to be adequately accurate. An open *wire frame* view-finder or one of the *Albada* type is a convenience because with it one can see what is *just* outside the limits of the picture field, at all times.

On a cruise somewhat different requirements exist. The principal interest in the pictures made will be according to how well they illustrate the happenings on board and the places visited. For this reason, it is well to try to produce a definite series of exposures, which will make up into an album record of the complete trip and which, when referred to in conjunction with the "log", will once again bring the whole holiday to life with all its joys and tribulations.

So far we have considered the photography of objects on the sea. Many of the most interesting marine pictures, however, have the land itself for their motif.

The cruising photographer will welcome the appearance of land as something on which to train his lens—and shutters will be heard clicking while other members of the party are busily engaged in trying to recognise details in the landscape through their binoculars. After days at sea the appearance of a strange coastline exerts a singular fascination over the camera owner, warping his judgment so that he commences exposing film long before the narrow belt of land on the horizon is close enough to be recognisable in the photographic interpretation of that word. Distances over an expanse of water are very deceptive, and objects a mile away look very near indeed in the absence of other objects nearer by as a basis of comparison. The photographer who starts shooting at this, and greater range, would never attempt such an impossible task with both feet on dry land; and, unless he is working with a really long focus lens, he will be well advised to curb his impatience until the range can be measured in hundreds of yards at the most, as otherwise he will secure little more than an immensity of sea and sky, divided by a thin dark line that he will have to explain to his friends as "the coast of ——" The safe guiding rule is thoroughly to study, assess and compose *every* view in the finder before pressing the button. Only this way can disappointment be avoided.

Photographing the sea itself can be a fascinating pursuit; but again there are disappointments in store. Breaking waves that assume considerable proportions in one's imagination have a disconcerting habit of appearing on the film as the faintest of undulations on the surface of the water. It is all a matter of scale. The sea is immense. Even the portion included by the camera is tremendous—

190

and against this expanse the biggest, angriest wave appears puny. The only solutions lie in contrasting the size of the waves with that of a known object, e.g. a passing ship or staunchions on one's own deck; or by isolating the waves from their immense water background by depicting them from so low a viewpoint that their serrated tops are visible in profile against the sky. A combination of these two methods will probably produce the most effective results.

Based, perhaps, on experience on land, there is always a tendency to try to hold the camera level in relation to one's own immediate surroundings—the ship itself. This may be quite satisfactory as far as deck scenes are concerned; but if any sea is visible in the picture it must be remembered that the horizon *always* is level and should be depicted as such, whatever effect this may appear to have on the ship itself. It is very easy to fall into this trap, particularly when one is concerned with adequately presenting a foreground object; but it should be given attention if a satisfactory and truthful result is to be secured.

Sunsets and—more rarely—sunrises at sea are irresistible. It is, however, fatally easy to be carried away by the glorious riot of colour, and to expect a result which is photographically impossible. Intensely bright red or orange clouds may have no greater photographic (actinic) brilliance than the blue sky against which they stand in such visual contrast. To exploit such a subject to the full the film must be panchromatic and a filter be carefully chosen which will produce the necessary contrast between the principal colours (see page 94). Only in this way can one hope to produce an attractive result. When the sunset is less colourful and is composed mostly of varying shades of light and dark, its photographic potentialities are much more easily estimated by eye. As with distant landscapes, one must ever be on guard against expecting too much. The interest is apt to be so centred on the phenomenon itself that the photographer all too readily overlooks the fact that it occupies but a fraction of the picture space on the film. For sunsets, a long focus lens has considerable advantages, unless a very wide area of sky is covered with attractively-lit clouds. Exposures should be short. There is no question of securing shadow detail. Any foreground object will necessarily have to be rendered in silhouette, as if too generous an exposure is given there will be insufficient differentiation between the sky tones and they will be almost unprintably dense in the negative.

PICTORIAL WORK

BEFORE considering the technical requirements of the pictorial photographer, as distinct from those of the dozen-and-one other specialist users, it is perhaps desirable to ask a few questions, and to establish in one's mind just exactly what pictorial photography is. Just when does a photograph cease to be a snap or a record and become dubbed pictorial? What constitutes a pictorial print? In what way, if any, is it distinguished from its brothers? How does one start to make real "pictures" with a miniature camera? Is there any technical difference in procedure or presentation that characterises the pictorial work? All these queries are easy to propound, but difficult to answer, and any interpretation offered is by necessity largely personal and in no way universally true.

Relatively few of us are blessed with the skill needed to become artists working in oils or water colours, but fortunately the camera takes care of the drawing, and by its aid almost any photographer with average technical ability can exploit any latent artistic urge he may possess in the production of so-called pictorial photographs. The pictorial photograph, then, can be described as *a pictorial expression of a personal interpretation of a scene, or subject*, and though this may sound both vague and fulsome, I find it difficult to find a more precise definition.

Given a good camera, an exposure meter, suitable materials, and the necessary care and skill, anyone can make a photograph that will command admiration because of its *technical* quality, but to come within our description

192

the picture must also have some personal characteristics which will identify it as a subjective interpretation of a subject.

One worker will photograph a village street scene so that it is a perfect representation of that particular place; a photograph in which those who live there will identify every familiar detail with ease. Another photographer will produce, from the same material, a picture on examining which one does not become conscious of any desire to know where it was taken, but is very much aware of the shimmering heat of a summer day, and can almost experience the sensations of the man who was there when the exposure was made. This second picture seems to convey to the beholder what *every* village is like on a hot day. So a pictorial photograph, I think, frequently depicts moods and sensations, rather than people and places.

Pictorial work is very much a matter of imaginative outlook. The photographer will have to ask himself how he can depict more or less abstract qualities like heat, cold, weariness, joy, sorrow, peace; or conditions such as fog, rain, snow, etc., all of which, while they do not necessarily form the primary subject of his picture, decisively affect its appearance. He will usually find that, in this sense, he will have to cultivate an indirect approach; that is, instead of concentrating on any particular subject as divorced from its surroundings, he will strive to emphasise the effect of moods, sensations, conditions on that subject; for example, the *effect* of the heat on the village street, or the rain on a city square. He should strive to produce prints which cause corresponding reactions in those to whom they are shown. A print which makes an observer say, "How horrible—you can almost feel the rain!" is well on the way to hanging on the exhibition wall.

What is a pictorial *subject?* I'm sure I don't know. I don't suppose there *is* such a thing. One thing of which I am sure is that, generally, a place, thing, or scene which is "pretty" in itself is not necessarily pictorial. I fall into this trap as often as anyone, I just can't resist photographing the beautiful things and places—but they seldom find their way on to the exhibition wall.

My own more successful work has been mostly pictures

of an "effect" rather than a place: the glint of sunshine or reflections of objects on water; the play of sunlight or clouds rather than pictures of people or places; and the successful portraitists generally give us pictures of moods rather than individuals (excluding celebrities, photographed for the sake of their name duly advertised in the caption).

Exhibition pictures must be *simple*; I would urge this necessity for simplification all the time. The best exhibitors often show pictures made from one small detail rather than from a whole landscape. The more one can simplify, the easier the task becomes. All extraneous matter conflicts with and detracts from the message. A photograph of one's house, as a whole, may be interesting because of personal associations; but the streaks of sunshine in the loggia or the play of shadows across the kitchen floor may easily furnish prints which would charm anybody—wherever that house may be. Never be afraid to concentrate on the "part"; it is frequently much more than the "whole".

Countless pages have been written on composition. Accepted authorities wrangle among themselves over the "rules" governing a well-composed picture. At the risk of appearing an agnostic I would go so far as to say that, in my opinion, there are no rules. I venture to suggest that "If it *looks* right, it *is* right". Some of the finest and most satisfying pictures I have ever seen depart widely from the normally accepted dictums. There may be, however, a few general hints one could give to secure a balanced, orderly appearance for the print. It is desirable to keep the interest within the "picture space". Avoid having prominent areas of exceptionally light or dark tone around the edges of the picture. They draw the eye, and make the observer conscious of the picture's borders. In a well arranged photograph, the beholder's interest should automatically circle round *inside* the picture, so that he is almost unaware of its edges. For a like reason, "lines" (roadways, paths, hedges, walls, the edge of a building, etc.) should lead the eye *into* the picture; preferably to the principal object in the picture itself. Similarly, the head, in a portrait, should look *into* the picture, i.e. one should allow more space in front of the head than behind it.

194

Walking figures and vehicles are always best shown as if moving *into* the picture. Some experiment along these lines will quickly convince the most hardened sceptic that there are a few general ideas that can usually be followed in the quest of pictures which appear satisfactorily "composed".

In the old days (say before 1930!) an exhibition print was often considered unsuitable for hanging if it was too sharply defined. It was "too photographic", and pictorialism became too closely linked with the graphic arts. Mercifully, we have passed the stage when if a photograph looked like a photograph it could not be considered to be "artistic".

Fuzziness is no criterion of pictorial value, neither is the use of a matt surface. There appears to be some long-standing aversion to the use of glossy papers for exhibition work. I suggest, however, that this viewpoint also is old-fashioned; and that if a better result can be obtained on this type of material—and it usually can—then there is no valid reason for not using it. In any case, most of the big exhibitions show prints under glass, and this alone makes it very hard to determine the actual surface of the paper.

At last we are getting proud of our chosen medium of expression; and the first concern of the budding modern pictorialist should be to see that he is master of the technicalities of his process. He must make his camera produce what *he* wants, just as much as he must make up his mind *what* he wants, and include just as much as he wants before pressing the button.

He must study the subject and should expose in accordance with its requirements. I will not attempt to recapitulate technical detail in this chapter, but I do recall the need for the exposure to receive most careful study with the view of securing the best possible rendering in the negative, *bearing in mind what is desired in the final print.* It may be that the subject contains dazzling sunshine and shadows on snow. Perhaps the whole "picture" depends on the presentation of the sunshine to the best advantage. To do so it may be—in fact *will* be—necessary considerably to under-expose darker objects, but this must be done if the sunshine is to be properly rendered and if the play of sunshine is to be the motif of the picture itself. I only cite this

195

as a bald example of the technical points calling for consideration before the button is pressed.

If there is any doubt about exposure, make several exposures at varying speeds or stops. Even though modern films have enormous latitude, you will thus place the various tones in relatively good or bad positions on the film curve and will probably find that one negative produces a print which *expresses* the atmosphere far better than the others, although likely enough all the negatives will yield a good print on a suitable grade of paper; and the subject matter in the narrower sense of that term— say, a group of trees—may duly be rendered as the same group of trees throughout the whole sequence of exposures. But its tonal relationship to the rest of what appears in the same negative frame may vary from exposure to exposure and only one of these will be such as to answer our pictorial requirements—however difficult it may be to state clearly enough just what these requirements be.

Good pictorial work frequently owes much to exaggeration of tone values. What would normally be just a pleasing landscape can often become an arresting and dramatic picture by, for example, accentuating the dark blue sky, so that the billowing white clouds stand out powerfully against their dark sky background. Similarly, the pale yellow of corn in sunshine can be emphasised by the choice of suitable filters. The pictorial worker is not greatly concerned with securing what is necessarily a *truthful* rendering; so long as his final print produces what he considers to be the desired effect.

For greater detail on the use of all common filters, I would again refer the reader to the appropriate chapter in this volume (p. 94), but to give an idea of those which I personally find most useful in pictorial work I would suggest the inclusion of:

1. "U.V." or very pale yellow—to secure true rendering of sky at high altitudes—also useful on snow in sunshine;
2. No. 1 yellow: used for general landscape pictures where it is not desired to exaggerate;
3. No. 2 or 3 yellow—for strong rendering of skies and to lighten yellow objects;

196

Pictorial photography is an all-embracing term. There is hardly a single subject that is not pictorial in some conditions or from some viewpoint. More often than not the lighting is of greater importance, pictorially, than the subject matter itself.

Page 197. NARCISSI—A subject which appeals because of its attractive pattern and on account of the excellent rendering of the blooms. The placing of the subjects in the picture space and the simplicity of the background contribute to success.—W. G. Briggs.

198

Page 198.   THE WOODMAN'S CHALET—*A delicate picture on conventional lines of composition. The dark trees in the foreground play a useful part in separating the chalet and its surroundings from the more distant trees.   This picture owes much of its charm to the beautiful quality of the shadowed snow.*—G. Underell.

Above.   THE WATER HOLE—*An intriguing picture taken facing into the light. The two dark tree trunks make a bold, if unusual, frame for the subject, which is well placed—walking* into *the picture space. The considerable value of the circular pattern of the ripples should be noted; it serves to join up the two otherwise separate tree trunks and to give unity to the picture.*—Felix H. Man.

199

LIQUID LIGHT—*This picture is one of a series of attempts to capture the oily ripples on the surface of a West Country harbour. Choice of exact camera position was important, as a movement of a foot or two one way or the other entirely altered the position of the brightest reflections. A choice of interchangeable lenses enabled the author to include just the desired amount from the most suitable viewpoint.*—H. S. Newcombe.

200

HOUSES OF PARLIAMENT—*A clever composition in which the floodlit building is emphasized by the dark figure and railings in the foreground. The considerable depth of focus of relatively short focus lenses is here again shown to advantage.*—Felix H. Man.

201

Above. THE STAIRWAY—*The composition is attractive. The stone balustrade leads the eye up the steps to the lamp which is the focus of interest in the picture. Many equally satisfactory subjects are waiting to be discovered in almost every town.*—F. Fiedler.

Page 203. GRECIAN LONDON—*A picture which has been created by the war and by the extremely wide angle of the 2.8 cm. lens, which dwarfs the background.*—H. S. Newcombe.

Page 204. LITTLE SHIP—*A subject which attracted its author by its simplicity of motif and delicate tone values. A pale yellow filter was used to lower slightly the sky and water tones. Otherwise the effect— immediately preceding a heavy thunderstorm—is quite natural.*—H. S. Newcombe.

202

4. Green for photographing foliage—particularly to differentiate between new fresh spring growths, and the darker green of more mature foliage (this filter is also very useful for outdoor portraiture in sunshine, when it is desired to retain the tone of suntanned flesh);

5. Orange or a "salmon" filter—to penetrate mist and to exaggerate the depth of dark blue sky, or its reflection in water;

6. Strong red filter—used just as the one above when a still more striking and exaggerated effect is desired.

With a range such as this, nature can be translated into any version of black-and-white according to the ideas of the man behind the camera. Assuming the possession of several filters similar to the above, I recommend taking the camera to a suitable scene and experimenting carefully to find out just what difference each filter makes. Technique *must* be above reproach—filters alone do not make pictures, and, in fact, *should not be used unless there is a genuine reason for so doing*.

The technically perfect print usually carries every tone from white to black. The pictorial print does not necessarily do so. For the heavy dark study, described as "low key", a satisfactory picture can often be obtained without using the lighter tones of which the paper is capable. An exception is usually the inclusion of a small "accent" highlight, which by contrast with the remainder emphasises the dark and strong, or mysterious, quality of the print. On the other hand a "high key" picture may well contain all the tones from white, down to quite a light gray, as its darkest tone. It is *not* possible to print a negative of a normal subject satisfactorily in either a low or high key manner. The governing factor is the nature of the subject itself: this is a definite rule which must be remembered. A well-lit child photograph, with light clothes and a light background, will produce a good high key print, in which all the available tones are adequately and accurately rendered—but the same child in dark clothes, photographed in contrasty sunshine, in front of a house, can *never* be printed properly as a high key picture. Any attempt to do so will merely falsify *all* the tones due to the under-printing necessary to avoid full blacks in the darker parts. In the same way, a "low key" effect cannot be obtained from a negative of a normal subject. It will look what it is, an over-exposed and degraded print.

It follows, therefore, that the print which is a technically correct rendering of the subject is the one for which to strive, and that, as a rule, "cooking" the result will seldom, if ever, produce a masterpiece. The tonal character of the picture should be considered with as much care *before* the exposure is made as is usually the choice of the motif; as, apart from cropping unwanted portions, one can do very little to improve the result after the picture is in negative form. The 35 mm. negative is already small enough; and as we are likely to enlarge it to 10 or 15 diameters in the production of our salon print, it is desirable to use the whole of the negative whenever this is possible, so as to reduce the necessary degree of enlargement to a minimum.

There is, unfortunately, no gainsaying that the user of a larger reflex or other camera with a ground glass focusing screen enjoys one very considerable advantage over us when it comes to this class of work. I refer in particular to the ease with which he can assess the three dimensional scene. He can *see* on the ground glass focusing screen the effect of opening or closing his lens diaphragm; and can adjust it until he has secured exactly the desired degree of sharpness or softness in the background. *We* have to rely on experience—and our depth of focus scale. I mention this because it is perhaps the one point on which at least the range-finder miniature is at a drawback when compared with its big brothers; but as has already been seen, no camera is perfect and ours enjoys so many advantages peculiarly its own that I think we can concede this point to the larger instrument.

The wide range of accessory lenses by the aid of which perspective can so largely be controlled (see p. 77) and the immensely rapid lens apertures that are *usable*, because their short focus ensures ample depth, enable the 35 mm. user to deal with many subjects denied to the larger camera: while even the differential focusing that is a feature of big camera work can easily be secured with the more rapid lenses, and particularly with those of long focus when used at full aperture. On balance, therefore, apart from the greater degree of technical skill required in processing and printing, I think that the miniature competes on quite favourable terms—even for pictorial work.

PORTRAITURE

PORTRAITURE with a precision miniature differs in few respects from portraiture with larger equipment. The greatest advantage—to my mind—is one that others of a more conservative outlook may consider to be a disadvantage; because retouching on the 35 mm. negative is practically impossible, the results are far more likely to be true to life than those produced in sizes which encourage the worker to interfere with nature. "Beautifying" is impossible. Because of this, the 35 mm. user will have to take care that retouching—as ordinarily understood—is not likely to be necessary at all. He will have to give more thought to his lighting, materials used, processing methods, and—last but not least—to his subject. This is all to the good: as, having done so, his results are likely to possess a freshness and appeal lacking in those prints that have relied on the pencil to eradicate defects and to smooth away to an unnatural extent the life lines in the sitter's face. Miniature portraiture lacks much of that artificial dignity of oldish photographs reminiscent of nineteenth-century painting, and has developed a typically photographic style of its own which Americans call "candid". Unfortunately there is occasionally some temptation to let "candid" work deteriorate to the level of indiscretion and bad taste.

One of the charms of 35 mm. portraiture is that it can be practised anywhere. With the immensely rapid lenses and films at our disposal it seems likely that the day of the old-fashioned type of studio is almost over, and that we shall soon consider ordinary portraits "dated" unless they are taken in the sitters' own homes—by natural home lighting. Studio conditions have an enormous effect on most (other than professional) models, and the home environment and familiarity with his or her surroundings go far to create the desirable natural expression or pose that is often so difficult to secure when the sitter goes to a strange studio expressly to be photographed.

Camera portraiture can obviously be practised by day or by artificial light. Each has its peculiarities. The open-air quality of *good* outdoor portraits is very hard to capture in work executed indoors, except when abnormally large and airy studio facilities exist. On the other hand, the possibility fully to control the lighting scheme and create definite actinic values by light are two points very much in favour of reliance on electricity.

Whatever method is adopted, the problems, as such, remain very much the same. They are: (*a*) The need for a comparatively unified source of light directed on to the model; (*b*) a background of suitable tone; (*c*) a method of "filling in" unwanted shadow areas; (*d*) a means of directing an accent light on to localised areas in order to bring out texture or highlights (e.g. in the hair).

Obviously such lighting control is hardly available to the outdoor man, who must necessarily make do with the sunshine—either direct or diffused—relying on the use of reflectors to illuminate the shadow side of the figure.

Backgrounds—out-of-doors—present a problem. Unless of the plainest character, they tend to become obtrusive, and to suggest the place where the picture was made, in which event interest is drawn from the subject in the narrower sense of the word. My own preference is for a plain sky background for outdoor work. If the sky is grey, it will, of course, be uncontrollable; but if blue in colour, a fair degree of control over its actual tone can be exercised by the use of suitable colour filters (provided always that they will have no adverse effect on the portrait) or by the use of a polarising filter (p. 100), by means of which the depth of the blue sky can largely be governed without affecting the colour balance of anything else.

For indoor work I am inclined to advocate the use of a

white background, at an ample distance—say 6 to 8 ft. behind the sitter. If the model, and the background, are illuminated by separate lamps, the tone of the background can be turned into anything from dead white to quite a dark grey, according to how well it is lit. One of the most popular writers on portrait lighting in America, *William Mortensen*, is a strong believer in this control of background brilliance; advocating that its luminosity should generally compare with the highlights in the face of the model. He also recommends what at first sight appears to be absolutely flat lighting; with a single lamp situated close to the camera lens: securing his modelling and plastic quality by cutting his exposure times to the minimum, and building up a sufficiency of contrast in the negative by considerably prolonged development.

I have used *Mortensen's* technique, and the results are all that could be desired, but I am not quite happy in recommending them to the 35 mm. photographer; because the very prolonged development—while entirely satisfactory in larger sizes—is productive of too coarse a grain for the results to be entirely pleasing. For this reason, therefore, I feel that, at least in this size, the more conventional lighting systems with two or more lamps are likely to yield a higher percentage of good results in average hands.

For the commencement I suggest that an outfit comprising 3 bowl reflectors, with adjustable stands, and fitted with 250 or 500 watt lamps, plus, if possible, a small "spotlight", is all that will be required.

One of these lamps will be used to illuminate the background only, the tone being controlled by the lamp (250 or 500) fitted, and its distance from the background. This lamp will *always* be behind or on a level with the subject, and so placed that on no account can any of its light spill on to the model, who relies solely on the other two lamps for illumination.

Natural light comes from above at a more or less oblique angle. Therefore for natural portraiture the main source of light should be from a point higher than the model's head. I suggest a 500 watt lamp 6 or 7 ft. up, a little to one side of the camera, as the main light, for a straightforward portrait.

209

The second lamp (possibly diffused by a piece of butter muslin draped over the mouth of the reflector) acts as a fill-in light, placed on the opposite side of the camera and somewhat lower, to illuminate (fill in) the shadows under the brows, nose, chin, etc., which are cast by the main light. It may prove that the fill-in competes with the main light. If so, a lower wattage (250) can advantageously be substituted; or the lamp moved away to a greater distance from the subject.

By following such a basically simple scheme as that outlined and by moving the main light up and down or to either side of the camera, while at the same time adjusting the second lamp so that it does its duty on the shadow side, an almost endless series of lighting schemes will be unfolded. A careful note of the positions, heights and distances of both lamps should be kept at least during the experimental period, as a guide to future work.

Many professional studios simply massacre the subject by turning on banks of lights from seemingly every conceivable direction, and then throwing in the effect of a couple of spotlamps for luck. This more often than not mainly serves the purpose of impressing the sitter, but quite often also confuses the photographer. Beyond a certain degree of intensity of illumination it becomes very hard if not impossible to judge subtle effects. Experimenting round a fundamentally simple scheme such as I have suggested will produce a far higher proportion of satisfying pictures.

We have not, so far, discussed the spot-light. I was even in two minds about advocating its acquisition. It is a valuable tool when used correctly *and with restraint*. It can be directed from one side, behind the model, to give a fringe of light on the hair, against a darker background— or from a more frontal position, to give lustre and modelling to the hair—and can be used to create patterned backgrounds. It can be employed as almost the sole source of light for some character portraits, or as an aid to "glamourising" female portraits of a film star type. It has many uses, and abuses; so, if I may be forgiven the repetition, treat it with restraint.

As I have said, natural lighting comes from above. Lighting a portrait from below will sometimes give it what is supposed to be a mystic character. More often the result will look macabre!

If your portraiture is likely to be of the casual variety, you may not care to face the cost of the 500 watt lamps. In this case, at the expense of longer exposures, you can do a lot with ordinary 100 watt household lamps, or with *Photoflood* No. 1 lamps costing only a couple of shillings each. These consume about 275 watts each, but only last for approximately two hours when run at their full intensity. It is not difficult to arrange a "double pole-double throw" switch in the circuit, however, by means of which one can use two such lamps "in series" while preparing the exposure and throwing the switch into the "parallel" position, the lamps are brought to their full brilliance, only for the few moments of the exposure itself. Used in this way *Photofloods* have an incredibly long life.

Camera position naturally has a very great effect on a portrait. We are accustomed to viewing people from their (or our) eye level—and a portrait from such a level is likely to be far more natural than one from, say, waist level, when the camera will be looking up underneath the chin and nostrils, presenting a viewpoint to which we are less accustomed.

Occasionally an inordinately low or high viewpoint may have advantages—for example, a very receding chin can be made less apparent by choosing a low viewpoint, while a model with a tendency to a double chin will probably better appreciate the portrait if the photographer has the good sense to keep the camera on the high side. There are many other parallel cases.

Study your sitter: decide what (if anything) requires emphasis or what should be played down and choose your viewpoint level accordingly. If you are taking a profile or semi-profile, bear in mind that no two halves of a face are ever the same. Examine the sitter from both angles, and then decide which is likely to be more "typical".

With a 35 mm. camera you will find the best results are usually secured with 85 or 90 mm. lenses for head and shoulders or half-length portraits. A 50 mm. lens is useful for standing figures if space is limited, but the longer focus is definitely to be preferred for everything else. With a 90 mm. lens one is usually able to *fill* the negative with the required part of the subject. This should be done to get the best out of our medium. One cannot retouch 35 mm. film, and it has to be enlarged considerably, therefore the negative must be as perfect, in the technical sense, as one can make it; and the subject as large on it as possible so as to limit the degree of enlargement required as far as is reasonable.

A 135 mm. lens is occasionally useful for large heads. It renders them on a very satisfying scale, and with a wealth of detail. I do not care for its use when much more of the figure is included, as it has a tendency to foreshorten and flatten the modelling, which, I think, is better preserved with 90 mm. Some exceptionally fine head studies have been produced with still longer objectives; and provided that the modelling and contours of the subject are sufficiently bold—and of course the studio length adequate—there would seem to be definite advantages in the employment of a 20 cm. or even 30 cm. objective, particularly if used with a reflex focusing attachment (see p. 34) where the subtleties of differential focusing can adequately be exploited.

When Leitz introduced their *Thambar* 9 cm. *f* 2.2 lens they made a contribution to the 35 mm. portraitist that exists in no other make. The lens combines the advantages of soft and sharp definition controllable to a remarkable degree. The removable opaque "stop" enables the user to secure an image which is definitely soft (to a selected degree) all over; or to obtain a rendering in which a sharp and detailed image is surrounded by a controllable amount of softness. Because this diffusion arises from a spreading of the brighter lights into the shadow areas, it creates a luminous quality in the print which cannot be obtained by making a diffused enlargement from a sharp negative. The use of a *Duto* or other soft focus attachment lens enables normal lenses to produce practically the same result; and by using the weaker (No. O) series, the need for retouching—almost impossible on 35 mm. negatives—is eliminated, without undue loss of definition.

Choice of materials is a matter of personal taste. I

212

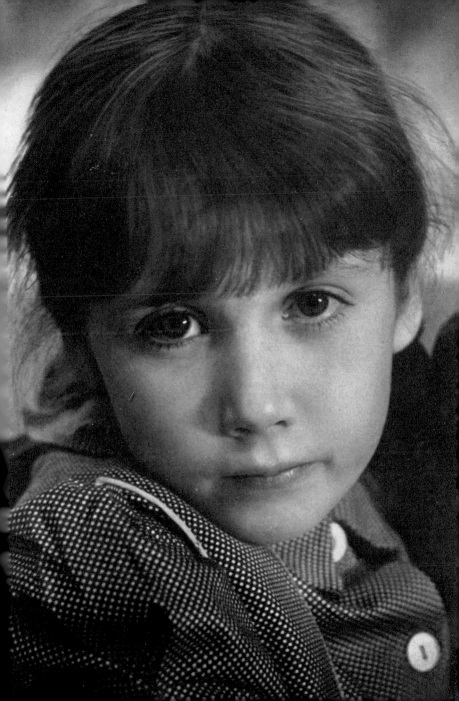

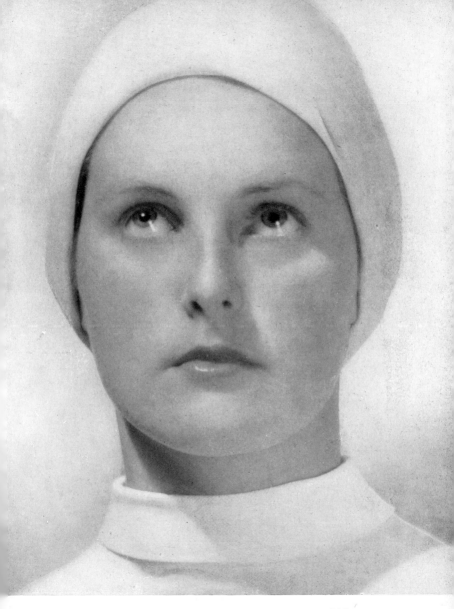

215

216

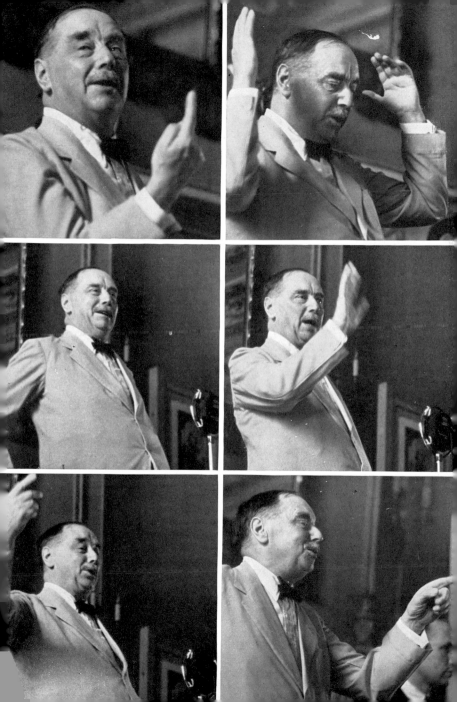

Miniature camera portraits frequently exhibit qualities seldom found in the work of large cameras. Owing to the speed with which the 35 mm. can be manipulated, characteristic poses are easily obtainable.

Page 213. PORTRAIT—An appealing picture which is an excellent example of work done in natural surroundings.—K. Hubschmann.

Page 214. THE HAT—Fashion photography is another branch where the 35 is a valuable tool.—K. Hubschmann.

Page 215. HIGH KEY PORTRAIT—A typical high key subject, suitable presented.—J. W. J. Underell.

Page 216. THE TRIBESMAN—An example of realistic portraiture. The sky makes a fine and suitable background.—J. Allan Cash.

Page 217. THE RT. HON. DAVID LLOYD GEORGE—This type of picture, shot "on the run", is available almost exclusively to the miniature.—K. Hubschmann.

Page 218.   THE ARTIST—*Another instance where the considerable depth of focus of the miniature camera has secured a picture that would have been impossible with a larger instrument.*—K. Hubschmann.

Page 219.   THE TOAST—*A slow exposure held in the hand. Illumination: one very weak and well shaded lamp.*—H. S. Newcombe.

Page 220.   WINDY DAY—*Spontaneous open-air portraiture.   An endeavour to portray the prevailing conditions.*—H. S. Newcombe.

Page 221.   MR. H. G. WELLS—*An amusing and characteristic series— a type of work which is exclusive to the miniaturist.*—Erich Auerbach.

Page 222.   THE CANTEEN—*One of a series taken to illustrate the work of a canteen, this picture typifies the so-called "candid" photography. A fast lens and steady hand are essential.*—K. Hubschmann.

Above.   THE ARCHBISHOP OF YORK—*Another fine example of a spontaneous portrait of very dramatic quality.*—Erich Auerbach.

Page 224.   UTTER AMAZEMENT—*A picture caught just at the right moment.   Again the ideal job for the fast working miniature.*— K. Hubschmann.

recommend avoiding the extremely rapid films on account of their relatively coarse grain, and would advise the use of films such as *Panatomic X., Isopan F, F.P.*3, all of which enjoy exceptionally fine grain and are capable of preserving "brilliance" without producing a harsh result. For male portraiture, there is something to be said for the use of orthochromatic material, particularly if the rugged characteristics of the model are to be emphasised, and as long as the sitter's eyes are not light blue, when they might be rendered too light.

By artificial light, on pan films, a pale blue filter is frequently desirable to prevent red lips, etc., appearing over-light and toneless. By daylight it should not be necessary. Out of doors, however, a green filter has its uses in preserving a good skin tone if the subject is tanned. Incidentally, if it is desired to *reduce* the tanned appearance, an orange or red filter will assist considerably.

Semi-profile or three-quarter views of a model wearing spectacles are always a problem. It is seldom possible to record the eyes satisfactorily, and frequently the glasses themselves appear as almost opaque white discs. This is where a polarising filter can most usefully be employed. If its angle is carefully adjusted, the spectacles will become transparent and the eyes be clearly visible through them.

As a last warning, do not forget that you should be filling the frame at a distance of perhaps only 5 or 6 ft. Remember therefore to adjust your view-finder accurately for the parallax correction, or you may lose an important part of the picture!

AT THE SHOWS

IF THERE is any one place more than another where the 35 mm. camera really comes into its own, it is in taking theatrical pictures during an ordinary performance. Above all, for this work a large lens aperture is essential, and only with the 35 mm. camera lenses are we able to enjoy such speed while, at the same time, securing sufficient depth of focus satisfactorily to depict the whole stage setting, as distinct from one solitary figure or group.

Stage photography, during the performance, is usually a continuous battle with under-exposure, and for this reason it is advisable to load the camera with one of the fastest films, such as *H.P.*3 or *H.P.S.*, *Tri X, Isopan Ultra,* etc., so that we are at least free from disturbing doubts, during the actual performance, as to whether it would not have been wiser, after all, to have a more rapid film than the one actually chosen.

Of course, these fastest films are relatively grainy; but if the show proves to be much better illuminated than was at first expected, this can be turned to account by exposing generously and then processing the film in one of the "fine grain" (p. 125) developers, thus again avoiding some of the grain that might otherwise be too apparent. If, however, the lighting proves to be—or even becomes, in the course of the performance—disappointing, then the fast film chosen will at least enable the user to secure the best results possible in the circumstances.

Picture making by the amateur during an ordinary performance is not generally encouraged, and application to the management for a permit is usually necessary. Even then permission is not always granted, as there is some fear that promiscuous snapshotting during the performance will interfere with its enjoyment by other patrons, apart from any questions of infringement of copyright that may arise. For this reason, if the photographer *is* fortunate enough to obtain the desired permission, it behoves him, or her, to work discreetly and to cause the minimum inconvenience and annoyance to other members of the public. It is also very desirable to submit copies of all photographs taken during a performance to the theatre management, for their approval, before publishing or exhibiting the results.

Having considered the preliminaries—now for the job in hand. The best position for camera work is usually in the front of the dress circle—preferably just off centre. The stalls are usually no good photographically, as the eye

226

(and the camera) is generally just on or below the level of the floor of the stage and consequently the performers' feet are liable to become predominant. The exact centre of the circle should also be avoided, as it frequently houses a battery of lights, the beams of which are very visible in the smoke fumes which come up from the ground floor. It is for this reason, and to avoid flat lighting, that a position somewhat to one side is advocated. A stage box has some advantages, but as the performers necessarily play to each side of the house in turn, it obviously cuts down photographic opportunities by about 50 per cent. Other boxes are usually worse than useless, as they view the stage at far too steep and awkward an angle.

Producers are anxious to make their productions attractive to the eye, and so they often rely on coloured illumination; this is where our greatest difficulty arises. Many of the more attractive scenes are lighted only by green or metallic blue "floods" which, whatever their artistic quality, are exceedingly poor photographically. The only saving grace is that such lights are usually associated with the quieter scenes where movement is often leisured, and relatively long exposures can be given. Films such as those recommended possess a proportionally better sensitivity to red, orange and yellow light, so that subjects so lit are more easily dealt with.

Another reason for choosing the most rapid emulsions lies in the fact that they possess a reasonably gentle gradation. Stage shots, particularly when spot lights are trained on the principal performer, can be extremely harsh; and an exposure which is right for the face on to which the "spot" is directed will be hopelessly short for everything else; while similarly, an exposure adequate for the stage as a whole will burn up anything on which the spotlights fall and make it unprintably dense. The advantage of a film with a sufficiently long scale to do justice to such lighting extremes is therefore obvious.

What are the best lenses for stage photography? The 5 cm. $f1.4$ or $f1.5$ lens is the most useful, except in a very large theatre, or where the photographer is rather far from the stage; but a slightly longer focus, high speed lens is also a very desirable accessory. An 8.5 cm. $f2$

227

or similar lens is an ideal second string and will be extremely useful if the subject matter occupies only a portion of the stage.

As far as the pictorial aspect of stage photography is concerned it does no harm to appreciate that the producer has carefully composed his picture within the limits of the stage itself; and frequently the complete stage is, in consequence, a more satisfying composition than any arbitrary selection of part of it made by the photographer with his longer focus lens. Or to put it another way: the picture covering the whole of the stage is ready made; the selective shot must be composed by the photographer himself—composed, one should remember, within a matter of seconds, i.e. much shorter time than usually is at one's disposal for that task.

Exposure is perhaps the hardest problem on which to proffer advice. One cannot generalise. Large and small stages, immense and intimate auditoriums, the lighting facilities of the house—they all have such appreciable bearing on the light that reaches the performers that I find it hard to make really useful suggestions. I have seldom found an exposure meter of much use, except when working from a stage box or a circle very close to the stage; and in the main prefer to rely on judgment—*and then to give twice that*! As I said at the outset, we are fighting against under-exposure; and while there are variety stages, particularly in London, where 1/200 second at $f\,1.5$ or even $f\,2$ will produce a well-exposed negative, the majority of plays seem to be so lit that 1/25 at $f\,2$ is more likely to result in a negative of good quality than anything faster. The majority of my own exposures on this type of subject are made at $f\,2$ with exposures between 1/20 and 1/60 second; but I often repeat the shot at 1/8 second (also at $f\,2$)—choosing a time when movement is at its minimum—and not infrequently find that this gives me a far better negative than that secured at a higher speed.

The worker who is limited to an $f\,3.5$ or slower lens should remember that there is still ample opportunity for successful stage photography if he chooses his time for exposure. Dances and many other stage actions, too, are rhythmic: and any such movement—up and down, or from

228

side to side—must in some sense of the word necessarily *stop* at the moment when it changes its direction. If the exposure is made at this precise moment, quite a slow speed (1/8 or ¼ second) may easily arrest apparently rapid movement. The timing must be of a high degree of accuracy: but careful study of the movements *before* making an exposure will give a clue to the length of time that the shutter may safely be left open at the conclusion of the next rhythmic swing.

Working at such slow shutter speeds is a test of camera-holding technique. It is advisable to use one of those one-legged stands, supported by a strap round the neck—alternatively supporting the elbows on the front of the rail or ledge of the circle: and in any case liberating the shutter by the most gentle pressure of which you are capable.

It is worth while learning how to adjust shutter speeds by feel alone; and, almost more important, to remember which way you have to turn the iris ring to set it wide open.

There is, unfortunately, no standard direction in which lens aperture rings open and close; and when one is working in the poor light of a theatre auditorium, it is not always easy to see small engraved figures. I would therefore advise the reader to familiarise himself with his particular lenses so that he may be able to "open up" the stop to maximum by turning the ring in what he *knows* to be the right direction. If the lens is fitted—as so many are, nowadays—with click-stop positions, it is then quite easy to move down, step by step, relying solely on feel, to any desired stop. But you must know, for certain, which end of the scale is wide open.

This kind of work can very well be dealt with with the reflex models—particularly those which are fitted with a lens with pre-set, or auto-pre-set aperture control. Nothing could be more suitable for work in a poor light.

Another thing of importance to the theatre-goer is the ability to select any desired shutter speed by feel alone. There will be times when he is forced to use a fast exposure: others when he can use something slower, and gain in depth of sharpness. But he will seldom be able to *see* what he is

229

doing, and the ability to adjust to any required speed by touch is inestimable in such conditions.

With the current M Leicas and many modern diaphragm shutters this is an easy business. The speeds are clearly "felt" by the click positions as one turns the speed dial or ring. It is easy to turn it right round to one end or the other, and then to "work back" from this position, counting the clicks until the desired speed is set. But you *must* know which way to turn the dial in the first place to reach "B" (or top speed—if preferred). It is wise always to work the same way.

In the earlier Leicas there are some slight differences. On the earlier models—up to IIIb—the adjustments are as follows. As far as the rapid speeds are concerned, one has merely to wind the shutter, and then, *lifting* the setting dial, turn it anti-clockwise, as far as it will go (until it reaches a springy resistance), and then allow it to drop in its slot. This sets the shutter for "Bulb". If the dial is now lifted, and turned gently, and allowed to drop into each of the seatings in turn, as described above, the shutter can easily be set for 1/20, 1/30, 1/40, 1/60 and so on in turn. If slow speeds only are to be altered, the process is even simpler. The dial on the top of the camera will of course be set to its 1/20 position, and after this the speed will be controlled *solely* by the knob on the camera front. If the camera is a IIIa or IIIb, this front dial engages a small spring catch at each speed setting. If it is remembered that with the front dial turned as far to the left as it will go (as seen from the front of the camera) it is set for 1/20 second; obviously, as it is then turned to the right, one will feel a "catch" at 1/8, $\frac{1}{4}$, $\frac{1}{2}$, and finally 1 second in turn. If the dial is turned *all* the way, the shutter will be set for "Time". The Leica IIIc and IIIf have a different slow speed dial, the sequence of speeds being 1/10, 1/15, 1/20, 1/30, 1/4, 1/2, 1, the "change over" from fast to slow speed dial being made at the 1/30 position. Leica IIIF models with a red synchronizing dial are calibrated 1/10, 1/15, 1/25, 1/5, 1/2, 1; the change-over point being 1/25 second. The Leica IIIg reverts to a slow speed dial that is very similar to the pre-war models with 1/30, 1/15, 1/8, 1/4, 1/2, and 1 second markings. The change-over there is the 1/30 position.

It is useful to sit down with the camera sometimes and spend a quarter of an hour getting used to setting to a variety of speeds, without actually looking at the markings. It is a most valuable accomplishment—not only in the dark but when one wants to re-set the camera to take a picture and does not want the preparations to be too apparent to the victim.

Processing stage pictures does not seriously differ from other developing methods. If the subject is known to be under-exposed a semi-fine grain developer should be employed even at the expense of grain. If possible, I use a normal fine grain formula which contains paraphenylene diamine metol and glycin, or others which are of somewhat similar character; while if I have been lucky enough to meet a *really* well-lit stage, I banish my grain troubles once for all by developing in one of the super-fine grain developers.

When the subject photographed includes much in the way of spot lighting, I invariably cut down development by 20 per cent, or so to avoid patches of absolutely unprintable density, and then make the best of such over-exposed patches as there are by careful "spot printing" as described in the chapter on enlarging (p. 294). With stage subjects in which there is *extreme* lighting contrast, much can be done by using one of the compensating two-bath developers described on p. 154.

The grain, however, will not be quite so fine as with the developers advocated above.

ACTION PHOTOGRAPHY

THE photography of moving objects and of sporting events appeals to every camera user. The owner of a 35 mm. instrument is very fortunately placed in attempting such work—the short focus of his normal lens equipment allows him to work at relatively large apertures without sacrificing depth of focus (p. 66) which in turn means that he can

231

employ an adequately fast shutter speed to arrest movement far more easily than can the user of a camera producing a larger negative.

The essentials of *good* action photography are: that the subject be on an adequately large scale, that it be sharply defined and free from blur, and that it should *convey* the impression of being in rapid motion.

To illustrate what I mean by the last phrase, consider an express train travelling at 60 m.p.h. down a gradient. The driver has temporarily "shut off"—there is no smoke or steam visible and a perfectly sharp picture of it will differ hardly at all from one of a stationary train. To secure an equally good picture which does suggest speed, the photographer will choose a position where the train is *climbing* a slight gradient—against the wind. Its speed may now be 10 m.p.h. slower than before: but the billowing clouds of smoke and steam produced as the driver strives to maintain speed up the bank, blown backwards by the prevailing wind, give an *impression* of high speed entirely lacking in our first picture.

The minimum shutter speed which is necessary to arrest motion and secure adequate sharpness depends on many things: the actual speed of the object over the ground; the secondary speed of moving limbs in the case of, for instance, a racehorse or runner; the distance of the object from the camera; the direction in which it is moving in relation to the camera; the focal length of the lens used and the extent to which the picture will be enlarged. In the appended table I have tried to indicate shutter speeds which are likely to be safe in arresting *continuous* movement directly across the field of view. These exposures can be increased if the movement is oblique or towards the camera.

The slower shutter speeds indicated for objects at a distance are only usable because the object will be small on the negative and any blur will not show. To enlarge from only part of such a negative in order to increase object size will result in a blurred image.

When more than a normal degree of enlargement is likely to be required, the exposure should be that indicated for a proportionally closer distance.

232

233

Stage and action photography offer a wide variety of subjects and many problems, particularly in relation to lighting.

Above. WINDMILL THEATRE—*An apparently well lit scene which taxed the film to the utmost. The whole set was illuminated by very weak coloured light plus a trifle of apple green light rising from the translucent stage floor.*—H. S. Newcombe.

Page 233. ROBERT AITKIN AND HELEN CHERRY IN *HENRY IV—This is a fine example of close up work such as can sometimes be secured with one of the more rapid long focus objectives. The arrangement of heads against the dark background is particularly satisfactory.*—K. Hubschmann.

Above. BALLET—*A rapid action shot. To secure so successful a composition demands a foreknowledge of the movements and a quick trigger finger.*—Felix H. Man.

Above. SPANISH DANCE—*A slow exposure at a moment of comparative rest.*—H. S. Newcombe.

Page 237.   AUTUMN CROCUS—*A* "Full Frame" *shot with an 8.5 cm. lens—from a stage box.*—H. S. Newcombe

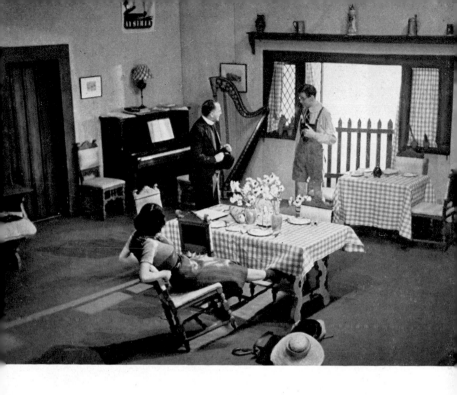

Page 238. THE DANCERS—*An interesting close-up by normal stage lighting. A somewhat high camera viewpoint has resulted in some fore-shortening of the figures.*—Felix H. Man.

Page 239. THE JUGGLER—*A fine specimen of really rapid action photography by stage lighting. The trimming has produced a most attractive composition and the effect is heightened by the plain back-ground.*—Unknown photographer.

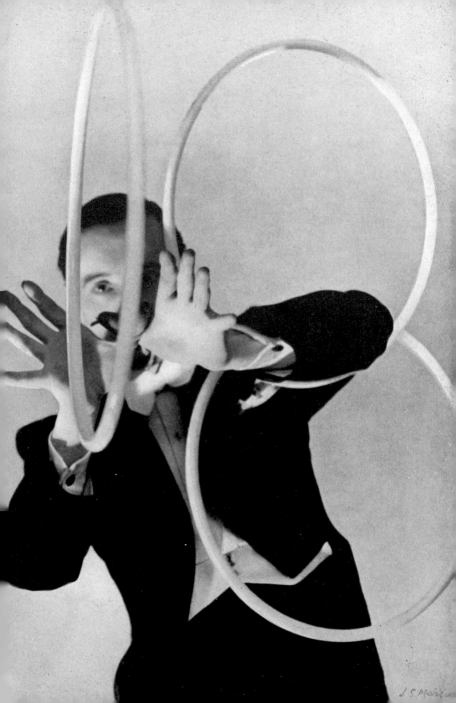

Page 240.   BALANCE—*An extremely well composed shot of a thrilling moment. With ringside seats one can seldom choose the lighting conditions and a lens which is reasonably free from flare is an asset.*— F. H. Sharman.

Above.   THE JUMP—*With a subject of this nature the camera can previously be focused on the fence in readiness for exposure immediately the horse and rider come into the picture.*—Doguibérie.

241

Above. THE CYCLE RACE—*A subject where it is usually more satisfactory to focus on a spot over which the riders will pass, and then expose when a satisfactory grouping exists.*—H. S. Newcombe.

242

Page 244. WINTER SPORT—*A fast shutter speed, careful anticipatory focusing and a good lens hood are the essentials for successful work in the snows. The blue sky is nature's own background.*—Hein Gorny.

Above. A SMART RETURN—*Even the fastest shutter speed will seldom arrest a ball in flight, but its elongation sometimes adds to the sensation of speed.*—Hein Gorny.

243

SHUTTER SPEEDS TO ARREST MOVEMENT

FOCAL LENGTH	DISTANCE BETWEEN CAMERA & SUBJECT					
3.5 cm.	7'	12'	17'	30'	60'	115'
5 cm.	10'	17'	25'	42'	83'	165'
7.5 cm.	15'	25'	37'	63'	125'	250'
10 cm.	20'	34'	50'	84'	166'	330'
13.5 cm.	27'	45'	66'	110'	220'	440'

SPEED OF SUBJECT m.p.h.	SHUTTER-SPEED IN FRACTIONS OF SECONDS					
3	1/100	1/60	1/40	1/25	1/12	1/6
4	1/125	1/75	1/50	1/30	1/15	1/8
6	1/200	1/100	1/75	1/50	1/25	1/10
8	1/250	1/150	1/100	1/60	1/30	1/15
10	1/300	1/200	1/125	1/75	1/60	1/30
20	1/600	1/400	1/250	1/150	1/75	1/40
40	1/1250	1/750	1/500	1/300	1/150	1/75
60	1/2000	1/1000	1/750	1/500	1/250	1/100
80	1/2400	1/1500	1/1000	1/600	1/300	1/150
100	1/3000	1/2000	1/1250	1/750	1/400	1/200

The minimum shutter speed necessary to arrest the movement is found by tracing vertically from the approximate "Distance" in the column of the appropriate focal length to the column "Speed of Subject". This shutter speed applies when photographing at right angles to the subject movement.

It should be realised that there is a wide difference in actual speed between, for example, a trotting horse and an express train—but both may require about the same shutter speed to arrest movement on account of the "secondary" (limb) movement of the horse.

When the object is moving obliquely at about 45° the speeds quoted in the table can be increased by about 50%. When the movement is directly to or from the camera at least twice the indicated exposure can safely be given.

Occasions arise when, because of weather conditions, it is impossible to give as short an exposure as is really necessary. In such cases—where there is only object movement in one direction—much can be done by swinging the camera so as to follow the moving object itself, releasing the shutter while the subject is held accurately in the view-finder. In this way an object moving at, say, 50 m.p.h. becomes virtually motionless as far as the *camera* is concerned and can be sharply defined with, say, an exposure of 1/50 or 1/100 second. The *background* will, however, now be rushing past the camera at 50 m.p.h., and will in consequence appear absolutely blurred: which often accentuates the apparent speed of the sharply defined moving object. This technique can most effectively be employed on motor or motor cycle subjects and the like. It is essential to keep the camera accurately lined up on the subject and to release the shutter without the slightest check in the instrument's smooth swinging travel.

At sports meetings, football matches and elsewhere the amateur sports photographer is often justifiably envious of the facilities and freedom afforded to his professional counterpart. It is unfortunately inevitable that he cannot enjoy the same freedom of movement; but this limitation need not spoil his photography. At the worst it only means the area in which his subject will occur is smaller, and that in itself makes his task easier; while from the stand he may get a very much better viewpoint than that enjoyed by the newspaper man on the touch-line or against the edge of the track. Obviously the use of a long focus lens is an asset in such conditions, and by its aid quite large and satisfactory groupings of relatively distant happenings can easily be secured; and because they *are* all relatively far off he will not be bothered by depth of focus problems.

When the viewpoint can be chosen at will, it will almost always prove best to select a spot where an oblique aspect can be obtained: to one side and well back from the tape in running events; low down so as to secure sky background, well past the hurdles, and to one side, for jumping and steeplechasing. At motor races a position where the banking looms up as a background is frequently advantageous. For cycle racing a point on top of the banking is always productive; and so on. Actually there are very few positions at any track event where good pictures cannot be made *provided* that the photographer contents himself with what he can secure from his chosen site.

Always compose the picture so that the direction of movement is *into* the picture space. Try to avoid shooting at awkward moments. Nothing looks worse than a horse apparently balancing with extreme difficulty on one foreleg.

The speed with which a 35 mm. camera can be operated may often enable a short series of pictures to be made to illustrate the various phases in a particular happening.

Every person and every camera has a certain reaction period, which is measured from the time the brain says "Fire" until the shutter has actually "gone off". It may be only a small fraction of a second, but it is there and has to be allowed for if the exposure is to take place at *precisely* the correct instant. It means pressing the button a split second *before* the subject is in the required position, and careful practice—even with an empty camera—will do much to co-ordinate mind and muscle so that there is a good chance of consistently accurate timing.

Apart from the photography of action for its own sake, there is endless opportunity for the camera in connection with every outdoor sport and pastime, either to make pictures for their own appeal or to illustrate various activities: fishing, stalking (a telephoto lens here at all cost!), on the golf course, tennis or shooting. At the local bowling club there is action photography and very good action too, although at first sight it may not appear rapid.

The more experience one can get in the photography of action the better it is for one's general work. There is very little that we photograph in which there is no living and moving interest, and the experience gained in firing the shutter at precisely the right instant to secure exactly the pose desired is invaluable even when the only moving object is a pedestrian in a landscape subject.

Reference to p. 27 in connection with direction of shutter travel is recommended; this matter should also receive consideration where rapidly moving objects are concerned.

FLASH WITH A MINIATURE

ESSENTIALLY, we have to deal with two basic forms of flash photography:—

(a) *Flash bulbs*. These are glass containers resembling small electric light bulbs and are usually filled with microscopically thin metal wire. They also contain oxygen, which enables the wire to burn with extreme rapidity when a suitable electric current is passed through the bulb.

(b) *Electronic flash*. Here a condenser containing stored electrical energy is discharged through a glass tube filled with one of the rare gases.

In the first case, the photograph is taken either by igniting the flash bulb during the period in which the shutter is open, or alternatively causing the shutter to open during the period in which the flash bulb is burning at its maximum brilliancy. In the case of electronic flash, the duration of which is so brief, the obvious way of exposing is to permit the flash to occur while the shutter is fully open.

An electronic flash tube will last for many thousand exposures, whereas the flash bulb is used once and then thrown away. Electronic flash equipment is necessarily bulky, heavy and somewhat more expensive, and it is therefore generally limited to the professional or to the keen amateur who intends to do a lot of flash photography. Its great advantage over flash bulbs is the incredibly short duration of the flash itself, usually of the order of 1/1000 second or less. Such a speed effectively arrests even the most rapid movement, enabling pictures to be taken of things which simply could not be photographed by any other method.

248

Many flash bulbs, on the other hand, give an exposure in the region of 1/50 second; but the bulbs themselves have widely varying characteristics. Naturally, any bulb which is ignited by an electrical current must, of necessity, take a definite time to reach its maximum brilliance, after which the illumination dies away. Flash bulbs vary considerably in the time (or *delay*) taken to reach this maximum brilliance and also in the duration of the period in which the bulb is furnishing useful and uniform light. Some bulbs ignite almost instantly, rise to maximum brilliance with great rapidity and then die away quickly. Others, including the majority of bulbs available, require a delay of anything up to 20 milliseconds to reach their peak and then continue for something like the same time to furnish a useful light before fading out.

One of the problems that we have to face with miniature cameras fitted with focal plane shutters is that the shutter itself takes anything up to 20 milliseconds to cross the whole of the film. The shutter is completely open only at some of the slower speeds, thereby exposing the whole of the film surface at any one instant.

A little thought will make it clear that flash bulb photography can only be carried out with cameras of this sort in two ways:—

(*a*) The bulb must go off at the precise moment when the shutter is completely open so that the effective light may fall on the whole of the film at the same instant, or

(*b*) The bulb must have a long burning period (long peak), the ignition of which is synchronised with the release of the shutter so that it reaches its maximum brilliance when the shutter commences to move across the film, and maintains this brilliance until the shutter has run down.

If, therefore, the shutter is used at its slow speeds (up to 1/25 or 1/30 second, according to the camera type and model), then any type of bulb may be used if suitably synchronized. The faster shutter speeds can, however, only be used with a long peak bulb.

The duration of an electronic flash is immeasurably short so the exposure can obviously only be made when the shutter is wide open. A miniature camera fitted with a Compur or similar shutter is in some ways more convenient for

249

flash photography, because whatever the duration of the exposure, the whole of the film is lit simultaneously.

Provided one is taking flash pictures in dark surroundings, or at night, it does not usually matter if the focal plane shutter has to be set at 1/20 second, because the exposure on the film will be derived from the light of the flash itself. But some problems arise when the flash is used as a means of augmenting daylight, e.g., to lighten over-dark shadows (a practice referred to in America as *synchro-sunlight*). If there is any movement, the comparatively long exposure of 1/20 second may allow ghost images to be formed on the film. For this type of work, therefore, the Compur type of shutter has distinct advantages.

When flash photography first became popular, the principal problem was that of determining the correct exposure, but fortunately this is capable of very simple solution. All flash bulbs of a given type have a practically uniform light emission, and it is now customary to quote a *flash factor* or *guide number* for these bulbs. This is a purely arbitrary figure from which the required lens aperture can be determined to ensure correct exposure of objects at any given distance. The method of employment is simple. To find the correct aperture, divide the flash factor by the flash-to-subject distance. For instance, with a bulb, the flash factor of which is quoted at 120 with a particular film, an object 10 ft. from the flash would be correctly exposed with the lens set at $f12$; or 20 ft. away at $f6$; and so on. Such a flash factor, of course, presumes that the whole of the light emission of the bulb would be used; that is, that the shutter will be working at 1/20 second, or thereabouts. With a long peak bulb and a faster shutter speed the flash factor is correspondingly reduced. The factor, of course, also varies with the speed of the film being employed.

The table on p. 251 indicates speeds, settings, and flash factors for Leicas If to IIIf with red or black delay dial.

The guide numbers in the table can also be used at the appropriate shutter speeds with the Leica models Ig and IIIg as well as the M.1, M.2, and M.3 (use the M-socket), although of course no setting of delay is necessary.

On the Leica M there are two outlets: one for electronic flash at 1/50 second and small flash bulbs at 1/30, the other

SYNCHRONISING SETTINGS ON LEICA If TO IIIf

Flash Bulb Used	Red Delay Dial / Black Delay Dial	Shutter Speed													
		1/25	1/30	1/40	1/50	1/60	1/75	1/100	1/100	1/200	1/200	1/500	1/500	1/1000	1/1000
Philips PF 1 G.E.C., Mazda No. 1	Factor	50	50	*	40	*	*	*	*	*	*	*	*	*	*
	Delay	7	15		10										
Philips PF 24	Factor	95	85	80	75	65	60	50	50	35	35	25	25	20	20
	Delay	16	20	15	13	10	7	7.5	5	5	2	4	1	3	0
Philips PF 5 G.E.C., Mazda No. 5	Factor	100	100	85	80	70	70	*	*	*	*	*	*	*	*
	Delay	10	16	11	11	9	6								
Philips PF 38	Factor	130	115	110	100	95	90	75	75	55	55	33	33	*	*
	Delay	14	16	11	11	9	6	5.5	4	4.5	2	4	1		
Philips PF 45	Factor	125	110	100	100	80	80	65	65	45	45	33	33	25	25
	Delay	16	20	15	13	10	7	5.5	4	5	2	4	1	3	0
Philips PF 60 G.E.C., Mazda No. 22	Factor	200	165	160	150	130	120	105	105	80	80	50	50	35	35
	Delay	10	16	11	11	9	6	5.5	5	5	2	4	1	2.5	0
Philips PF 100	Factor	250	230	190	180	160	150	120	120	80	80	*	*	*	*
	Delay	15.5	20	15	12.5	10	6.5	7	7	4.5	2				
Electronic Flash	Factor	*	*	*	*	*	*	*	*	*	*	*	*	*	*
	Delay		2.5												

*These flash bulbs should not be used at these shutter speeds.

All the above factors are calculated for 26° BS (32 ASA) film, and normal development, or 29° BS (64 ASA) film and super-fine grain development.

Use 1 stop larger for super-fine grain development or slow ultra-fine grain film (group AA, p. 59).

Use 1 stop smaller for 29° BS (64 ASA) film and normal development, or 31–32° BS (100–125 ASA) film (group C, p. 95) and super-fine grain development.

Use 2 stops smaller for 31–32° BS (100–125 ASA) film and normal development.

for large or focal plane bulbs (e.g. PF 45) at all speeds. The flash factors are the same as given on p. 254.

Flash bulbs are mostly ignited by small dry batteries, and many commercial flash lamps employ ordinary torch batteries as a source of power. These lamps are light, portable and in some cases fitted with a shoe or bracket by means of which they can readily be attached to the miniature camera. One of the best designed units of this nature is that made by Messrs. Leitz, known as the *Chico*. On this model the reflector, which has an effective diameter of 6½ in., is made to fold up like a fan.

Dry batteries inevitably lose their strength with storage, even if not used. Moreover, a comparatively high output of current is required to ensure perfect ignition of flash bulbs, particularly if more than one are fired simultaneously. Lately, therefore, many people have started using capacitors in place of batteries. A typical capacitor unit, while not very much larger than the ordinary pocket torch, consists of a very small dry battery of long life (the type used in hearing aids is very suitable) of about 20 to 25 volts. In series with this, is a comparatively high resistance and an electrolytic condenser of anything from 50 to 150 mfd. capacity. In series with this circuit is the plug leading to the flash lamp or lamps.

The condenser receives a small but steady charge through the resistance, without appreciable drain on the battery. On closing the flash contact, the condenser is connected directly across the lamps, and the whole of its available current passes through the flash bulbs instantaneously, ensuring immediate ignition. The amount of current used is small, as it only lasts a fraction of a second.

This form of flash equipment is considerably more reliable than any ordinary dry battery, the internal resistance of which may limit the amount of current available on demand. Dry batteries used in capacitors appear to have an extremely long life, and for the photographer who intends to work with flash bulbs, I think that one of these devices is by far the most dependable equipment.

Turning to electronic flash equipment, a variety of models and makes are available on the market. They all work basically on the same principle.

252

A battery charges a large capacity condenser and this in turn is made to discharge through the gas-filled tube in a very brief flash. The various lamps are rated in *joules* to indicate the strength of the available light (1 joule is the equivalent of 1 watt for a period of 1 second).

From this it will be seen that the light from, for example, a 100 joule lamp, the discharge time of which may be about 1/1000 second, is intensely brilliant. But as it lasts for such an infinitesimal time, it may safely be used for portraiture, figure and animal studies, without any risk of strain on the part of the model, such as might occur with very bright continuous studio lighting. Even the eyes, which normally adapt themselves immediately to very bright lights, are not affected by this form of flash photography, as the picture is taken long before the almost instantaneous physical reaction on the iris of the eye can take effect.

Early electronic equipment was bulky and heavy. The latest models—now employing transistors—are powered only by a few U.2 torch batteries, which last for hundreds of exposures. These models weigh around 3 lb. and take up little more space than the camera itself. They open up a completely new field of photography, in monochrome and colour and are worthy of investigation by every keen worker.

Flash photography generally is one of the most automatic processes, in that everything is uniform and under control. Therein also lies its greatest drawback. The use of a flash gun on or near to the camera, inevitably results in flat lighting. For artistic portraiture, as distinct from straight-forward record work, an extension unit carrying a second flash bulb or flash tube is desirable as a modelling light or background light.

One final word on electronic flash. Some films behave abnormally under the special conditions of such extremely short high-intensity exposures. Many materials give very soft negatives, and therefore need increased development (up to 50 per cent more). Certain films even lose speed, though the extent to which they do this does not seem to depend on the normal film speed. For this reason it is difficult to give reliable flash factors for electronic flash, and the user is advised to make his own tests to find the best factors for any particular film.

COLOUR PHOTOGRAPHY

Practical colour photography now exists, for the 35 mm. worker, in two basic forms: processes designed to produce transparencies, and processes which produce colour negatives from which colour prints may be made.

CURRENT COLOUR PROCESSES

Maker	Material	Balanced for	Type	Processed by	Produces
PRIMARILY FOR PROJECTION					
ADOX	Adox Color C18	Daylight	} Reversal	Makers	Transparencies
AGFA	Agfacolor CT18 Agfacolor CK	Daylight Art. light	} Reversal	Makers' appointed stations	Transparencies Also makers' service for prints
ANSCO	Ansco- chrome Super Ansco- chrome	Daylight Daylight Tungsten	} Reversal	User and Trade	Transparencies
KODAK	Ektachrome Ektachrome F H.S. Ekta- chrome	Daylight Flash Daylight Tungsten	} Reversal	User and Trade	Transparencies
	Kodachrome Kodachrome A Kodachrome F	Daylight Art. light Flash	} Reversal	Makers only	Transparencies Also maker's service for paper prints
ILFORD	Ilfachrome	Daylight	} Reversal	Makers only	Transparencies Also service for prints
FERRANIA	Ferrania- color	Daylight art. light	} Reversal	User and Trade	Transparencies
GEVAERT	Gevacolor	Daylight; or art. light with correction filter	} Reversal	Makers	Transparencies
PERUTZ	Perutz Color	Daylight	Reversal	Makers	Transparencies
PRIMARILY FOR PRINT-MAKING					
AGFA	Agfacolor CN14 Agfacolor CN17	Universal	} Negative	Makers' appointed stations	Colour prints, or b. & w. prints
KODAK	Kodacolor	Universal	Negative	Makers, and appointed stations	Colour prints, or b. & w. prints
PAKOLOR	Pakolor	Universal	Negative	Makers, user and Trade	Colour prints, transparencies, or b. & w. prints
GEVAERT	Gevacolor	Universal	} Negative	Makers' appointed stations	Colour prints, or b. & w. prints

The current types of colour film carry three separate

emulsions, each one of which is sensitive only to *one* of the primary colour sensations—red, green and blue. In the case of Kodachrome they are arranged so that the upper layer is sensitive only to blue light; the one below it to green and the final layer to red. Thus each colour forms its image in the appropriate emulsion; or, if it is not a *pure* colour, to a varying degree in any two, or even all three of them. In the processing a negative silver image is formed initially in the first development; the film is then re-exposed successively to red, blue and green light and re-developed three times, once after each re-exposure. Exposure to X-radiation or chemical fogging may be substituted for green. Together with the positive silver images, dye images are produced. These dye deposits are created by combination of the developer oxidation product with a colour coupler present in the developer. In each layer the dye image is in the colour complementary to that which the layer records in the exposure; thus the blue sensitive emulsion carries an image in yellow, the green layer magenta, and the red sensitive coating becomes blue-green in colour. The original silver image formed in developing is removed by bleaching during the process, leaving only the stained gelatine layers, which, being in absolute contact with each other, are perfectly defined, and free from colour "fringing". The processing of Kodachrome has to be entrusted to its maker.

Some keen workers are rather averse to surrendering their films to the maker for processing; they feel they are missing part of the fun of their production—or even losing caste, photographically, by failing to do everything for themselves. These are now well catered for by the Ferrania process outlined above, for which home processing kits are provided.

It will be noted from the above list that Agfa, Kodak, and Ilford offer a service for colour enlargements from their transparencies. This is a comparatively new innovation, and one which is proving extremely popular. Users of these processes get the best of both worlds—they have superb transparencies for projection, and without prejudicing their safety in any way, they may also have tolerably good colour prints for mounting in the album. I say "tolerably good" deliberately, and I do not think that the makers would criticise me for so doing. These services have been evolved to meet the demand for album prints at a modest price. By the very nature of the process (which resembles that which produced the transparency itself) the results are unlikely to be as perfect as can be obtained by more complex negative-positive methods; but they meet a need which has existed since colour films were first invented. In the Kodak process the enlargements are on a "nearly glossy" paper support, while Ilford favour a fully glazed white plastic material instead of paper.

The processes designed solely for the production of colour prints (Agfa—Gevaert—Kodacolor) are also based on "subtractive" principles, but after development they are not reversed as is done in the previous processes. They exist in their finished state as *colour negatives*—that is to say they are negatives in the sense in which we already understand the term, with the lights and darks of the original subject reversed; but in addition they are in colour, which also is reversed in relation to the subject.

This means that the colours of the original are represented by their *complementaries* in the negative, so that reds are depicted by a blueish-green; greens are purple-red in colour; and so on.

Such negatives are used for the production of prints, in colour, by printing them on a material which is coated with a similar set of three superimposed emulsions, although they can also be printed on ordinary bromide or contact paper to give a black-and-white image, if required. Because of the coloured image of the negative, this print may not be completely accurate as to tone, but it is entirely adequate for normal purposes. Many workers make a practice of having their colour negatives "proofed" in monochrome first to ascertain those that are most likely to warrant the expense of colour printing.

Thanks to the excellent and simple exposure guide furnished with each roll of film, there is a tendency to believe that the production of satisfying colour transparencies is simpler than it is. In reality there are quite a number of contributory factors that require constantly to be borne in mind. For instance, accurate exposure is desirable in a black and white negative if the best print is required, but a reasonable latitude exists above and below

256

the theoretically perfect level which will result in a thinner or denser negative; still by choosing a suitable printing paper this will yield quite a good print. With colour transparencies, however, exposure *must* be accurate. The film has to stand or fall by itself. If it is over-exposed it will be thin and too empty to project satisfactorily, while if the error is towards under-exposure the transparency will be too dense, have clogged-up shadows, and, in addition, in both cases the colours will not present a true reproduction of those in the original subject. So, exposure *must* be correct—within half a stop.

How can the exposure be determined with this extra degree of accuracy? A good, well-tried photo-electric meter is essential. You will recall how, when discussing negative making (p. 107), I insisted on the necessity for taking care that the meter will read the light reflected only from that part of the subject that was to be in the picture? The same rule holds good again, but is even more important now than with black and white. It is worth spending some time ascertaining the exposure before taking any colour shot, by making a number of readings with the meter on varying parts of the subject in order to learn something of its contrast range. Owing to the film's relatively limited latitude, a subject which is too contrasty will have to sacrifice something in either the shadows or highlights, at the worker's discretion.

One of the published "rules" for colour work, of course, is that the subject should, in the main, be flatly lighted, i.e. that the source of light should be mostly behind the camera. In black and white work we are making our picture out of the contrasts between light and shade; in colour work, it is the contrasts between the *colours* that matter most. I do not want to induce anyone to make a fetish of "sun over your shoulder" pictures—they are too apt to be devoid of modelling; but I would counsel, at least at the outset, to avoid strong against-the-light effects.

Suppose we are taking a normal landscape scene—in good bright sunshine, with the sun more or less behind the camera. Our picture includes a whitewashed cottage, moorland background, dark trees, strong blue sky, and a foreground group of people. Let us go round the subjects and see what amount of light they reflect. A close-up reading on the whitewash will probably send a *Weston* meter soaring to 1,000 or 1,600. The foreground group, in average clothing, may record as 100. The moorland (if we can measure it without including the sky) may easily reach 200, while the blue sky itself has a value of possibly 500 and the dark fir trees at the edge of the picture will probably be as low as 25. With the foreknowledge that colour film will only satisfactorily record over a relatively limited contrast range, it will be evident that the *whole* scheme *cannot* be given any one correct exposure. If we analyse our readings, it will be seen that *a* the group (100), *b* the moorland (200), and *c* the blue sky (500) *just* come within these limits, but *d* the dark trees (25) and *e* the whitewash (1,000) are definitely outside the range; thus any exposure suitable for *a*, *b*, *c* *cannot* be correct for *d* and *e*. Over-exposing *any* colour makes it lighter and weaker, in the same way that pouring water into a solution of coloured dye dilutes its intensity and lightens its colour. In our example the whitewash will be over-exposed, but as one cannot make pure white *lighter*, this will not matter much. We shall undoubtedly lose some of the *texture* of the white stonework, but at least it will remain white. At the other end of the scale the dark trees will be so grossly *under*-exposed that they will register almost black, instead of in their true dark greeny-brown colour. As, however, they appear to the eye almost as a silhouette, this too is acceptable. We are therefore concerned mainly with estimating the exposure which will best bracket the values 100–200–500. Which, using the *Weston III* meter, and accepting the speed of Kodachrome as "10", gives about 1/25–1/30 second at *f*8. Now I always try to keep within limits of 1 : 4 if possible, and in this particular example I would consider it more important that the group (100) be adequately exposed than that the blue sky (500) be perfect, and in favouring the group and the moorland would be prepared to accept a *slightly* over-exposed blue sky, with its resultant loss of depth of colour, and would compromise at an exposure of 1/25 at *f*8. Using the meter in the direct way—i.e. pointing it at the subject and exposing according to the aggregate reading—may result in a very different and far less satisfactory exposure, as it will depend solely on the *relative areas of light and dark* tones, instead of on their brilliance; and with a large proportion of the reflected light coming from the white house, sky and moorland, all of which are "high reading" subjects, the exposure indicated will almost certainly be one which will be totally inadequate for the fore-ground group.

Assuming that this care and forethought is given to every colour exposure, there is no reason why a consistently satisfactory standard of results should not be obtained. If facilities for individual tone measurement such as I have suggested do not exist, I, at least, would prefer to be guided by the printed instruction sheet issued with each film than by *any* form of meter.

Many colour pictures are of prepared subjects: portraits in attractive costume and settings, made at leisure, at home or in a studio. In such cases one is not faced with the extremes of contrast common in nature and can contrive to keep the range within the desired limits, by suitable choice of coloured costumes, and by the expedient of using reflectors to cast additional light on to those parts that would otherwise be over-dark.

There is such a thing as composition in colour, as well as in form. In "composing" our ordinary photograph, we arrange it so that it is in satisfactory balance, and ensure that its lines and the shapes of its component parts are pleasing. We avoid harsh angular shapes and distracting arrangements. In colour pictures we have all the above to consider; and, in addition, the actual choice of the colours themselves, whether they shall blend, or contrast. I have heard it said that "in Nature, colours never clash". I am afraid that man-made colours are not so considerate, and while the decision must of necessity rest with the good taste of the photographer, it is perhaps worth considering again the spectrum of colours that combine to make white light. It is common knowledge that the various shades can be roughly divided into those which are "warm" and those which are "cold", and perhaps the easiest colour compositions are arrangements where the main colour scheme is based on one or the other group. Unless one is deliberately seeking a violent or garish arrangement because it is "colourful", it is well to try out schemes in which the principal colours are in a close series, such as red–orange–yellow, or a variety of blues and greens, or even a green-yellow and orange. As an "accent", a small amount of the colour which is the complementary of the one predominating can be very useful as emphasising the principal colour itself, and a trick worth remembering is that the brilliancy of *any* colour is enhanced by displaying it in company with its complementary, while a narrow separating band of black (in the case of light colours) or white (with darker colours) invariably increases the apparent luminosity and strength of both. Black is a most useful foil to any strong light colour, and it can frequently be employed as a background where the maximum colour effect is desired. Lest it should appear that I am advocating strong colour contrasts as desirable features in a picture, I would like to impress on the reader that in my experience those subjects that appear to the eye to be of a more or less monochrome character frequently produce the most pleasing colour slides.

When you photograph a child in a white frock you may be disappointed to find that the frock is pale green—or overcast by some other hue—in the slide. Please don't blame the processing. It is quite likely that the frock *was* pale green at the time of exposure, but that you, *knowing* it to be white, made some kind of mental adjustment and *saw* it as white. If, for example, the child stood on a lawn, quite a considerable amount of green light was reflected on to the clothes—and even the face. You must make a point of considering this possibility before making any exposure. There is no cure for the trouble, except to move the model to less colourful surroundings.

What colour are the shadows of sunlit snow? If the sky is blue, the shadows will also be blue, because they receive their illumination *only* from that source. I would hazard a guess that your eye sees them as grey, even if only because you know that snow is white, and that shadowed white generally *is* grey. The eye has to be trained to see these reflected colours, and it can be done by practice and logical reasoning.

Daylight varies enormously in its colour—from almost orange at sunrise and sunset to a strong yellow in direct sunshine during the day, while on a grey day the light may

The following pages show far the most common technical problems in miniature work.

Above. FLARE SPOTS, GHOST IMAGES AND HALATION— *Remedy: avoid unscreened lights in the picture area; and protect lens against those outside with lens hood.*

Page 262. LATITUDE *is a valuable characteristic in films. The prints in the* upper and centre rows *are from negatives exposed* 1, 2, 4, 8, 16, 32 *units. The prints in the* bottom row *are from normally exposed negatives developed for* $\frac{1}{2}$, 1 *and* 2x *normal time. All prints are on the same grade of paper and received the same printing exposure time.*

Page 263. GRAIN AND DEFINITION. *Definition becomes less crisp and grain more apparent in the really large sizes. These small sections of original print are enlarged* $4\times$, $10\times$, $15\times$, $25\times$.

Page 264. DISTORTION DUE TO TILTING CAMERA *can largely be corrected in printing, although this introduces a slight vertical elongation which, however, usually goes unnoticed.*

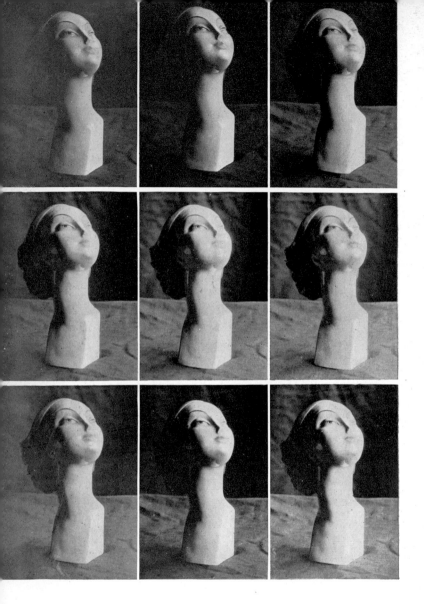

262

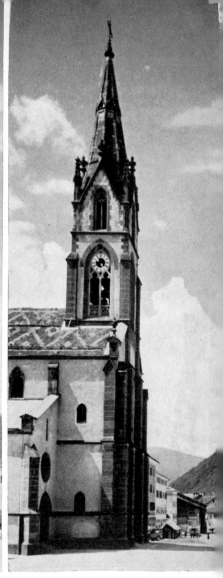

264

be of almost a blue-white colour, and—as we have seen—
under a blue sky, but out of the rays of the sun, the light
will be actually blue in colour. These variations of nominally
white daylight are measured by their "colour temperature"
and are quoted in degrees according to the *Kelvin* scale
(K). To give an indication of the range that can exist
it is worth noting that midsummer sunshine frequently
registers at 5,000 to 6,000 K, while a cloudy sky can bring
the reading up to 7,000 to 8,000 K, and the unobscured
light from a blue sky may easily top the 12,000 mark.
Artificial light is much richer in red rays than any form of
daylight, and this manifests itself in the fact that *Photoflood*
lamps usually give readings of only 3,000 to 3,500 K,
which, of course, is the reason why a different type of film
has to be used by artificial light.

35 *mm.* Kodachrome is made in two forms. "Daylight"
for daylight use, and "Kodachrome A", which is intended
for use with Photoflood and similar photographic lamps.
The speed to their appropriate light is ASA 10 and 16.
Kodachrome A can also be used in daylight if exposed
through a special filter provided by its maker for this purpose. Similarly a filter exists to enable the daylight type to
be exposed by artificial light, but in this case its speed is
reduced to about ASA 4.

The Ilford Ilfachrome film exists only as a daylight type,
but can be used in artificial light with a compensating
filter.

Agfacolor CT 18 reversal film (for daylight) has a speed
of about 50 ASA, while the type CN 17 negative film is
about 40 ASA (27° BS).

Ektachrome 35 mm. film is also fairly fast—32 ASA,
while a flash emulsion (type F) is rated at 25 ASA (25°
BS). High-speed Ektachrome at 160 ASA is so far the fastest
colour film in existence. Also of importance are the Gevacolor negative and reversal films—both daylight types—at
25 and 40 ASA.

Obviously any colour film can only depict colours
accurately if it is exposed in light of the colour temperature
for which it is intended. Daylight Kodachrome is designed
to be truthful in midday summer sunshine of temperate
climates; i.e., at about 5,400 K, and any *considerable*

variation from this will result in a "warmer" or "colder" transparency unless corrected by means of a suitable filter on the lens at the time of exposure.

There are Colour Temperature Meters, by means of which the light can be accurately assessed; and for the worker who takes his colour very seriously, provide a range of gelatine filters in a series of very pale blues to raise the temperature and a comparable set of suitably graded straw colour to lower it in light which is too blue.

Colour transparencies are physically frail. They are extremely sensitive to abrasion, and should be cut up and mounted between cover glasses *immediately the processed film is received from the factory*. Do not be tempted to display them to friends, until they are so protected.

To bind colour slides, two plain cover glasses 49.5 mm. square are required for each slide. It is worth noting that these slides are regularly referred to as being "2 in. square". This is only approximate, and if you use cover glasses measuring 2 × 2 in. you will probably find that they jam in the carrier of several of the projectors on the market to-day. To bind the slides the cover glasses must be carefully cleaned and warmed to ensure that they are dry. They should then be examined for flaws, and rejected if not absolutely clear. An opaque paper mask with a *clean cut* rectangular aperture 36 × 24 mm. is taken, and the transparency attached to it by fragments of gummed paper (or the permanently adhesive Cellophane tape). Care must be used to see that all edges are masked (and that the horizon is horizontal). Then, having shaken the mask and film, and tapped the two glasses on their edges on the table to dislodge any dust that may have settled on them, they are brought together, sandwiching the film and mask, and are bound round all four edges with four separate strips of 3/8 in. *Kodaslide* binding—or the Cellophane tape. It is a good plan to mark a white spot on the black paper mask before enclosing it in glass. This should be near the bottom left corner when the picture is the correct way up and the right way round. The spot enables the operator to ensure that the slides are loaded into the projector correctly. The slide is inserted "spot" at the top, and facing away from the screen.

266

HAVING reached the point where a *negative* of satisfactory character is—or should be—a foregone conclusion, we have arrived at by far the most interesting, and provocative part of the 35 mm. process. In order to secure, on paper, all the delicate and subtle tones that are available in the negative involves attention to similar details to those which concerned us in the production of the negative itself.

Because we are about to enlarge our negative considerably—remember a 15×10 in. print is *one hundred times* the area of the original—we must devote scrupulous care to the choice of equipment as well as to all the details of the process, if really flawless results are to be obtained.

The actual process of enlarging—denuded of the frills—is simplicity itself. The enlarger is little more than a "magic lantern" by means of which the negative is projected on to a sheet of photographic paper. The size of the print—or the degree of enlargement—is determined by the distance between the negative and the paper, while adjustment of the lens ensures that the projected image is as sharp as can be obtained from the negative itself.

Let us run over the ordinary steps in producing a straightforward print with any normal enlarger. First there is the darkroom safelight—yellow or bright greenish yellow—to provide adequate illumination for working; then the necessary chemicals—a dish of prepared paper developer (at not less than 68° F.), a dish of plain rinse water, and a dish of freshly made acid fixer—laid out ready.

Now, the negative is examined to see that it is clean and free from drying marks (on the back) and from dust (on both surfaces). The enlarger lens and condenser have already been cleaned, together with the negative carrier.

Having inserted the negative in the carrier *very* carefully, to avoid risk of surface scratching, the image projected on a piece of white card is examined and the lamphouse raised or lowered until the picture is of the required size. The lens is now adjusted to secure accurate focus and its iris diaphragm stopped down a trifle, if the projected image is very bright. The enlarger is then switched off.

A sheet of suitable printing paper (see p. 281) is selected and secured on the enlarger baseboard by means of pins or the masking paper holder if one is used; and the enlarger switched on for what is estimated to be the correct exposure (p. 287).

The print is then removed from the enlarger and placed in the developer by tilting the dish and sliding the paper under the solution in one smooth movement, so as to ensure the developer reaching all parts of it at the same instant. The dish is briskly rocked to assist in this, and to keep the paper covered with solution. A pair of developing tweezers (of stainless steel or plastic) are used to move the print about and to turn it over so that no part is left dry, and to dispel any obstinate air bells that may adhere to the surface.

If the exposure has been correctly estimated, the image will begin to appear in *about half a minute* and development will be completed in *not less than two minutes.* When this point is reached the print is removed with the tweezers, passed through the rinse water and dropped in the fixing bath, where it should be doused and moved about briskly for several seconds with *another* pair of tweezers. Fixation will take 10 to 15 minutes in a fresh bath. After this the print may be examined in a bright light. Washing for 20 to 30 minutes in running water completes the process, after which the print may be allowed to dry.

ENLARGING EQUIPMENT

I SHOULD like to stress at the outset the need for a *good* enlarger. There are several splendid instruments on the market, and while it is hardly practicable to recommend one or the other makes, I mention the *Leitz Valoy* and *Focomat, Kodak Precision, Blumfield Masterprinter,* the *Reid,* and the *Solar* models as being representative of the type of enlarger best suited to critical miniature work. There are other equally good models by other makers. There are also hosts of flimsy, inaccurate, tawdry enlargers hardly worthy of the name; but which, because they are more or less similar in appearance to the good instruments and are offered at a little lower price, are bought in large numbers by photographers who somewhat later not unnaturally come to the conclusion that 35 mm. work, in their hands, is not really a satisfactory proposition.

What do we expect of an enlarger? To my mind the essentials are that it should be absolutely rigid, should hold the negative flat and exactly parallel to the baseboard, and that the lighting and optical system should ensure perfectly even illumination and uniformly good definition over the whole of the negative area, at all degrees of magnification. Whether the enlarger has the convenience of automatic focusing does not matter, for this is a convenience and nothing more.

In order that the illumination over the negative be even, makers employ either a condenser—a lens which collects the light rays from the lamp and spreads them uniformly over the negative—or a diffusing system of, say, opal glass which serves the same purpose. Both these methods are satisfactory and both have slight drawbacks of their own. The condenser enlarger yields sharper and more contrasty prints than one employing diffused light, while the latter has the merit of suppressing to a large extent any mechanical flaws (coarse grain, scratches, etc.) that may exist in the negative. Because of these slight differences, it is desirable that negatives should be developed to a trifle higher degree of contrast when diffused light is to be used, or kept a shade less contrasty than normal if they are to be printed through an enlarger employing only a condenser. Combining the best features of both systems, enlargers such as those specifically mentioned utilise a "diffused-condensed" lighting source, which on balance seems to be almost ideal for our class of work.

The lens of the enlarger must be suitable for the job. It should be of about 2 in. focal length if the best results are to be obtained. Besides purely optical reasons, there is this objection to the use of a lens considerably in excess of this focal length, that it would involve a greater working distance between the negative and the bromide paper which always seems adversely to affect definition.

Sliding films into an enlarger's negative carrier will often cause minute scratches which will vary in direction according to how the enlarger has to be loaded. With care to ensure that the film surface does not touch anything over which it is moving this can largely be avoided. Most of the better class enlargers provide some protection by their design, but with *Leitz* instruments I find it safer to insert the film from the *side* (i.e. end first) rather than to slide it over the polished ramps provided for the purpose of "front" loading. A glassless negative carrier is quite safe in this respect as the film is first placed in the carrier and then the latter inserted in the enlarger. Here, the only warning I would offer, is to avoid moving the film when it is in the carrier and the latter closed.

Dust on the negative in the enlarger is an ever-present trouble. If your carrier consists of two glass plates, you have just four more surfaces on which dust can collect, and you will do well to see if some form of glassless holder can be substituted. If not, you must keep the glasses very clean and free from scratches. Cleaning the glass by rubbing it with material frequently electrifies its surface, so that it *attracts* dust particles from the air and the cure is then worse than the disease. This charge can often be dispersed by breathing on the glass immediately it has been cleaned, deferring its use for a moment or two to allow the steaming to evaporate.

These comments apply also to exposed condenser lenses which come into physical contact with the back of the film.

Be careful not to use an enlarger of this type immediately after cleaning the condenser in any case. If it is not *absolutely* bone dry it will probably cause those odd oyster shell markings called *Newton's rings*, on the enlargement. This is by no means the only cause of Newton's rings—but it is a fairly sure way of getting them! I have found them most troublesome when using very new film—whether it is that the base is "green" and has some moisture content when apparently quite dry, I do not know, but it is a

270

trouble that occurs only when the film is in physical contact with glass and will therefore not worry those using the double metal carriers. The *Focomat* user who is bothered in this way can usually overcome the trouble by inserting a thin card or metal mask, with an aperture $1\frac{1}{2} \times 1$ in. between the negative and the lower face of the condenser so as to avoid their making actual contact. The film is not likely to bulge sufficiently to cause any loss of sharpness.

For all ordinary purposes, that is, for enlargements from $2 \times$ to $10 \times$ (3×2 in. to 15×10 in.) the commercial enlarger as usually supplied is adequate and you will find that there is little if any room for improvement within these limits. For the larger sizes, the makers generally recommend that the enlarger "head" be turned round to the back of the baseboard, which is then stood on the edge of the table so that the picture can be projected on to the floor; the base board being suitably weighted with a pile of heavy books to eliminate the possibility of the whole assembly over-balancing.

One can, undoubtedly, do work of the highest possible excellence in this way, and I have no doubt that many outstanding exhibition pictures have had their genesis while their producer groped about the floor on hands and knees. I do not, however, feel that such makeshift methods contribute to the best work—or to the greatest comfort on the part of the worker—which, incidentally, may easily have some bearing on the quality of the results. Having suffered much in this way, and being blessed with a permanent darkroom, I set out, some years ago, to "improve" my Focomat. The result has been so successful, that I am tempted to describe the method as a guide to those who have also found the production of "Twenty-sixteens" something of a problem.

Apart from the limit of magnification imposed by the length of the enlarger upright column, the two great difficulties with almost all commercial enlargers are (a) that the baseboard is not large enough, and (b) that the optical axis of the enlarger head is too near the column. Thus—there is difficulty in holding the paper in any case and—if the *whole* of the negative is to be enlarged to a really big

271

size—it is usual to find that the lower part of the column gets in the way of both the paper and the projected image. To overcome this I chose the somewhat unusual way out of securing the baseboard of my enlarger to the *ceiling* of the dark room immediately over my workbench, so that there was about 6 in. clearance below the top (now the bottom) of the column, and the bench itself. This prevented the base of the column casting a shadow, and allowed room for me to move the paper about on the bench as required. The lamphouse was, of course, remounted so as to project down on to the bench. This curious arrangement worked well as soon as I had found the correct position for the lamphouse to be clamped so that the automatic focusing would operate properly.

After some weeks use, I decided that I was definitely on the right track and that a more permanent installation on somewhat similar lines could usefully be devised. I therefore obtained some lengths of 2×2 in. timber and some "matching" and built up a new enlarging stand. The three 2×2 columns were secured to the wall, reaching from floor to ceiling. The right hand pair are a trifle over 3 ft. apart, the distance between the centre and left hand post being somewhat less. A framework extends forward just over 2 ft. and the upright sides which are made of ordinary $\frac{3}{4}$ tongued and grooved wood carry a series of rails 1×1 in. at intervals of about 6 in. from their top (which is at about breast height) down to the false floor—about 10 in. from the ground. A baseboard 3×2 ft. can be placed on *any* pair of these rails, so that the position of the bromide paper can conveniently be varied within very wide limits in relation to the lamphouse without moving the top part of the enlarger on its column at all. The false floor referred to above, was fitted with a flap door secured by a ball catch to provide storage space for really large bromide paper. It accommodates flat packages up to 25×20 in. with ease. I decided on a 3×2 ft. baseboard, not so much because I might expect to enlarge to this size, but rather to allow a sheet of 20×16 or 25×20 in. to be placed out of centre, if only a part of a negative had to be enlarged to fill it. A normal 40 in. Focomat column is employed — the original baseboard being removed. The column is sup-

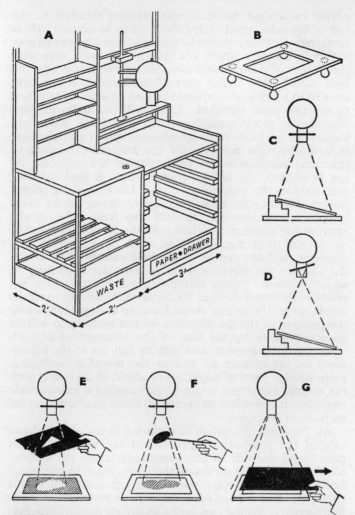

(A) *Enlarger mounted on framework permitting of* very *big enlargements.*
(B) *Hollow frame carrying lamps to illuminate subject when copying.*
(C) *Tilting printing paper.* (D) *Tilting negative and paper.* (E) *Spot printing.* (F) *Shading.* (G) *Flashing.*

ported on a rigid wooden cross member attached to the top of the sides which carry the 3×2 ft. baseboard. (It is important that the column be mounted 6 or 8 in. away from the main uprights which are close to the wall, otherwise the degree of enlargement possible will be limited by the wall itself.) The upper part of the column is similarly secured to a block of hardwood carried on a batten attached to the two main uprights. Leitz drill two holes in their columns to accommodate a metal peg which accurately locates the position of the lamphouse support arms, so that it is in the right position for the automatic focusing to function; one hole serves when pictures are projected on the baseboard, the second (higher) hole is used to compensate for the thickness of the Leitz masking paper holder. As the column was no longer resting on the baseboard, it was necessary to drill two fresh holes in the appropriate position in relation to the baseboard when in its normal (top) position. The holes have to be 5 mm. diameter, and the centre of the hole exactly 17 in. above the face of the baseboard or paperholder according to which is used. Unless this distance is correct, it is *not* possible for the Focomat to focus automatically over its whole range. With any visual focusing enlarger, obviously the position of the lamphouse does not matter and will be governed solely by the size of the enlargement desired. With this arrangement, and making full use of the adjustment on the column as well as the movable baseboard, I can enlarge parts of negatives to about 40 diameters with the normal 5 cm. lens, while by substituting a 35 mm. wide angle lens it is possible to exceed 50 diameters from selected sections of negatives.

An "on-and-off" switch is mounted at the top left-hand side of the baseboard support, and the wires from this pass round the side of the framework, along the support for the column and up inside the latter, reaching the lamphouse in the customary way. The left hand half of the enlarging stand is purely for convenience and anyone whose floor space is limited can easily secure all the facilities that I enjoy, without using more than about $3\frac{1}{2} \times 2\frac{1}{2}$ ft. of darkroom space. If, however, space is available the shelves are very useful for storing boxes of bromide paper in the smaller sizes, while the draining rack for dishes and the waste box also have their uses.

The one thing that puzzles me now, is how I ever managed comfortably to do *really* big work with the original enlarger as supplied by its maker—good though it was for smaller sizes.

CONTACT PRINTING

IF, as I do, one wants to see results on paper with the least possible delay, it is economically sound to make "strip" contact prints, on the specially perforated 35 mm. bromide paper which the makers provide, preferably using a device such as the *Leitz Eldia* printer, or British equivalent, which allows individual exposure to be given to each negative.

In the absence of this machine, or if one is not unduly worried about securing exact exposure for each small print, it is easy to make a set of record prints by putting 6 strips of 6 films, face down, side by side, on a 10 × 8 in. or 12 × 10 in. sheet of bromide paper on the baseboard of the enlarger, holding them in place (and in contact with the paper) by laying a suitable sheet of plate glass on top.

Obviously one cannot thus give each negative individual attention, but if their exposures are anywhere near accurate, all the negatives in one strip of film should be similar enough for some average exposure to yield a passable print, which is at least good enough to enable one to estimate the pictorial and technical possibilities of any given frame.

These contact prints can be cut up into strips and ultimately filed with the negatives as already recommended.

If it is thought that such prints are too small to give a fair indication of the negative's possibilities, I would suggest making a proof enlargement of every frame. The most convenient and cheapest size that I have found satisfactory for these, is obtained by cutting half-plate paper in halves. The resulting $4\frac{3}{4} \times 3\frac{1}{4}$ in. is large enough to examine closely, and approximates more closely in shape to the original film proportions than does the commercial quarter plate size. For such trial prints, I seldom bother to make test exposures for more than the first sheet. I find that I can estimate what negatives require by the appearance of the projected image, and have proved to my own satisfaction that the easiest way to do this is to expose every negative for a *constant* time—say, five or ten seconds. I select one or other of these times according to the average density of the film, a thin film naturally being tried out for the shorter time at whatever seems likely to be a suitable "stop". In the event of the first print being satisfactory I then switch on the enlarger again and study the *appearance* of the projected image, and try to *carry this in my mind*. When subsequent negatives are projected, I endeavour to match their image with my recollection of the first one; making whatever adjustments may appear necessary by altering the stop of the lens—thereafter exposing for the standard five (or ten) seconds. I find that my percentage of bad prints is extremely low, by this method; and consider that it is far easier to carry the appearance of a certain "standard" in mind, than it is to assess accurately the *exposure* required by a number of different negatives.

For large prints, however, I advocate one or other of the more positive methods of determining exposure to be described further on.

THE IDEAL DEGREE OF ENLARGEMENT

SIZE is not everything. In fact, print size must depend on the purpose which it is supposed to serve.

At first sight it would seem to be simple enough to

determine the extent to which the picture should be enlarged, and I can imagine the majority of workers saying, for example, "I always make quarter-plates for the album and enlarge to 15 × 12 in. for club exhibitions". On the face of it this sounds reasonable enough.

Everybody has heard, however, at some time or other someone comment that, "So-and-so's print looks too wide angled and the perspective is distorted," or that, "That large head seems too flat, and is lacking in modelling". More often than not there is really not much reason for such criticisms. Every photograph will appear right under suitable conditions, and these conditions depend on three things: the distance from which the picture is viewed, the degree of enlargement and the focal length of the lens with which the negative was made. To obtain in a print what appears to the eye to be natural and correct perspective we have, first, to decide on the distance from which the print will most probably be viewed. In the case of an album print, this will probably be about 10 in. A framed enlargement for home decoration will generally be examined at a range of about 20 in. At exhibitions, the majority of visitors take up a position about 40 in. away from the wall —only approaching it more closely when it is necessary to examine in detail an exhibit of less than average size, or, of course, to seek imperfections in some of the larger examples. Armed with these basic probable viewing distances, how can we best exploit this knowledge and enlarge our prints to the most suitable and satisfactory size?

This brings us to Variable No. 2: the focal length of the camera lens used. Let us assume for the moment that we are concerned only with a picture taken with the standard 2 in. (5 cm.) lens *and that the whole of the negative will be used.*

The human eye has a natural close focusing distance of about 10 in., i.e. the majority of people read or examine small things most easily at that distance, and it has been found that a photograph taken, with say a large stand camera using a 10 in. focus lens appears to yield "natural" perspective when viewed at that distance—i.e. *at a distance corresponding to the focus of the lens used.* There then is the basis on which we can calculate the extent to which

277

we should enlarge our pictures so as to retain satisfactory perspective.

How can we interpret these figures? Our standard lens is 2 in. focus, while the theoretical "ideal" focus seems to be 10 in. If, therefore, we enlarge our 35 mm. negative 5 times ($10 \div 2$) we shall produce a $7\frac{1}{2} \times 5$ in. print such as would have been made with a 10 in. focus lens. This print will "look right" in every respect from 10 in. distance. If, however, we were to frame this picture and view it on the wall at, say, 20 in. it would appear lacking in modelling and perspective. For it to look right (in the sense it did at 10 in.) at double the distance, it should be enlarged twice as much, i.e. $20 \div 2 =$ ten times. The resulting 15×10 in. print at 20 in. will appear just as satisfactory as the smaller print at 10 in. distance. If, similarly, we are to cater for the exhibition wall with its 40 in. probable viewing distance, the print of the whole negative should measure 30×20 in. If only part of the negative is used, the print should be proportionally smaller.

All this presumes that we are using the normal 2 in. (5 cm.) lens. If the original negative was made with a $1\frac{3}{8}$ in. (3.5 cm.) wide angle lens, then the magnification required to yield the ideal print for viewing at 10, 20 and 40 in. respectively will be $7 \times$, $14 \times$, and $28 \times$, which in turn means an album print measuring about 10×7 in., a framed enlargement 20×14 in., and a picture on the exhibition wall of no less size than about 40×30 in.!

At the other end of the scale, with a long focus lens, the degree of enlargement should be less, again in proportion to the focal length. This may not be practicable, and in any case I would like to make it clear that these rules are intended to secure theoretically *perfect* perspective, and quite appreciable liberties can be taken before the result really shows signs of being "out of drawing". To simplify the matter I append three tables showing the "ideal" size to which the *complete* negative should be enlarged, according to the lens used, for each of these viewing distances.

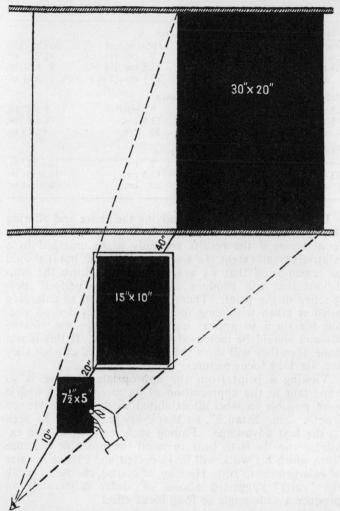

30"×20"

15"×10"

40"

7½"×5"

20"

10"

Print size should vary according to viewing distance. Dimensions shown ensure natural perspective when the whole of a 35 mm. negative taken with 5 cm. lens is used. For different lenses, or if only part of the negative is enlarged, sizes should be altered accordingly.

279

Sizes—to be viewed at 10 in. distance.

Focus of lens	Size of Print	Focus of lens	Size of Print
2.8 cm. (1⅛ in.)	13½×9 in.	9 cm. (3½ in.)	4½×3 in.
3.5 cm. (1⅜ in.)	10½×7 in.	13.5 cm. (5⅜ in.)	3 ×2 in.
5 cm. (2 in.)	7½×5 in.	20 cm. (8 in.)	2 ×1¼ in.

Sizes—to be viewed at 20 in. distance.

2.8 cm.	27×18 in.	9 cm.	9×6 in.
3.5 cm.	21×14 in.	13.5 cm.	6×4 in.
5 cm.	15×10 in.	20 cm.	4×2½ in.

Sizes—to be viewed at 40 in. distance.

2.8 cm.	54×36 in.	9 cm.	18×12 in.
3.5 cm.	42×28 in.	13.5 cm.	12× 8 in.
5 cm.	30×20 in.	20 cm.	8× 5¼ in.

I can imagine the reader studying the above and offering the opinion that there seems little value in the use of long focus lenses if the results are only to be enlarged to a relatively small extent. In a sense that is true; but it should be remembered that we are, here, laying down the conditions that will produce conventionally "perfect" perspective in the print. There is no objection to enlarging pictures taken with long focus lenses to any desired size, but for them to appear natural to the eye the *viewing distance* should be increased in proportion. If this is not done, then they will show the typical qualities of what they are, viz. long focus pictures.

Viewing a print from the appropriate distance is so important to the appreciation of its merits that I wish it were possible to label all exhibited work, "To be viewed from . . . in. distance", so that every print might be seen to the best advantage. Failing such a guide, all the exhibitor can do is to bear in mind the probable distance from which his work will be inspected and choose his size of enlargement to suit. He may, of course, choose to break the "rules" suggested above, in order deliberately to produce a wide angle or long focus effect.

THE first thing that calls for consideration in making the enlargement is the negative itself. What is a negative? We may describe it as a series of varying opacities, composed of metallic silver, representing, in reverse, the lights and shades of the object photographed. I say "representing" advisedly, because the varying tones in the negative may, and probably will, seldom correspond exactly to those in the original. Depending on whether the negative is over- or under-exposed—or over- or under-developed—and whether the subject was lit by an intense or a diffused light, the steps in the negative will vary, and the total *range* of the negative will be *long* or *short*.

We may, or may not, *want* to reproduce the tones of the negative accurately. If the subject is somewhat lacking in contrast, or shows too much of it, it will be better somewhat to compensate for such shortcomings in the final print. To take care of these problems, paper is produced in a variety of *grades* (degrees of contrast). It is in suiting the paper to the requirements of the negative to produce either an accurate reproduction or to secure a particular effect where the skill of the operator comes into its own, and where a clever worker will produce a *picture* while his opposite number may get nothing better than just a "print".

Unsurmountable confusion sometimes seems to exist among beginners between paper *grades* and paper *surfaces*. All the regularly used surfaces—Glossy, Matt, Velvet, Lustre, etc.—are usually to be had in all the usual grades or degrees of contrast. The choice between the *surfaces* is merely one of personal preference and has little to do with technique proper. Broad effects are usually most pleasingly rendered on the rougher papers. Velvety papers are a good general choice for average work, while dead matt papers are attractive on occasion for the more delicate results. To get the best possible print from any negative, from a purely technical standpoint, there is nothing to approach glossy papers.

A glossy paper is capable of producing a much "blacker" black than can be produced on a matt paper, which on account of its surface reflects a great deal of the light by which it is viewed, with the result that its darkest black is always some sort of grey. Any paper between glossy and matt will similarly yield a result in which the black is less intense than that on glossy, but much darker and richer than what could be secured on a dead matt. It is for this reason, largely, that pictures for reproduction are commonly printed on a shiny surfaced paper. But let us repeat: paper surface is ultimately a matter of taste; paper grade is a definitely technical distinction.

Let us consider now what these various grades of bromide paper can do. *Normal* (sometimes called *Medium*) paper will generally require about sixty times as much exposure to light to secure an absolute black as it requires to produce the lightest visible tone of grey. *Soft* paper, on the other hand, may possibly need as much as a hundred times the minimum exposure before the image is truly black, while a *Hard* (or *Vigorous*) paper may yield a good dense black tone with possibly only twenty times the exposure that produced the first grey tone. Some makers give as many as five or six grades of contrast in their range of papers, including *Extra Soft* and *Extra Contrast*.

It is simple for the user to determine the "scale" of the paper used, if he feels that the makers' classification is insufficient. It is only necessary to find what exposure to light will produce the first visible grey deposit, after normal full development, and what exposure produces the first true black. This can be done by placing a strip of paper on the enlarger baseboard (without a negative) and exposing it progressively in steps, by covering up the strip with an opaque card, a step at a time so that each successive step receives twice the exposure of the one before it. It will be seen that if exposures have ranged from, say, 1 second over 2, 4, 8, 16, etc., up to perhaps 512 seconds, we have a series which, on development, will tell us everything that we want to know of the paper's character. Suppose that the 1 second exposure does not produce a tone but that the 2 seconds does, and that the 128 seconds exposure produces a black which does not get any blacker in the steps which follow, we can then say that that particular paper has a scale of $128 \div 2$ or 64 to 1. In other words, it is a fairly soft type of *normal* paper. If these steps are carried out with all

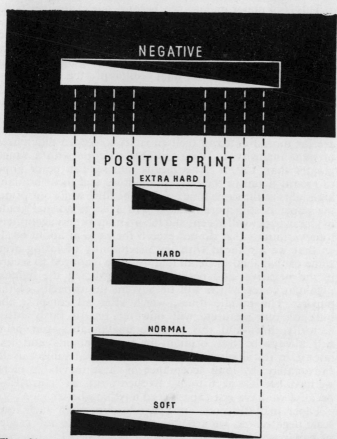

SUBJECT

NEGATIVE

POSITIVE PRINT

EXTRA HARD

HARD

NORMAL

SOFT

The subject scale may be greater than the film's capacity to record tone differences. The paper's tone capacity is still lower. Normal paper will preserve the tone separation of the negative. Soft paper will include a wider range (with less contrast between tones). Contrast or extra hard paper will spread a small part of the tone range so that it ranges from black to white in the print.

283

the papers that are likely to be used, their different characteristics will be more fully appreciated; but whether this information can be put to the fullest use naturally depends on our ability to judge the contrast of the negative itself.

This is of major importance, because one of the inevitable things about photography is that the subject often has a considerably wider range of tones than can possibly be properly recorded on the film; and to make matters worse, the film has a far greater capacity for recording tones than has the paper on which the final result is printed. This naturally introduces complications. Put into plain English this means that, while a subject such as a brilliantly-lit landscape or seascape with dark foreground objects may have a contrast range of about 500 or even 1,000 to 1, films are far more limited in their capacity to record differences of light intensity and few are able to cope with a range greater than 150:1. This means that we can never hope to record detail in the darkest shadows and most brilliant highlights at the same time even on the film, while our printing paper is still more limited. An average normal grade of glossy paper will accept and record more or less accurately tone variations that do not exceed the ratio of about 60:1, so that we are faced with the inevitability of losing even some of that shadow detail that we have managed to secure in the negative, and perhaps also sacrificing the lightest highlight tones which will lie beyond the capacity of the paper. The middle tones, which after all compose the bulk of our pictures, will however record fairly satisfactorily, but—and this is quite unavoidable—our print will always be less brilliant in the highlights and less intense in the shadows than was the original subject itself. Fortunately, by long acceptance of these inevitable facts, we have become accustomed to such prints as "correct"—because we have not experienced anything better.

Paper manufacturers, in order to cope with such long scale negatives as we are now discussing, make *soft* grades of paper which have an exposure range of 90:1 (or even in some cases as high as 120:1). At first sight, the use of such a paper would seem almost to solve our problem; but it must be remembered that any paper's range is only from white to black, and whether we divide that range

284

into 10, 20, 60 or even 120 steps of tone we cannot get a greater *difference* between the extremes of white and black. To use such a soft paper will undoubtedly allow us to secure *detail* in the highlights and in the shadow areas that would be plain white and black respectively were normal paper to be used; but it will do it at the expense of compressing the entire range of tones, so that there is less difference between any two tones than there is in either the negative or the original subject, and so the resultant print will inevitably appear *flat* and lifeless. The choice between accuracy over most of the tones and omissions at both ends of the scale, or the inclusion of a wider band of tones and a flattening of the contrasts throughout, is something that will have to be decided by the individual. Some objects respond best to one treatment, some to the other.

I am not suggesting that every negative inevitably presents such difficulties. The majority of normal subjects have a much shorter range of tones and, unless they have been falsified by considerable over-development of the negative, will probably print quite well on a paper of medium contrast. If, however, the contrast, for some reason or other, is too great to reproduce on even a soft paper, then difficulties are bound to arise and the only remedies are either to reduce the contrasts by *reducing* the negative (see p. 160) or to print the negative in such a way that detail is secured in the shadows at the expense of empty highlights; or, the other way round, to print (by giving more exposure) until the highlights are satisfactory, even though this means that the shadow areas will be blocked up through over-exposure and are consequently devoid of detail.

Let us just go back for a moment. Suppose, that for some reason—flat subject, over-exposure, under-development—we have a negative which is *lacking* in contrast, and which, if we could measure its range of contrast, would prove to be only 15 to 1. If we were to print this on a normal paper, which has a range of about 60 to 1, we should be able to use only about one-quarter of its range—that is to say that, although the whole range of tones on the negative could be printed on this paper, the result would be entirely unsatisfactory because it would accurately reproduce the flatness of the original negative. To deal successfully with this type of negative it is necessary to use a harder paper—one with a shorter scale—which requires fewer tones in the negative to reach from white to black. The use of such a paper will *expand* the steps between the tones of the negative, so that those parts which should print white (but for the flatness of the particular negative) will remain reasonably light in tone, while the darker parts of the picture print up to a satisfactory depth of grey or black.

Similarly, if we have a negative which has been over-developed and is too contrasty in consequence, the remedy is to use a printing paper which *requires* a very long scale between the lightest and the darkest tones in the negative in order to give a satisfactory print—in other words, a soft paper.

If we now presume that our negatives are satisfactorily exposed and developed—and after all there is no reason why they should not be, at least for the majority of subjects—a print on paper of a normal contrast will probably be all that could be desired; but cases will arise where for pictorial reasons we do not necessarily wish the print to be an exact replica of the negative and may desire to exploit the darker tones at the expense of the highlights. In this case it may pay to choose a harder paper and to expose it so that the tones that we desire are expanded to fill, more or less completely, the paper's tone capacity; letting the lighter half-tones, together with the highlights, be crowded off the paper's scale, where they will print white.

This is perhaps the right place to draw attention to the futility of attempting to achieve more than is possible solely by means of printing. One hears a lot about *high key* and *low key* prints, as though they were something controllable in the act of enlarging. It must, however, be kept in mind that a high key print can *only* be made from a high key subject—i.e. one in which there are no large dark areas; and similarly a low key print also requires a subject suitably lit. To attempt to make a high or low key print from a *normal* negative will produce either a flat, under-printed and "washed out" print, or a badly over-exposed and degraded one, according to the result attempted. It can be nothing more. The key of a subject is determined before even the film is exposed.

286

PRINT EXPOSURE AND PRINT PROCESSING

UNLIKE most of the modern films, printing paper has relatively little latitude. That is to say, the exposure must be just about right, or the print will be unsatisfactory. If the exposure is excessively short the highlights will look empty; whereas if too generous the lighter tones will be degraded by the time that development is completed, while the shadows will have clogged up.

Well-tried methods exist for determining the nominal enlarging exposure. Photo-electric meters have been employed to measure the aggregate light transmission of the negative, but this approach of course takes no account of the contrast of the negative itself, and personally I do not care for it. Balancing photometers such as the well-known *M.C.M.* are used successfully by many careful workers, but this involves a preliminary paper speed test and I must confess to a preference for the old-fashioned "test strip" for my own work. By this method a series of exposures are made on a strip of paper and then developed for the normal recommended time; reference to this, if it has been made from a representative part of the negative— i.e. contains samples of all relevant tones—gives a very good guide as to what exposure is required, and has the added advantage that one's estimate of the particular grade of paper to be used is checked up definitely.

With the majority of bromide papers the choice of developing formulæ is not very important. Obviously that recommended by the maker is always safe; but I have found no objection to interchanging various makers' recommendations as far as Metol-hydro-quinone developers are concerned. The following formulæ are recommended from personal experience:

ILFORD I.D.20					
	Metol	1.5	grm.	15	gr.
	Sodium sulphite (cryst.)	50	grm.	1	oz.
	Hydroquinone	6	grm.	60	gr.
	Sodium carbonate (cryst.)	80	grm.	1½	oz.
	Potassium bromide	2	grm.	20	gr.
	Water	1000	c.cm.	20	oz.

For use dilute with equal quantity of water.

KODAK			
D.163	Metol	2.2 grm.	80 gr.
	Sodium sulphite (anhydrous)	75 grm.	6 oz.
	Hydroquinone	17 grm.	1 oz. 160 gr.
	Sodium carbonate (anhydrous)	65 grm.	5 oz. 80 gr.
	Potassium bromide	2.8 grm.	100 gr.
	Water	1000 c.cm.	80 oz.

For use take one part and add three parts water.

KODAK			
D.170	Sodium sulphite (anhydrous)	25 grm.	2 oz.
	Potassium bromide	1 grm.	35 gr.
	Water	200 c.cm.	16 oz.

This is kept as a stock solution. For use, dilute the 200 c.cm. with water to make 1,000 c.cm. (16 oz. with water to make 80 oz.), and then dissolve 4.5 grm. (or 160 gr.) Kodak Dolmi (amidol) immediately before use. The mixed solution does not keep.

PRINT QUALITY

IN the course of the year I have the privilege of examining literally thousands of amateur prints and enlargements made from 35 mm. and larger negatives, and frequently wish that their authors could study professional and commercial work. The tone range of the paper is hardly ever fully exploited. Besides, instead of the pleasing neutral black and greys that give a print charm and richness, these prints so very often are greenish-grey in colour—due possibly to over-worked developer—and seldom have any *real* black in them anywhere. Such criticism may sound harsh and intolerant, but if it makes some reader look into the general quality and colour of *his* prints it will have done good.

The real root trouble seems to be—besides the somewhat haphazard choice of the paper grade—in print *under-development*. I know that most of the paper makers' instructions say that somewhere about two minutes in the developer will produce a satisfactory result, but they do not forbid you to leave the print there longer; and it is often in the *following* two minutes or so that the best prints gain all their subtle quality. Most bromide papers, provided that they are not stale, can be left in any normal *Metol-hydroquinone* or *Amidol* developer for 3 or 4 minutes at normal temperatures without appreciable fogging; and the longer they are left there, within reason, the better the colour of the blacks will be. I am afraid that many workers could not leave their prints in the developer in this way; they would go too dark. *This means that they have been over-exposed.* To get the best out of any paper the exposure must be adjusted so that the print will develop up to about the right extent in about the recommended two minutes; but the exposure should be sufficiently short for it to be possible to leave the print there for *at least* another one minute without it going appreciably darker. Adherence to this rule will pay handsome dividends in that elusive thing that we call "quality".

This technique applies only to *bromide* papers. *Bromesko*, *Plastika*, and similar papers should be handled according to the maker's recommendations.

It should be remembered, too, that some developers, notably those containing hydroquinone, will never produce a good black if used at too low a temperature. I advocate working at anything from 68° to 73° F. A few specific tests, during the winter, at normal room temperatures, and at those suggested above, will convince the sceptic once and for all. I may be criticised for placing such stress on securing "blacks" which are above reproach. I quite realise that not every picture has or needs any intense black. I do however wish to emphasise that the treatment which secures this black tone is also the one which ensures good quality in all the other tones of the picture as well.

Paper which has passed its heyday will not stand the degree of development which I have advocated, without the whites going grey, and I suggest adding some Developer Improver (*Johnsons* 142, *P.A.C.* Latitol, *Kodak* Anti-Fog). These new chemicals, which are simply added to the developer, almost eliminate any form of chemical fogging. They enable one to use paper otherwise too old to produce satisfactory results. It is necessary to increase the exposure slightly when Developer Improvers are used.

If, for any reason, you are cursed with some negatives which are so contrasty that they will not print satisfactorily on the softest grade of paper available—and it does happen sometimes, as I have found to my cost—I recommend the use of the following formula for very soft results which works admirably with all the more general makes of paper. Again, there is of course no merit in using it if one can secure the desired result with soft paper in the normal way.

KODAK D.165			
	Metol	6 grm.	105 gr.
	Sodium sulphite (anhydrous)	25 grm.	1 oz.
	Sodium carbonate (anhydrous)	37 grm.	1½ oz.
	Potassium bromide	1 grm.	18 gr.
	Water	1000 c.cm.	40 oz.

For use take 1 part of above and 3 parts water.

If your negatives are so flat that you cannot get bright prints from them even on the most contrasty paper, the proper remedy is intensification (see p. 159). If, however, for any reason you do not wish to give them this treatment, it might be worth trying the following developer before giving it best.

DEVELOPER FOR INCREASED CONTRAST

KODAK D.72				
	Metol		3.1 grm.	110 gr.
	Sodium sulphite (anhydrous)	45 grm.	3 oz.	265 gr.
	Hydroquinone		12 grm.	420 gr.
	Sodium carbonate (anhydrous)	67.5 grm.	5 oz.	175 gr.
	Potassium bromide		1.9 grm.	65 gr.
	Water to make		1000 c.cm.	80 oz.

For use dilute with *equal quantity of water*.

Prints which are a trifle flat and degraded, as the result of *very slight* over-exposure, can sometimes be improved by clearing (after they have been thoroughly washed) in the following solution. Only a brief immersion is required, and the print must be kept on the move the whole time, and withdrawn *just before* it has reached the desired stage, when it should be washed promptly and well in running water, as the clearing (or reduction) will go on for a short time after removal by virtue of the amount of the solution absorbed by the gelatine and the paper itself.

290

CLEARING	A.	Hypo crystals	5 grm.	¼ oz.
BATH		Water	100 c.cm.	5 ozs.
	B.	Potassium ferricyanide	5 grm.	¼ oz.
		Water	100 c.cm.	5 ozs.

For use take 1 part A—1 part B—10 parts water and mix thoroughly before immersing the print. The *mixed* solution will not keep.

Prints which are a shade flat or lacking in contrast can sometimes be improved by intensification. For this they need to be very thoroughly washed before treatment. The prints are immersed in the bleacher given below, and kept moving until the entire image has disappeared. They are then washed *thoroughly* to *remove all the stain of the bleacher*, after which they are re-developed in full daylight in the normal print developer, and finally washed and dried.

BLEACHER	Potassium bichromate	5 grm.	87 grs.
	Hydrochloric acid	1 c.cm.	20 minims.
	Water	500 c.cm.	20 ozs.

Bleaching should take place in a subdued light.

Before you use a new darkroom, or a different brand of paper to that which you are accustomed, make sure that your "safelight" lives up to its name with that particular material. An incredible number of pictures are just "below par" because their highlights are degraded to just that trifling extent that robs them of all the brilliancy and snap that they might have possessed. Some of the more recently introduced papers are by no means insensitive to light which is safe enough with older types of emulsions, and it seems therefore negligent not to make a simple test to ensure that all is well. The easiest way to be really sure of any darkroom illumination is to cut a piece of the paper to be tried—about 3 in. square—and to lay this, face up, on the workbench underneath the safelight. A coin should lie on top of the paper, and the safelight should then be switched on, and left on for, say, a matter of three minutes. It should then be extinguished again, and the paper developed, in total darkness, for the maximum time that one is ever likely to develop—probably four or five minutes. Once the paper is in the fixing bath, the light should again be put on; when, if the light is in any way unsafe the shape of the coin will stand out white against a slightly (or considerably!) darker grey surround. If the whole paper is uniformly white all is well. If not, you must substitute a safer light filter, or reduce the power of the lamp—or even move it a greater distance from the work-bench. *And repeat your tests* until the desired result *is* obtained. Only then can you be sure that any loss of brilliancy in your prints is due to some other cause.

DRYING THE PRINT

ONE of my own earlier problems was always the difficulty of drying prints so that they were reasonably flat when I came to collect them. I have tried all sorts of methods but have now standardised on the elementary system of wiping the print, back first, then front, with a "viscose" or other absorbent sponge, and then leaving it *face down* on a towel overnight. A refinement is to substitute butter muslin stretched over a frame of wood, but even rough towelling serves quite satisfactorily, and any few traces of lint adhering to the face of the print can be easily removed with the finger directly the print is dry.

If the print is in any way "cockled" after this treatment, which is most likely to occur with prints on "single weight" paper, this can be easily remedied when dry by the simple expedient of stroking the back of the print with a flat wooden ruler. The paper is placed face down on a clean surface, and held by one corner; with the other hand a ruler is placed diagonally across the centre of the print, and, as it is stroked to a corner away from the centre, the rest of the print is lifted up by the hand which holds it. On *no* account should the print be *pulled* from under the ruler. This treatment, repeated four times (to each corner in turn) will remove all but the most stubborn curl or cockle, and placing the prints under a weight or between the pages of a book for an hour or two does the rest.

Even when a white margin has been left by the printing mask, all the edges should be trimmed. After washing and drying the edges of the paper are always slightly rough and to remove them improves the appearance considerably.

CORRECTIVE PRINTING

IF THE photographer is faced with the necessity of photographing the whole of a tall building, and cannot move far enough away to include it while his camera is held on an even keel, he is forced to tilt the camera uphill, to get the top of the building into the picture. By doing this he will secure a negative in which the vertical lines converge slightly (or considerably, according to the degree of violence with which the camera was tilted). A straight enlargement from such a negative will reproduce its failings, but the fault can to some extent be remedied by tilting the paperholder on the baseboard of the enlarger, so that the image of the *top* of the building is farthest away from the negative. When this method is employed it is necessary to focus on somewhere about the middle of the sloping board, and adjust the tilt so that the converging sides of the house become parallel, after which the lens must be stopped down to a very small aperture to secure sharp definition at both ends of the picture. For users of the *Leitz Focomat* and *Valoy* enlargers a special negative carrier is available, the design of which allows the *negative* also to be tilted. This should be used in conjunction with the tilting paperholder, but in the reverse direction. Tilting the negative in addition to the paper has two advantages: it increases the degree of correction possible; and, as the two opposite "tilts" compensate for each other, it is not necessary to stop down so far to secure satisfactory definition as when the paper alone is tilted. Correction by these methods causes some new distortion—it must do, because the image is being thrown on to a sloping surface instead of one at right angles to the axis of the lens. This distortion takes the form of some elongation of the vertical lines, but it is hardly of importance in any but scientific work, and frequently unnoticeable. (See p. 264 and p. 273, C and D.)

It is quite common to find that some part or other of even a technically excellent negative is inclined to print too dark; perhaps not too dark for accuracy, but darker than is desired. This can be remedied largely by holding back the appropriate part for a portion of the exposure,

293

while allowing the remainder of the negative to continue printing. It is desirable to memorise carefully what we are doing, so that the process can be repeated, or modified, in successive prints. Test strips should be made of the portion of the negative in need of such treatment, and the exposure for that particular portion be ascertained with as much accuracy as that of the whole of the remainder of the picture. This *shading* is accomplished by holding an opaque object between the lens and the projected image for part of the exposure time. It is important that the shadow cast on the paper should not have too sharp or well defined an edge, and for this reason it is desirable to keep the object moving slightly the whole time it is in use. For all except very small areas I find that I can do most of my shading with my hands alone. They can be made to follow almost any shape desired; but it is quite worth while practising for a moment or two with the negative in position before the bromide paper is placed on the easel, so as to determine how best to arrange the hands to secure the desired result. If only a small area has to be held back—particularly if it is in the centre of the picture—a small piece of cardboard torn roughly to the desired shape, or a piece of cotton-wool teased out to the shape, will meet most needs; to avoid encroaching on the other part of the picture while using it, it is generally mounted on the end of a piece of wire, which, if kept moving slightly, will cast no harmful shadow itself. (See p. 273, E and F.)

To meet the opposite requirement: a portion of the picture which prints too light, *dodging*—additional localised exposure, sometimes also called *spot printing*—becomes necessary. The hands, again, are a very flexible means of directing a beam of light to any one particular spot, and if they are kept well away from the paper the edge of the cone of light will be sufficiently soft to avoid a harsh line showing where the extra printing has taken place. I keep a number of pieces of opaque card (out of whole-plate packets of paper) in my own darkroom; most of these have been torn to a variety of curved shapes with which I can more or less match any desired outline. I have others in which I have torn and cut holes—circular, crescent-shaped, triangles, etc., and with these, modified sometimes by placing the hand or fingers partly over or through one or other hole, it is quite easy to lead a beam of light on to almost any part of the picture. Again, tests may have to be carried out to determine just how much extra exposure is necessary to a particular part to secure the desired effect.

Sometimes I find that my negative has far too many highlights round the edges of the picture, so that, if printed in the normal way, the picture does not "hang together", and one's attention is for ever being drawn from the real subject matter to these conspicuous light spots at the edges or corners. Dodging these spots down does not always prove a remedy; often enough it seems rather to draw attention to them. In such a case it is worth while to tone down the edges of the paper by *flashing*, which is really nothing more than fogging the edges by exposure to light. To make successful use of this technique as a means of localising interest in the centre of the picture, some definite system must be followed, otherwise the effect is likely to become far too apparent, and the final result less pleasing than a straight print. The prime essentials are that flashing always be done with the same light source, and that this be weak enough to necessitate an exposure of an appreciable number of seconds, so that the process is at all times under control. The choice of light source is one of personal convenience. There is much to be said for a lamp of low wattage, mounted in a box close to the dark-room ceiling and immediately over the work table. If this be installed, it will be wise to have the sides of the box opaque, and the mouth (facing downwards) covered with several layers of tissue paper or its equivalent. Some workers—I am one—manage very well with the enlarger itself. My practice is to raise it to the top of its 40 in. column, and to stop the lens down to the smallest opening. This ensures a constant and controllable light source. Before attempting to employ the process on an enlargement, tests should be made to ascertain the degree of darkening that can be obtained with various exposures. It is desirable to make the tests on a sheet of the paper that is normally used—in much the same way as one would find the exposure for an enlargement, but of course, in this case, without a negative in the carrier. A series of exposures should be made, by gradually moving a mask over the sheet so that progressive "steps" have received, say, 5, 10, 20, 40, 80 seconds exposure. The strip is then fully developed, fixed, washed and dried and should be kept as a guide for future work. (See p. 273, G.)

When it is desired to lower the tone of the edges of a print, comparison of a straight print with this test sheet will indicate approximately what additional flashing exposure will be necessary to reduce the edge tones to the required extent. Armed with this knowledge, one can set about the task with some certainty of result. Assuming that the print has now been exposed, the additional treatment is accomplished by (a) removing the paper to a safe place (marking it so that the top of the picture can be identified), (b) removing the negative from its carrier, (c) setting the enlarger to the pre-chosen position on its column, and (d) stopping the lens down to the desired extent. With the enlarger light off, the paper is placed on the baseboard and completely covered with an opaque card. The enlarger light is now switched on; and, noting the time exactly, the card is raised and moved backwards and forwards so as to allow the light to spill over one edge in order to fog the appropriate part of the paper below. To avoid hard lines the card must be kept moving so that the fog is vignetted into the image, and the extent of the movement necessary can best be estimated by having a straight print nearby for comparison while the job is in progress. As soon as one edge has been dealt with the light is switched off and the time once again noted and another edge similarly treated. After all four edges have had the requisite amount of flashing the light is extinguished and the print developed and finished in the usual way. A uniformly straight flashing line is hardly ever desirable, and the most satisfactory results are usually obtained by moving the card in such a way that the corners get a trifle more exposure than the centre of the print edge, by allowing the light to spill farther in at the corners than elsewhere. This is most easily accomplished if the card is twisted on its axis, a trifle to left and to right alternately, as it is moved backwards and forwards.

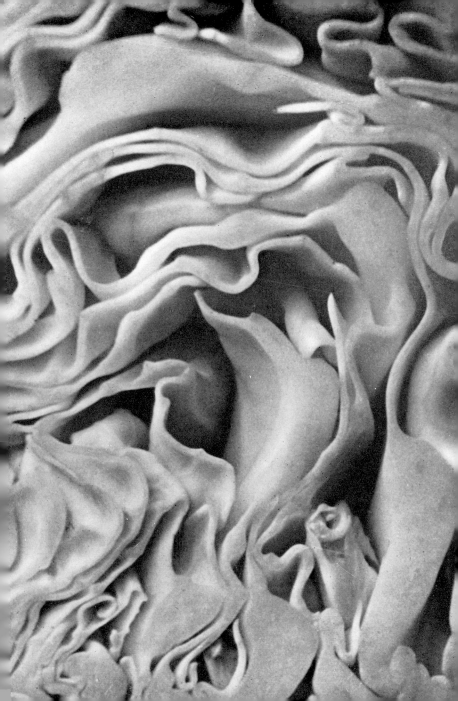

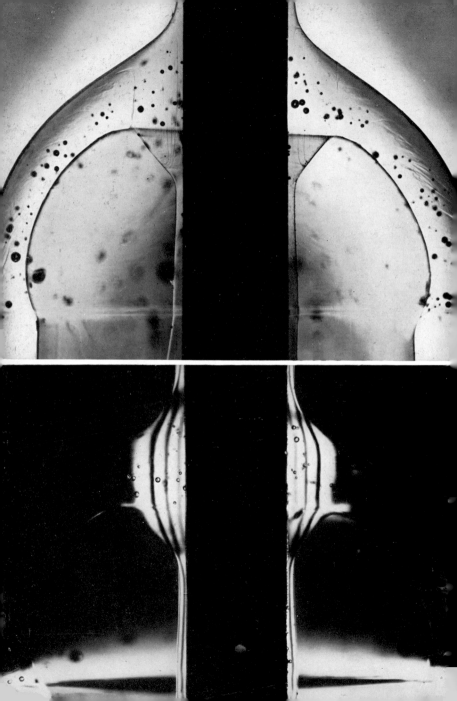

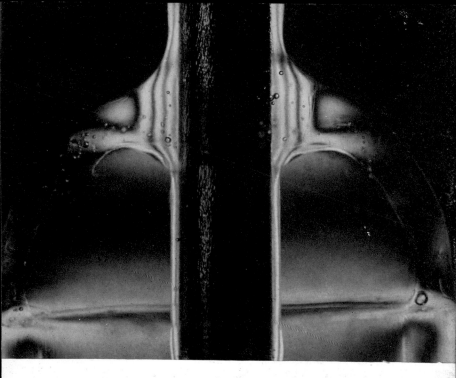

The photographs of this section offer a last glimpse into the immense scope and versatility of the 35 mm. camera.

*Page 297. JUST A CABBAGE—An example of close-up photography using a near focusing device (Contameter). Reproduced on this scale (over life size) the picture enters the field of Macro photography.—*Lancelot Vining.

Above and opposite. STRAIN IN SILICA GLASS SEALS—*Pictures show 3 mm. tungsten rod passing through glass seal. For examination the seal is placed in carbon tetrachloride (which has the same refractive index as the glass) thus showing the seal as a section. A background mask gives dark reflections in the edges, showing the shape to the best advantage. To show "strain", the immersed seal is placed between crossed polaroid filters. This reveals strain reaching the third order surrounding the tungsten, little strain in the dome walls, and some strain at the join to the tube. Focusing attachment and a 100 mm. extension tube were used on the camera. The* first *picture was taken without filters, the* second *picture with correctly oriented polaroid filters each side of the seal, the third (above) had in addition to the polarised light some slight oblique illumination to show the glass shape and rod surface. The exposures with the polarised light were 7½ times the exposure used in straight light.—*D. Andrews (by courtesy, *M. O. Valve Co.*).

PANORAMS *increase the interest of landscape and travel photography. In the absence of a "panoram head" for the tripod, such pictures
can easily be made, by hand, provided that an adequate "overlap" is*

300

ensured. Prints to form a panoram must *have exactly the same exposure and development, otherwise they will not make up satisfactorily. The above panoram is from two negatives.*—H. S. Newcombe.

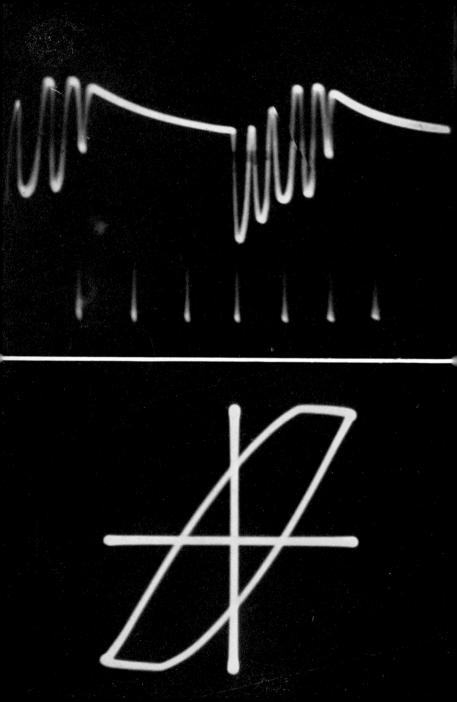

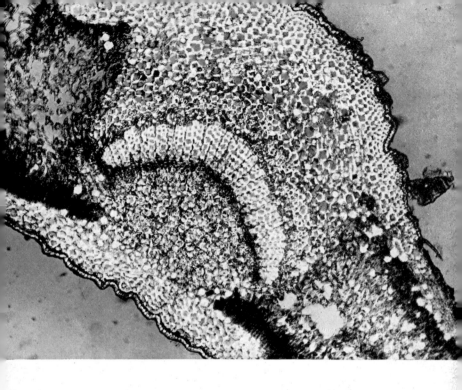

Above. PHOTOMICROGRAPH—*A cross section through an oleander leaf by polarised light.*—A. Niklitschek.

Opposite. OSCILLOGRAMS—*The top oscillogram is of* 10 *k.c. wave obtained from* 100 *k.c. generator using an electronic divider superimposed time scale* 2 *microseconds per division, double exposed on to the negative. The* bottom *oscillogram is of amplifier characteristic showing output-input curve with slight overload at* 30 *cycles/sec. Ordinates printed in by multiple exposure on negative. In both cases focusing attachment and the* 60 *mm. extension were used.*—D. Andrews (by courtesy M. O. Valve Co.).

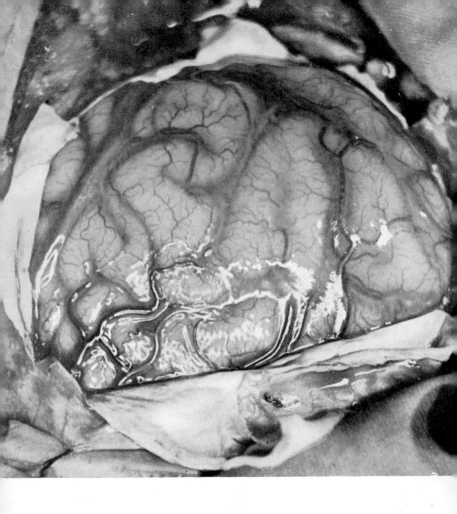

Above. THE HUMAN BRAIN *taken during an operation. A form of camera work for which the 35 mm. instrument is invaluable—its small size, and the ability to work at large lens apertures, while still ensuring adequate depth of good definition are important advantages to the photographer whose requirements must ever be secondary to the needs of the surgeon. A short extension tube was used for near focusing.—* Jean Straker.

THE shortcomings of the paper print—its inability to cope simultaneously with the highlight and shadow ends of a long scale negative—have induced many workers to experiment with a view to finding some way round this apparently insurmountable problem.

It has long been realised that, while admittedly the greater part of every photograph is composed of half-tones—varying shades of grey—which (at least on a normal paper) are well separated, the shadow tones and the highlights are always somewhat compressed, because they lie on the toe and shoulder of the film curve. To this must be added the fact that printing paper also suffers from a further flattening of contrast at both ends of the scale, and so the total loss in tone separation at these extremities in comparison with the original subject can well be imagined (p. 284).

As we have already seen (p. 294), a great deal can be done by masking part of the projected image for a portion of the exposure time—to hold back the shadow areas so that they do not overprint and to allow the denser highlights time to record themselves. But this method can necessarily only deal with *areas*—not with details. A method mainly practised in continental Europe and America by a few specialists exists, however, by means of which the highlight and shadow areas can be separately printed on to the same sheet of paper. Acknowledgment must be made to *Alfred Person* for the part he played in making a practical process of what had previously been of a very experimental character.

The essence of the process is in the production of a suitable original negative, which is preferably made on a film with thin emulsion and of only moderate speed. This should be exposed only just sufficiently to secure adequate *shadow* detail and then developed fully so as to obtain all possible contrast in that area while disregarding the highlights, which are bound to block-up considerably.

From this negative a soft contrast transparency is made by contact on *positive* film. The exposure for this is adjusted so as to secure the utmost detail in the highlights and kept to only moderate contrast by dilute development. When the transparency is dry it is in turn printed by contact on positive film; this time exposing only just enough to record the highlight detail while the shadow areas should be so under-exposed that they are practically plain celluloid. Development of this second negative should be very full and is preferably carried out in a vigorous developer, with the object of building up all possible contrast in the highlights. We now have (*a*) the original (somewhat contrasty) negative in which there is good separation between the shadow tones and some half-tone detail, and (*b*) the second negative which is glass-clear everywhere except in the extreme highlights where it should be moderately dense, and in the slightly less brilliant highlights in which there should also be some appreciable silver deposit.

If the original negative be printed on a normal or hard grade paper with a suitable exposure to record the shadows satisfactorily, and the second negative then be substituted and *its* image also printed with an exposure just sufficient to differentiate between the highlights and the *extreme* highlight tones, the combined print will show satisfactory tone separation at both ends of the scale, thus securing brilliance, gradation and plasticity, while there will be sufficient overlap in the half-tones for these also to be rendered in a satisfactory manner. This method necessarily makes the shadows and the highlight areas each occupy more of the available black–white tone range than they would and thus actually brings them closer together in tone; but to offset this, the consequent gain in sparkle and quality makes the relative shortage of the half-tones proper almost unnoticeable. This separation business is *not* an easy process. It requires laboratory conditions of care and cleanliness at all stages of the proceedings. Contact printing must be done with extreme care to avoid trouble due to dust and scratches. In the absence of a machine such as the *Leitz Eldia*, a well-made printing frame, with a flawless sheet of glass, is quite satisfactory. It is most desirable that the positive film be of anti-halation type with soluble backing. In the absence of this, some other *very slow* film of this type should be chosen.

To secure the requisite quality in the original negative,

it is desirable to develop in a double or triple strength solution, when, if the exposure is correct, there will be sufficient differentiation between the separate shadow tones. If the original negative is at all veiled in the shadows, this fog should be removed with *Farmer's* reducer (p. 160), while, should there be insufficient contrast between these shadow tones, the use of the chromium intensifier (p. 159) is recommended. A suitable extra soft working developer for the intermediate positive is the following:

SOFT DEVELOPER				
	Metol	3	grm.	45 gr.
	Sodium sulphite (anhydrous)	15	grm.	225 gr.
	Potassium carbonate (anhydrous)	15	grm.	225 gr.
	Potassium bromide	0.4	grm.	6 gr.
	Water	200	c.cm.	7 oz.

Dilute one part of this solution with three parts of water and develop for about 15 *seconds only* at 68° F. (20° C.).

When making the second negative from this transparency, it is necessary to cut the exposure to the *minimum that will secure detail in the highlights* and then to develop in a strong Metol-hydroquinone solution (as used for bromide printing) and to develop until the extreme highlights and the ordinary highlights are well contrasted. It is worth while making several transparencies and reserve "second" negatives with trifling exposure differences in order to secure the best possible separation of tones. The film is cheap enough and the additional labour of no consequence if they are all done at the same time.

In making the print, one has to ascertain the exposure for the shadows (original negative) and the highlights (second negative); but to add one to the other will necessarily produce too dark a print, as the clear celluloid part of the second negative will allow light to pass to *all* parts of the image except the highlights. For this reason, if the shadows require, say, 10 seconds and the highlight negative, say, 3 seconds as tested separately, the final print will probably be most satisfactory if the shadow negative is given 7 or 8 seconds only—the balance being made up with the 3 seconds that the highlight negative will add when its exposure is added.

Probably the greatest difficulty that the user will find in

attempting this fascinating process will lie in the problem of securing exact registration of the two separately projected images. The best method is to scratch two minute crosses in diagonally opposite corners of the original negative somewhere where it will not affect the picture. This should be done prior to making the transparency so that it prints through on to it, and thus on to the second negative. When the original negative is in the enlarger, the red glass safety cover in position and the bromide paper in place on the easel, a sharp-pointed pencil should be used to mark the exact intersection of the two crosses, and the same marks be used to locate the paper in precisely the correct position for the second negative.

Because of their lower speed and their emulsion characteristics, papers of the chloro-bromide class are particularly suited to this work; but if ordinary bromide paper is preferred, it is usually desirable to select a hard or contrasty grade.

Prints made in this way are usually slightly veiled in the lightest parts: and a brief immersion in weak Farmer's reducer (p. 160) is generally beneficial in clearing up the highlights and increasing the brilliancy of the result.

The foregoing is only the outline of the process. It is one which lends itself to personal control to a degree and, unlike all the so-called "control" processes, it is pure photography at every stage.

There is no need to confine oneself to working with only the two negatives described—much attractive work has been done by separating the tone areas of a subject into three or even four parts; making negatives for each one via suitable transparencies so that the final built up picture has a "poster-like" character based on three or four more or less uniform tints representing the extreme highlights, lighter tones, mid tones and shadows respectively. This is delving into more complex forms of control, but the basic principle remains the same, and enough has been said to indicate the method to be followed by the worker keen enough to desire to extend his work beyond the limitations of ordinary photographic printing routine.

THE bulk of our considerations, so far, have been directed to taking and making pictures for their own sake. There is, however, a very wide and ever growing field of use for the 35 mm. camera in more serious pursuits. Curiously enough, many of these begin where the normal camera user leaves off; that is, at distances closer than the $3\frac{1}{2}$ ft. to which the majority of miniature cameras are scaled.

We can divide the close-up use of the miniature into, roughly, three headings: *copying and reproduction* on a reasonable scale up to life size; *macro photography*, embracing reproduction from life size up to a small magnification; and *photo-micrography*, the production of a negative at a considerable degree of magnification—usually taken through a microscope.

The makers of those cameras normally fitted with interchangeable lenses have catered for these needs.

For example, for Leica models up to IIIf, the *Nooky* device, attached to the camera front, takes the lens and employs a prism device which allows the normal range-finder and view-finder to be used to focus objects at any distance from $3\frac{1}{2}$ ft. to $16\frac{1}{2}$ in. Other makers tackle the problem differently, and provide a separate range-finder with a set of supplementary lenses, which permits of accurate focusing and view-finding at set distances. Special lenses, usually for 35 mm. reflex cameras, are available with close-focusing mounts going from infinity to about 4 or 6 in. All these devices enable close work to be done, even when the camera has to be held in the hand.

When the camera can be securely supported, even simpler means can be employed to cover a still wider range. As most focusing mounts will not extend beyond the $3\frac{1}{2}$ ft. mark, there are two methods available for increasing the range: (a) to mount *extension tubes* between the lens and the camera, thus providing the necessary extra extension, and (b) to shorten the focus of the lens itself by the addition of weak positive *front lenses* (*Proxar, Focar*)—so that what was the normal $3\frac{1}{2}$ ft. setting with the 5 cm. lens becomes the appropriate extension for focusing a much closer object when the focus of the lens is reduced. For moderately close work, say 3½ ft. down to 10 in., the supplementary lens is a simple and satisfactory method; and although focusing must now be done entirely by rule, the respective makers provide adequately detailed measurement tables for such lenses. When still closer work has to be done, extension tubes become necessary and, while again tabular data is provided, some method of visual focusing on a ground glass screen is obviously a considerable asset.

An alternative method is the use of *distance gauges* which are provided by the makers of several 35 mm. cameras. They are available for use either with fixed extension tubes, or with specified supplementary lenses, according to the type of instrument and the camera for which it is designed. The principle is that if the camera can be held at a fixed distance from the subject, corresponding to the lens or tube used, the picture will be sharp. The distance gauge therefore consists of a suitable camera fitting with two or four legs or rods projecting in front. The length of the rods is designed so that the plane of their tips is in fact the plane of sharpest focus of the subject. Where four rods are used, their tips also correspond to the corners of the subject area. The device thus acts both as a distance gauge and a viewfinding frame.

Copying stands exist in several forms. Fundamentally they all provide a baseboard on which the subject lies, and an upright with some provision for carrying the camera parallel to the base.

It is worth noting that 35 mm. instruments of the reflex type lend themselves admirably to this class of work as the full size focusing screen is constantly available whatever lens, extension tubes or supplementary lenses are used.

For really serious work, however, the greater versatility of a visual focusing stand is desirable even if the column and baseboard are those normally used for the enlarger.

The basic design of such accessories is simple, and includes a stationary lower plate of metal into which the lens and possibly extension tubes are screwed. On this plate slides (or rotates) another somewhat similar plate pierced with two holes, over which are mounted, respectively, the camera body (without lens), face down, and a permanent ground glass focusing screen adapter in which a 36 × 24 mm.

ground glass is fixed to correspond exactly with the plane of the film.

In use, the image of the object is accurately composed and focused on this screen, after which the upper plate is allowed to slide along (or is rotated) until the camera is in position over the lens, when the exposure can be made with certain assurance of good definition and accurate placing.

This type of plate, mounted on a ball and socket joint to provide universal adjustment and supported by a really rigid tripod stand, provides the ideal apparatus for clinical work and is largely employed for dental and surgical record photography, while it is equally suitable for the majority of industrial research and record subjects.

During the war an immense number of official and business documents were recorded in this way, on 35 mm. film. Whole libraries are similarly being copied and are becoming available for study in the form of easily portable positive 35 mm. strips on which the book pages are clearly readable under a magnifier or by projection. Police departments all over the world have found the "35" invaluable. Its employment in connection with mass radiography is now common knowledge. The philatelist will find his own use for such equipment, as will also the naturalist interested, for example, in insect life.

This class of work may well enter the macro range, where really long extension tubes or even a bellows extension unit, may be used. Various makes of these have become available. It is worth noting here that when the lens is thus extended to a greater than normal distance from the film the engraved f values cease to have their usual significance so far as exposure is concerned. It is necessary to calculate the lens aperture in relation to its increased working distance—e.g. a 2 in. f 2 lens (approx. 1 in. diameter) used on the end of a 6 in. extension tube works as an 8 in. lens (1 in. diameter) which gives a maximum aperture of about f 8, and if it is stopped down for use its working aperture will be proportionately lower than the markings on the aperture scale.

The illumination of objects or documents when copying is sometimes tricky. It must be governed by the result required. If texture is to be recorded, fairly oblique light from one side will best serve. If texture is undesirable, as in copying ordinary printed or written matter, the light should come equally from both sides, preferably at about 45° to the surface to avoid any chance of light reflections into the lens.

For really close work at a fairly high scale of magnification the shadowless *ring illuminator* is to be recommended. This takes the form of a saucer-shaped, hollow metal reflector containing several small electric lamps mounted round its periphery. It is supported over the small object to be photographed at a distance of a few cm., so that the light reaches the object uniformly from all sides. The centre of the reflector is pierced with a hole through which the lens can obtain an unobscured view of the subject matter, and a turned down rim, surrounding this aperture, protects the lens from direct light from the lamps. Similar units exist with a curved electronic flash tube.

From "macro" to the higher realms of "micro" is but a step—but in making this step, we make one fundamental change. Instead of increasing the working distance between the lens and the camera still more, to gain greater magnification we employ an ordinary microscope to secure a magnified image, and then photograph what the eye sees through it. It is possible to do this in two ways: either to focus the microscope visually through the eyepiece in the usual way, and then to mount the camera with its own lens focused at infinity immediately over the eyepiece, or to allow the microscope eyepiece itself to project the image on to the sensitive film. This is done by mounting a suitable light-tight adapting tube, containing a focusing screen, over the eyepiece and focusing the image carefully on the screen with a magnifier. After this preparation, the focusing screen adapter is removed and the camera body substituted, so that the image is projected on to the film as soon as the shutter is opened.

Both methods have certain advantages. The first system is, of course, open to all 35 mm. users, as nothing beyond a suitable light-tight tube coupling between the lens and the eyepiece is necessary; the second one, however, is more generally used where a suitable attachment such as the Leitz *Mikas* is available. With this particular device the camera is screwed by its flange on to a tubular adapter about 6 cm. long, which carries at its lower end a 10× micro eyepiece. At a suitable point in the tube is a prism by means of which the image can be examined through an eyepiece projecting at 90° to the axis. This prism is transparent and an exposure can be made through it while the reflected image is still under observation, which is of considerable value if photographing a living specimen. The prism is, however, movable under the control of a flexible wire release and can be put out of the way if not required. This, of course, enables shorter exposures to be given. The exposure itself, in this device, is controlled by an *Ibsor* diaphragm shutter mounted at the top of the tube, also wire operated, the Leica shutter, of course, being left open on "T."

This same basic method can be used with any camera with removable lens if a focusing screen adapter is available. For this work the miniature reflex is particularly suitable, as nothing but a tube adapter to connect camera and microscope is required.

Any desired size of objective can be used according to need, but a 10× eyepiece is definitely best suited to 35 mm. camera work as it produces an image of suitable area on the film. In passing, it is useful to remember that a three diameter enlargement from a negative made in this way will produce a print on a scale similar to that obtained visually through the microscope.

Where coloured originals have to be copied with some semblance of accuracy, a panchromatic film is essential. This may well be one of the first group (page 92), if the subject contains a variety of tones, as this type of material will ensure adequately fine grain and reasonable tone rendering. If, however, a line subject in either black-and-white or colour is to be reproduced and contrast is of more importance than half-tone rendering, the most suitable material is one of the very slow panchromatic emulsions such as *Microfile*, *Ilford Micro-neg*, etc. Such films will yield very brilliant negatives, even with our normal developers, but if the maximum contrast is desired the following formula is to be recommended.

313

Page	Title	Author	Camera
9	An Anxious Moment	F. H. Sharman, F.R.P.S.	Contax II
10	A Policeman's Lot	C. C. B. Herbert	Leica III A
11	Out of the Window	Paul Wolff	Leica
12	Theatre	Felix H. Man	Leica
13	The Statue		Contax
14	Penguin	E. Auerbach	Contax
15	Quite a Handful	E. Auerbach	Contaflex
16	Going Down	Hugo Wadenoyen, F.R.P.S.	Contax
84	Springtime	Herm. Ebel	Leica
84	Derwent Water	W. A. Poucher, F.R.P.S.	Leica III A
101	"Rex"	G. Schuh	Contax
102	The Road to Tyro	H. S. Newcombe, F.R.P.S.	Leica
103	The Icefield	H. S. Newcombe, F.R.P.S.	Leica III B
104	Skye Landscape	H. S. Newcombe, F.R.P.S.	Leica
113	Lions	K. Hubschmann	Leica
114	Black Forest Village	H. S. Newcombe, F.R.P.S.	Leica
115	Christmas Eve	P. Damm	Contax
116	Street Lamps	H. S. Newcombe, F.R.P.S.	Leica III A
117	Grosvenor House Cabaret	Lancelot Vining, F.R.P.S.	Contax
118	Snow Blossom	H. S. Newcombe, F.R.P.S.	Leica III
119	Starting Back	Paul Wolff	Leica
120	Alpine Village	H. S. Newcombe, F.R.P.S.	Leica II
169	The Fountain	G. Schuh	Contax
170	A French Road	H. S. Newcombe, F.R.P.S.	Leica III A
171	The Bay	H. S. Newcombe, F.R.P.S.	Leica III B
172	The Mousky, Cairo	J. Allan Cash, F.R.P.S.	Leica
173	Evening	E. Loose	Contax II
174	The Night Traveller	G. Schuh	Contax
175	Two Reflections	Paul Wolff	
176	The Bartender's View	K. Hubschmann	Leica
185	Waiting for the Tide	H. S. Newcombe, F.R.P.S.	Leica III B
186	In Harbour	C. Croeber	Contax
187	Fitting Out	H. S. Newcombe, F.R.P.S.	Leica III A
188	The Small Class	C. Croeber	Contax
197	Narcissi	W. G. Briggs	Leica
198	The Woodman's Chalet	G. Underell, F.R.P.S.	Leica
199	The Water Hole	Felix H. Man	Leica
200	Liquid Light	H. S. Newcombe, F.R.P.S.	Leica III B
201	Houses of Parliament	Felix H. Man	Leica
202	The Stairway	F. Fiedler	Contax
203	Grecian London	H. S. Newcombe, F.R.P.S.	Leica III B
204	Little Ship	H. S. Newcombe, F.R.P.S.	Leica III
213	Portrait	K. Hubschmann	Leica
214	The Hat	K. Hubschmann	Leica
215	High Key Portrait	J. W. J. Underell, F.R.P.S.	Leica
216	The Tribesman	J. Allan Cash, F.R.P.S.	Leica
217	David Lloyd George	K. Hubschmann	Leica
218	The Artist	K. Hubschmann	Leica
219	The Toast	H. S. Newcombe, F.R.P.S.	Leica
220	Windy Day	H. S. Newcombe, F.R.P.S.	Leica
221	H. G. Wells	E. Auerbach	Contaflex
222	The Canteen	K. Hubschmann	Leica
223	The Archbishop of York	E. Auerbach	Contaflex
224	Utter Amazement	K. Hubschmann	Leica
233	Robert Aitkin and Helen Cherry	K. Hubschmann	Contax
234	Windmill Theatre	H. S. Newcombe, F.R.P.S.	Leica III B
235	Ballet	Felix H. Man	Leica
236	Spanish Dance	H. S. Newcombe, F.R.P.S.	Leica III B
237	Autumn Crocus	H. S. Newcombe, F.R.P.S.	Contax II
238	The Dancers	Felix H. Man	Leica
239	The Juggler		
240	Balance	F. H. Sharman, F.R.P.S.	Contax II
241	The Jump	Doguibérie	Contax
242	The Cycle Race	H. S. Newcombe, F.R.P.S.	Leica III B
243	A Smart Return	Hein Gorny	Leica
244	Winter Sport	Hein Gorny	Leica
261	Flare Spots	H. S. Newcombe, F.R.P.S.	Leica III A
262	Latitude	H. S. Newcombe, F.R.P.S.	Leica III B
263	Grain	H. S. Newcombe, F.R.P.S.	Leica III
264	Distortion	H. S. Newcombe, F.R.P.S.	Leica III A
297	Cabbage	Lancelot Vining, F.R.P.S.	Contax &
298	Strain in Glass	D. Andrews, A.R.P.S.	Leica III B
298	Strain in Glass	D. Andrews, A.R.P.S.	Leica III B
299	Strain in Glass	D. Andrews, A.R.P.S.	Leica III B
300/1	Panoram	H. S. Newcombe	Leica III B
302	Oscillogram	D. Andrews, A.R.P.S.	Leica III B
302	Oscillogram	D. Andrews, A.R.P.S.	Leica III B
303	Photomicrograph	A. Niklitschek	Contax &
304	Clinical Photography	Jean Straker	Kine Exakta

THE ILLUSTRATIONS

Lens	Focus, cm.	Stop	Exp.	Filter	Film	Developer
Sonnar	5	1.5	1/250		Plus X	D.76
Summar	5	2.8	1/20		Agfa I.S.S.	M.C.M.
Wide angle	3.5	9	10			
Sonnar	13.5	9				
Sonnar	5		2			
Sonnar	5	2.8	1/250		Plus X Pan	
Summitar		6.3	1/100	2 X Yellow		
Elmar	3.5	6.3	1/60	Yellow	Agfa F.F.	Final
Elmar	5	9	1/200	Yellow	Agfa F.	
Elmar	3.5	9	1/100	Red	Agfa F.	P.D.M.G.
		4.5	1/30		S.XX	
Elmar	3.5	6.3	1/30		Agfa F.	Sease III
Summar	5	2	1/20		Super XX	P.D.M.G.
Sonnar	5	2	1/125		Super XX	
Elmar	5	4.5	1/40	Yellow	Panatomic	P.D.M.G.
Elmar	3.5	8	1/200			
Elmar	5	6.3	1/60	Yellow	Agfa F.F.	Final
Elmar	5	6.3	1/60		Agfa F.	Sease III
Summar	5	9	1/100	Yellow	Agfa F.	Sease III
Summar	5	4.5	1/100		Pan film	
Sonnar	5	1.5	1/25			
Tessar		9	1/50	Yellow	Agfa F.	
Wide angle	3.5	9				
Elmar	5	9	1/200		Panatomic X	Sease III
Sonnar	5					
Elmar	5	6.3	1/100		Agfa F.	P.D.M.G.
Sonnar	5	2.8	1/125			
Astro		9	1/60		H.P.2	
Elmar	5	9	1/100		Agfa	Atomal
Hektor	13.5	6	1/200		Isopan F.	
Elmar	9	9	1/200		Panatomic X	P.D.M.G
Summar	5	2.8	1/4			
Sonnar	5	4.5	1/50		Agfa F.	
Hektor	2.8	9	1/40	Yellow	Agfa F.	
Hektor	13.5	4.5	1/60	Yellow	Agfa F.	
	9	6.3	1/10		Plus X	
	9	6.3	1/10		Plus X	
Elmar	9	4	1/8		Agfa F.	
Summar	5	6.3	1/100	Green		
	9	6.3	1/60		Plus X	
Elmar	5	9	1/4		Plus X	
Summar	5	2	1/8		Agfa I.S.S.	D.76
Elmar	5	6.3	1/60		Agfa F.	
Sonnar	8.5	2	1/25		S.XX	D.K.20
Summar		2	1/8		S.XX	
Sonnar	8.5	2	1/10			
Elmar	9	6.3	1/60			
Sonnar	1.5	2	1/50		S.XX	
Summar	5	2	1/8		H.P.3	P.D.M.G.
Summar		2	1/200			
Summar	5	2	1/8		Selo H.P.3	I D. II
Sonnar	8.5	2	1/10		Super XX	P.D.M.G.
Summar	5	2.8	1/40			
Sonnar	5	2	1/125		Plus X	D.76
Summar	5	2	1/200		Panatomic X	D.76
Summar	5	4.5	2 sec.		Isopan F.	Sease III
Elmar	9	6.3	Various		Panatomic X	Sease III
Elmar	5	6.3	1/60		Super X	
Hektor	2.8	6.3	1/100	Yellow	Isopan F.	Sease III
Contameter	5	16	1/10		Agfa F.F.	Meritol Metol
Summar	5	6.3	2 sec.		Panatomic X	Meritol Metol
Summar	5	6.3	15 sec.	Polaroid	Panatomic X	Meritol Metol
Summar	5	6.3	15 sec.	Polaroid	Panatomic X	Meritol Metol
Summar	5	9	1/60	Yellow	Panatomic X	Sease III
Elmar	9	6.3	I sec.		H.P.3	Meritol Metol
Elmar	9	6.3	I sec.		H.P.3	Meritol Metol
Miflex		9	I sec.	Bernotar (Polar)		
Tessar	5	4.5	1/50		Super XX	Meritol Metol

KODAK D.II	Water	500 c.c.s.	16 ozs.
	Elon (Metol)	1 gm.	15 grs.
	Sodium Sulphite (Anhyd)	75 gms.	2½ ozs.
	Hydroquinone	9 gms.	130 grs.
	Potassium Carbonate (Anhyd)	25 gms.	360 grs.
	Potassium Bromide	5 gms.	70 grs.
	Water to make	1000 c.cm.	32 ozs.

Time of development at 65° F. about 5 minutes.

Correct exposure is perhaps the most difficult matter on which to proffer advice. When copying documents, etc., it is fairly easy to use a photo-electric meter for a localised reading with some certainty of result; but with macro-photography the illuminated area is sometimes too small to permit of accurate measurement in this way, and although the meter may give an approximate guide it will be advisable to make a number of exposures above and below that considered to be correct.

If exposures are made by artificial light, the colour of the light itself will provide almost the same degree of correction as would a pale yellow filter—a point worth remembering if one is dealing with coloured originals.

With photo-micrography, experience alone will guide. The use of a meter is possible, but a trial and error method is usually adequate. Once again I would urge that conditions—distance of lamp and bullseye (for opaques), position of substage condenser, iris setting (for transparent specimens)—should be noted so that a repeat exposure may be made with confidence if the first attempts are not satisfactory. The density and stain intensity of a micro slide will also considerably influence the exposure required.

The immensity of the subject makes it impossible to do more than explore the fringe of this very close work, but the keen 35 mm. worker who sighs for fresh fields to conquer will do well to investigate more deeply the joys—and problems—of "getting closer still".

INDEX

	Page
Acceptance angle of meters	107
Action photography	51, 117, 231
Acutance	91
Adox films	92
Advertising photography	42, 99
Advocate camera	58
Agfa films	92
Agfacolor film	254, 265
Aggregate exposure calculations	108
Agitation in film development	141
Albada finder	53, 54
Alpa camera	22
Angle of acceptance	107
Angular finder	177
Angulon lens	35
Ansco film	92
Anscochrome	254
Architectural photography	42, 99
ASA Arith. Index speeds	111
ASA Log. Index speeds	111
Automatic cameras	58
Automation	57
Backgrounds	208
Bessamatic	22, 28
Between-lens shutters	57
Binding lantern slides	266
Biogon lens	35
Blacks, to obtain	281
Bloomed lenses	44
Bright-line finder	49
BS Arith. Index speeds	111
BS Log. Index speeds	111
Bulk packings, film	61
Cameras	17–31
Canon	22
Candid camera work	208
Capacitors	252
Care of camera	58
Carrying the camera	163
Cartridges, film	60, 121
Cassettes, film	61
Characteristic curve	89, 105
Choosing the camera	31
Chromium intensifier	159
Circle of confusion	72, 73
Cleaning dishes	145
Cleaning film	144
Clearing bath, print	291

	Page
Climbing, how to carry camera	163
Clinical photography	42, 99
Coated lenses	44
Color-Skopar lens	35
Colour composition	259
Colour, exposure for	112, 256
Colour photography	254
Colour prints	256
Colour rendering (table)	95
Colour sensitivity	87
Colour slides, binding	266
Colour temperature	265
Colour transparencies	266
Composition	194
Compur shutters	57
Condenser enlargers	269
Contact printing	275
Contaflex camera	22–28, 48
Contarex camera	37
Contameter	297, 309
Contax camera	22, 46 48, 61, 62
Contax lenses	46
Contrast filters	96
Contrast, negative	90
Contrasty films	90
Control of image size	78
Converging verticals	293
Convertible lenses	25
Copying	309
Copying stands	310
Corrective printing	293
Correx tanks	140
Coupled rangefinder	44
Cruising photography	190
Cutting part used film	122
Cycling photography	163
Darkroom, layout	138
Definition	72, 74, 133, 261
Depth of field	66
Depth of field charts	67–71
Depth of field ring	75
Depth of field scale	74
Developer and film	131
Developer improvers	289
Developers, basic types	123
Developers, maximum energy	156
Developers, normal fine grain	124, 125, 148
Developers, print	287

317

Page

Developers, semi-fine grain 123, 125, 147
Developers, surface 124
Developers, temperature of 127
Developers, two-bath 154
Developers, ultra-fine grain 124, 126, 150
Developing formulae 147
Developing tanks 140
Developing times 127
Development 123, 131
Diaphragm shutter 21
Diaphragm shutter Reflex 28
Dichroic fog 125
Diffused light enlargers 269
DIN speeds 111
Direct vision finders 54
Distance gauges 310
Distortion due to camera tilt 261
Distortion of image due to shutter 33
Dodging prints 294
Double-coating 90, 106
Drying film 142
Drying prints 292
Duplicate negatives 306
Duto lens 212

Ektachrome 254, 265
Eldia, Leitz 306
Electronic flash 248
Elmar lenses 35, 45
Emulsion characteristics 88
Enlargement, degree of 276
Enlarging equipment 268
Enlarging exposure 110
Enlarging routine 267
Ergol developer 156
Exakta camera 22
Exhibition pictures 194
Exposing colour film 257
Exposing routine 63
Exposure meters 107, 112
Exposure, negative 105, 113–120
Exposure, print 287
Extension tubes 309

Farmer's reducer 161
Faults, negative, correction of 159
Ferrania color 254
Ferrania film 92
Film characteristics 86, 89
Film gradation 93
Film, handling 121, 161
Film speeds 86, 111
Film storage 145
Film types 92
Films and developers 131
Filter factors 97, 98, 105
Filters 94, 196, 225
Filters, choice of 99
Finders (view) 51
Fine grain and definition 133
Fine grain, how to secure 130
Fixation 142
Flare spots 45, 64, 74, 261
Flash bulbs 248
Flash factors 250
Flash photography 248

Flashing prints 295
Flexilette camera 31
Focal depth 66–77
Focal plane shutters 57, 249
Focomat enlarger 268
Focomat, improving the 271
Focusing, depth 72, 84
Focusing, differential 84
Focusing, front cell 56
Focusing methods, presetting 51
Focusing methods, scale 56
Focusing, rangefinder 46, 57
Focusing systems 55
Focar lens 309
Formulae, developing 147
Formulae, post-development 157

Gamma 129
G.E. meter speeds 111
Genre subjects 177
Gevacolor film 254, 265
Gevaert film 92
Grain, size of 87, 261
Guide numbers 250

Halation 88, 89, 116, 124
Hard contrast print developer 290
Hardening film (formula) 142
Haze 97
Heating darkroom 138
Heligon lens 35
High key prints 286
High speed development 156
Holding the camera 59, 81

Ibsor diaphragm shutter 313
Ideal camera 19
Ilfachrome film 254
Ilford film 92
Image size 77
Indoors photography 76, 117
Industrial photography 44, 99
Intensification, negative 130, 159
Intensification, print 290
Interchangeable lenses 20
Iris, to adjust 229

Joule 253

Karat camera 57
Kine Exakta camera 313
Kodachrome 254, 265
Kodacolor 254
Kodak films 92

Landscape photography 42, 99
Latitude, film 88, 261
Leica camera 22, 46, 61, 62
Leica lenses 46
Leica M/2 and M/3
Leica If, IIf, IIIf cameras 48
Leica IIIg camera 48
Lens hood 64
Lenses, choice of 35
Lenses, comparison of 43
Lenses, Contax 36
Lenses (general) 35
Lenses, Leica 35

318

	Page
Lighting, artificial	209
Loading the camera	60
Long focus lenses	37
Low key prints	286
Macro photography	297, 309, 311
Marine photography	44, 99, 182
Masterprinter enlarger	286
Meritol	124, 126
Meritol Caustic developer	155
Meter settings	112
Meters, photoelectric	107
Meter; testing the	112
Metol-hydroquinone developer	287
Metraphot meter	110
Microscope, photography with the	312
Mikas, Leitz	312
Modulo lens	212
Mortensen technique	209
Motoring	167
Mountaineering	42, 99
Movement, arresting	51, 117, 231
Multiple finder	54
Nature photography	42, 99
Negative carriers	270
Neofin developers	137
Newton's rings	270
Night photography	115, 116, 174
Nikon camera	22
Nooky attachment	309
Object size control	78
Optical equipment	35, 44, 55
Ortho-phenylene-diamine	124, 126
Over-development, negative	130, 158
Over-exposure, negative	106, 157
Over-exposure, print	289
Pakolor	254
Panchromatic film	87
Panoram head	179
Panorams	179, 300–301
Panphot	54
Paper, grades of	282
Paper, scale of	283
Paper, surfaces of	281
Parallax	49–52, 225
Paraphenylene-diamine	124, 126
Pentax camera	22
Pentaprism	27
Person process	305
Perspective	77, 83
Persulphate, ammonium, reducer	161
Perutz color film	254
Perutz film	92
Photoelectric meters	107
Photofloods	211
Photometers	110, 287
Photomicrography	303, 309
Pictorial photography	192
Pictures from moving vehicles	178
Polarizing filters	97, 225, 299
Portraiture	42, 99, 207
Post-development formulae	157
Posterized prints	308

	Page
Precision enlarger	268
Press photography	42, 51, 99, 155
Print developers	287
Print exposure	287
Print processing	287
Print quality	288
Printing, contact	275
Printing, corrective	293
Printing, creative	305
Printing paper, choice of	281
Processing conditions	138
Promicrol developer	156
Prominent camera	22
Prontormat shutter	57
Proportions, control of	77
Proxars, Zeiss	309
Rambling	162
Rangefinders	23, 44–46
Rangefinders (screen)	28–48
Record photography	44, 99, 311
Reduction, negative	130, 160, 161
Refills, film	60
Reflected colour	260
Reflex focusing housing	26
Reflex cameras	26
Reflex models	26
Regattas	189
Reid enlarger	268
Releasing the shutter	63
Reloading cassettes	121
Reproduction	309
Resolution	88
Retina Reflex cameras	22–28, 48, 61
Ring illuminator	312
Robot camera	57, 61
Rotating stage plate	311
Sailing	189
Scheiner speeds	111
Scratches on film	143
Sea, the	190
SEI Photometer	108
Shading prints	294
Shooting	63
Short ends of film, handling	122
Shows, photographing	44, 225
Shutter, direction of movement	33
Shutter speed to arrest movement	245
Simplified 35 mm. cameras	55
Size of enlargement desirable	276
Snapshooting	42
Snow	118, 119
Soft contrast film developer	290
Soft contrast print developer	307
Soft focus lenses	212
Soft-working films	90
Solar enlarger	268
Solinar lens	35
Speed, film	86, 111
Speed photography	232
Speed settings, daylight	112
Spiral groove tanks	140
Sports photography	44, 54, 99
Spot printing	294

	Page
Stage photography	225
Stop bath	142
Storing films	145
Street scenes	177
Studio portraiture	207
Subject contrast	284
Subjects and lenses	43
Summarit lens	35
Summaron lenses	35, 309
Summicron lens	35, 309
Sunsets	191
Sunshade	64
Sunshine, rendering of	195
Swinging the camera	246
Synchro-sunlight	250

	Page
Tanks, developing	140
Telephoto lenses	37
Tele-Tessar lens	37
Temperature of developer (negative)	127
Temperature of developer (print)	289
Tessar lenses	35, 45
Test strip (print)	287
Theatrical photography	44, 225
35 mm. system, advantages of	8
Tone separation	305
Touring with a camera	162

	Page
Triotar lens	38
Tropical requirements	178
Two-bath developers	154
Under-development, negative	129, 158
Under-development, print	288
Under-exposure, negative	106, 157
Universal finder	53
Valoy enlarger	268
Variable focus finders	54
Vehicles, pictures from moving	178
Vidom viewfinder	53
Viewfinders, comparison of	51
Viewpoint	77, 82
Visoflex	54
Vrook viewfinder	52
Washing films	142
Weston Master meter	108
Weston meter speeds	111
Wetting agents	144
Wiping films	143
Xenon lens	35
"Zoom" lenses	41

MY WAY WITH THE MINIATURE
By Lancelot Vining

Ten years' more experience has gone into the thorough revision, ample additions and new illustrations of the present reissue of this work.

260 pp., 50 illus., 13th ed. **Price 19/6**
(U.S.A. price $4.50)

THE ROLLEI WAY
By L. A. Mannheim

A composite work, built from the experience and advice of leading photographers, dealing with essential points of Rolleiflex or Rolleicord practice.

232 pp., 245 illus., 6th ed. **Price 25/-**
(U.S.A. price $4.50)

THE RETINA WAY
By O. R. Croy

Will put the whole Retina technique safely in your hands and bring all the subjects of Retina photography within your easy reach.

240 pp., 214 illus., 9th ed. **Price 21/-**
(U.S.A. price $4.95)

LIGHTING FOR PHOTOGRAPHY
By W. Nurnberg

This book explains the principles, makes countless suggestions and shows over a hundred examples.

176 pp., 297 illus., 13th ed. **Price 21/-**
(U.S.A. price $4.50)

PHOTO-FLASH IN PRACTICE
By Geoffrey Gilbert

How flash works and how to work it. How to use it just to give light and how as a creative medium.

304 pp., 163 illus., 4th ed. **Price 17/6**
(U.S.A. price $3.50)

POSING PATTERNS
By L. E. Broome

A pictorial guide to posing for photographers, students and models. Text and diagrams help to analyse each pose, explaining how to photograph it and for what purpose it can be used.

208 pp., 1,226 illus. **Price 35/-**
(U.S.A. price $10.00)

BIRD PHOTOGRAPHY
By John Warham

Written for the reader with an elementary knowledge both of photography and of birds, documented and illustrated at every step.

200 pp., 100 illus. **Price 25/-**
(U.S.A. price $4.95)

THE LEICA WAY
By Andrew Matheson

Covers the whole technique and art of Leica photography both with the latest equipment and older models and accessories.

432 pp., 307 illus., 5th ed. **Price 25/-**
(U.S.A. price $4.50)

THE CONTAFLEX WAY
By H. Freytag

A handbook dealing exhaustively with Contaflex equipment and accessories, both for twin- and single-lens models. Invaluable to beginner and expert.

312 pp., 270 illus., 3rd ed. **Price 25/-**
(U.S.A. price $4.95)

THE CONTAX WAY
By H. Freytag

Up-to-date facts and authoritative advice on all Contax equipment applied to every conceivable Contax subject.

224 pp., 241 illus., 6th ed. **Price 21/-**
(U.S.A. price $4.95)

LIGHTING FOR PORTRAITURE
By W. Nurnberg

The wealth of possibilities in portrait lighting is broken down to a simple system of "how to do it" in this work.

192 pp., 500 illus., 3rd ed. **Price 21/-**
(U.S.A. price $5.00)

HOW TO TAKE PHOTOGRAPHS THAT EDITORS WILL BUY
By Ronald Spillman

A specialist in the field of feature photography shares his success secrets and shows the way to the fat fee market.

224 pp., 97 illus. **Price 19/6**
(U.S.A. price $4.50)

GLAMOUR IN YOUR LENS
By James Macgregor

This book shows what anyone can do anywhere with a camera and any pretty girl. Entertaining but practical, and illustrated by brilliant photographs.

160 pp., 80 photographs **Price 12/6**
(U.S.A. price $1.95)

CLOSE RANGE PHOTOGRAPHY
By C. H. Adams

Explains how to achieve large-scale photography of small subjects with home-made and inexpensive equipment.

192 pp., 63 illus. **Price 21/-**
(U.S.A. price $4.50)

CAMERA TECHNIQUES
By H. J. Walls
A textbook to serve the intelligent photographer, concerned with first principles and sound methods.
384 pp., 305 illus.   **Price 25/-**
                    (U.S.A. price $4.50)

DEVELOPING
By C. I. Jacobson
This is the best text and reference book on the basic facts and every practical aspect of negative processing and after-treatment.
328 pp., 150 illus., 14th ed.   **Price 19/6**
                    (U.S.A. price $4.50)

OPTICS
By Arthur Cox
The lens is the most precious part of any camera. So it pays to know how they work and how to handle them.
376 pp., 352 illus., 12th ed.   **Price 25/-**
                    (U.S.A. price $5.75)

SENSITOMETRY
By L. Lobel and M. Dubois
Explains basic facts about emulsions and their properties; methods used in measuring them and their practical applications.
264 pp., 102 illus.   **Price 25/-**
                    (U.S.A. price $5.00)

COLOUR FILMS
By C. Leslie Thomson
Deals with all aspects of working with colour film. Covering negative and reversal materials, exposure and processing.

296 pp., 150 illus. 2nd ed.   **Price 42/-**
                    (U.S.A. price $7.95)

COLOUR SEPARATION NEGATIVES
By Phillip Jenkins
Equipment, techniques, methods for separation negatives from the subject and from colour transparencies, masking and materials covered by an expert.

272 pp., 115 illus.   **Price 42/-**
                    (U.S.A. price $8.50)

THE COMPLETE ART OF PRINTING AND ENLARGING
By O. R. Croy
An encyclopedic volume in which every kind of print and every modern printing process is explained.
256 pp., 443 illus., 6th ed.   **Price 21/-**
                    (U.S.A. price $5.00)

EXPOSURE
By W. F. Berg
This work shows up the interdependence of equipment, materials, lighting conditions and subject matter.
448 pp., 200 illus., 2nd ed.   **Price 21/-**
                    (U.S.A. price $5.00)

ENLARGING
By C. I. Jacobson
This standard work shows how to choose and use enlarging equipment and materials so as to achieve perfect results.

312 pp., 136 illus., 17th ed.   **Price 21/-**
                    (U.S.A. price $4.50)

RETOUCHING
By O. R. Croy
Tells what to retouch and how to do it, which tools and methods will cope with any particular case, illustrating every step.
200 pp., 304 illus., 2nd ed.   **Price 17/6**
                    (U.S.A. price $4.50)

STEREO PHOTOGRAPHY
By K. C. M. Symons
Explains what stereo photography is and how it works. A complete guide for the practical photographer.

224 pp., 80 illus.   **Price 25/-**
                    (U.S.A. price $5.00)

COLOUR PRINTS
By Jack H. Coote
Covers negative-positive processes such as Agfacolor, Pakcolor, Gevacolor, Synthacolor, etc., as well as more traditional procedures.
328 pp., 4 colour plates, 40 diag. **Price 25/-**
                    (U.S.A. price $4.95)

THE COLOUR BOOK OF PHOTOGRAPHY
By Lucien Lorelle
Written for people who are interested in the technicalities of different colour processes only as far as they need them to obtain good results.
212 pp., 120 diag., 12 colour plates, 5th ed.
                    Price 15/6
                    (U.S.A. price $3.95)

AMATEUR CARBRO COLOUR PRINTS
By Viscount Hanworth
This book shows the way to do a first-rate job with amateur means.

188 pp., 33 diag., 3rd ed.   **Price 12/6**
                    (U.S.A. price $3.00)

FOCAL CINE BOOKS

HOW TO FILM	*by G. Wain*
HOW TO USE 9.5 mm. FILM	*by D. M. Neale*
HOW TO MAKE 8 mm. FILMS	*by N. Bau*
HOW TO USE COLOUR	*by C. L. Thomson*
HOW TO CHOOSE MUSIC	*by F. Rawlings*
HOW TO PRODUCE EFFECTS	*by Julien Caunter*
HOW TO DO TRICKS	*by Julien Caunter*
HOW TO CARTOON	*by J. Halas and B. Privett*
HOW TO ANIMATE CUT-OUTS	*by C. H. Barton*
HOW TO SCRIPT	*by Oswell Blakeston*
HOW TO WRITE FILM STORIES	*by Richard Harrison*
HOW TO WRITE COMMENTARIES	*by M. Kirsch*
HOW TO PROCESS	*by Leslie Wheeler*
HOW TO EDIT	*by H. Baddeley*
HOW TO TITLE	*by L. F. Minter*
HOW TO PROJECT	*by Norman Jenkins*
HOW TO ACT	*by Tony Rose and Martin Benson*
HOW TO FILM CHILDREN	*by Marcel Natkin*
HOW TO MAKE HOLIDAY FILMS	*by H. Baddeley*
HOW TO DIRECT	*by Tony Rose*
HOW TO ADD SOUND	*by D. M. Neale*
HOW TO FILM INDOORS	*by L. F. Minter and E. J. Chard*
HOW TO MAKE CINE GADGETS	*by H. Walden*

144 pages, case bound, fully illustrated

Price 10/6 (Postage 1/-)
(U.S.A. price $1.75–$2.50)

FOCAL CHARTS

FOCAL EXPOSURE CHART
By W. D. Emanuel

Anywhere, any time, any subject, any light, any camera, any film.

FOCAL FILTER CHART
By W. D. Emanuel

The right filter, film, light, stop, speed for any subject.

FOCAL FOCUSING CHART
By Arthur Cox

Sharp focus, safe depth, with any lens or attachment.

FOCAL STOP AND SPEED CHART
By E. Steffens

A whole library of facts on exposure, depth and action.

FOCAL LIGHTING CHART
By W. D. Emanuel

Lighting schemes, lamp positions, exact exposure values.

FOCAL FLASH CHART
By W. D. Emanuel

Flash exposure disc, sun-flash exposure disc, ten typical set-ups.

FOCAL DEVELOPING CHART
By W. D. Emanuel

The developing time at any temperature for any film and developer.

Price 4/6 each (Postage 6d.)

FOCAL CINE CHART
By W. D. Emanuel

All the technical data needed.

FOCAL COLOUR CHART
By W. D. Emanuel

Everything about colour film and your camera.

Price 5/- (Postage 6d.)

FOCAL ENLARGING CHART
By W. D. Emanuel

Measures exposure, ensures sharpness, defines magnification.

Price 9/6 (Postage 1/-)

324

CAMERA GUIDES

BESSAMATIC GUIDE

BOLEX 8 GUIDE

CONTAFLEX GUIDE

CONTAREX GUIDE

CONTAX GUIDE

CONTINA GUIDE

EDIXA REFLEX GUIDE

G.B.-B. & H.624 GUIDE

LEICA GUIDE

PAXETTE GUIDE

PENTAX GUIDE

RETINA GUIDE

RETINA REFLEX GUIDE

ROLLEIFLEX GUIDE

SILETTE GUIDE

VITO GUIDE

VITOMATIC GUIDE

Price 9/6 each

BALDESSA GUIDE

BOLEX H GUIDE

IKOFLEX GUIDE

IKOPHOT GUIDE

ISOLETTE GUIDE

MINOX GUIDE

MOVIKON GUIDE

NETTAR GUIDE

RETINETTE GUIDE

ROBOT GUIDE

ROLLEICORD GUIDE

SPORTSTER GUIDE

SUPER IKONTA GUIDE

Price 7/6 each

EXAKTA 35 mm. GUIDE

VITESSA GUIDE

Price 6/6 each

REGULA GUIDE

Price 5/6

COLORSNAP GUIDE

ILOCA GUIDE

KARAT GUIDE

Price 4/6 each

(U.S.A. prices $1.75–$1.95)

PERSPECTIVE

*A Quarterly Review of Progress in Photography,
Cinematography, Sound and Image Recording*

PERSPECTIVE is the only journal of its kind in the world.

Authoritative, accurate and concise—it presents the sum total of all the important, informative and interesting news on the economics, technology and research published by the leading periodicals throughout the world.

It reports on new products, their uses and their markets. It inquires into novel problems and applications in science, industry, medicine, commerce, education and administration. It offers intelligence from expert contributors and correspondents in research and industrial centres in every country.

Unique as a journal and reference book in one—it watches trends, publishes up-to-date surveys, analyses statistics, lines up digest summaries, abstracts new patents, signposts vital news. It translates messages of significance into words of common sense.

Published four times a year: March, June, September, and December. Fully illustrated by graphs, diagrams and photographs. 400 pages per volume. Size crown quarto (10 × 7½ in.) The annual subscription is £2 12s. 6d. ($7.50, DM 30.00, S.fr. 32.00) post free.

PERSPECTIVE is obtainable only through direct subscription exclusively, from the publishers Focal Press Ltd., 31 Fitzroy Square, London, W.1.

The Focal
ENCYCLOPEDIA
of
PHOTOGRAPHY

2,000 articles: 1¼ million words

1,468 pages, 385 photographs, 1,500 diagrams

Bound burgundy buckram, stamped silver

Price 5 gns   Desk Edition 35s

THE FOCAL ENCYCLOPEDIA will do the job of a whole library. This single volume holds the right answers to any question on photography—ready for prompt reference. It contains more information than many books put together. Much of it could not easily be found elsewhere. A great deal of it has never been published before.

THE FOCAL ENCYCLOPEDIA covers completely the vast technology of photography and follows up all its uses for picture making. It defines terms, identifies personalities and quotes rules. It recalls past developments and records the present state of progress all over the world. It sums up scientific theory and instructs in up-to-date practice. It presents all the facts that matter, explains "why" and shows "how". It hands out advice based on first-hand knowledge, expert skill and reliable authority.

THE FOCAL ENCYCLOPEDIA is specially written in plain, readable and commonsense English. It was carefully planned and set out in alphabetical order for easy reference. You will be able to find, instantly master and put to good use, all the information you need from whatever angle you look for it.

THE FOCAL ENCYCLOPEDIA is the only work of its kind in the world. A unique, up-to-date and universal source of photographic knowledge and an unfailing tool of practical help to any photographer, student of photography, professional and amateur, advanced and beginner alike.

THE FOCAL ENCYCLOPEDIA can take the place of a photographic library; and no library is complete without it.

See it at your bookseller's or photographic dealer's or write for full prospectus to Focal Press.

FOR THE BEST OF PHOTOGRAPHY

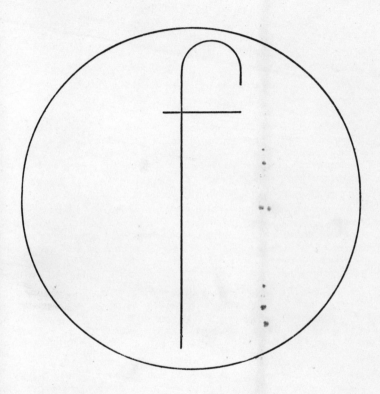

BY THE BEST OF PHOTOGRAPHERS